KING LABOUR

KING LABOUR

*The British Working Class
1850 – 1914*

David Kynaston

ROWMAN AND LITTLEFIELD
Totowa, New Jersey

First published in the United States 1976
by ROWMAN AND LITTLEFIELD, Totowa, N.J.

Library of Congress Cataloging in Publication Data

Kynaston, David.
  King Labour : the British working class, 1850–1914.

  Bibliography : p.
    1. Labor and laboring classes—Great Britain—History. 2. Labor and laboring classes—Great Britain—Political activity—History. 3. Socialism in Great Britain—History. I. Title. HD8390.K96 1976   331'.0941   76–22581
ISBN 0–87471–891–0

Printed in Great Britain

Foreword

In his already notorious *New Statesman* article of May 1975, 'A Brotherhood of National Misery', Paul Johnson described the wage-pulling trade unionists of the first half of the 1970s as 'dazed and bewildered', like 'medieval peasants who have burnt down the lord's manor' but have no idea what to do next. Much has happened since 1914, but in a very real sense, as Johnson himself suggests, the modern incomprehension is a direct result of the grittily defensive role which Labour out of necessity evolved for itself during the course of the nineteenth century. The manifold forms of social and economic control, the political retreat after Chartism, the continuing seduction of Gladstonian ethicalism for the influential minority, the alternative forms of inward burrowing for the passive majority – all these alone meant that a grasp of Marxian totalities, the ability to cope with a burnt-down manor, almost entirely by-passed the British working class during this period. The object of the book is to study this process in action and in so doing add the worm's eye perspective, the root of the modern bewilderment, to the half-truth embodied in the horny old phrase 'the rise of Labour'.

For my material I am largely dependent on the researches of others. The references show the extent of my debt. The coverage is in no way intended to be comprehensive either in a chronological or a region-by-region sense, though I do give certain phases (for example 1865–75) more detailed treatment as central working examples of particularly significant issues and attitudes. The book is concerned primarily with the second half of the nineteenth century, and it is to that time span that the middle 'background' chapters are related, but at the risk of a certain imbalance I have added a short postscript chapter in order to take the political narrative up to the formative event of the Great War.

My thanks to Keith Harling at the London Library and Miss Leslie at Senate House for bibliographical help; to Rosie Elgar for typing help; and to Jill Nicholls, John Wakefield and Dave Wilson for conversational help. The book is dedicated to Zvia.

King Labour

The wizard, King Labour, walked over the land,
   And the spade for a sceptre he bore;
And each step he took left an Eden behind,
   While the desert untamed frowned before.
He levelled huge mountains, and blasted the rocks,
   Where for ages vast treasures lay hid;
And shewed Heaven the coffer where Earth stored her wealth,
   And laughed loud as he shattered the lid.

J. B. LENO

Contents

Chapter 1

RETRENCHMENT

1850 — 1868

'Chartists, what is your duty? It is to organise. I tell you we are on the very verge of triumph.
'The Government are without funds – their expenditure is increasing . . . the middle class mistrust them – the working class despise them . . .' [1]

These hopeful words, addressed by Ernest Jones to fellow-Chartists soon after the mass meeting held on Kennington Common on 10 April 1848, proved sadly misplaced. Jones himself, along with five other leading London Chartists, was shortly to receive a sentence of two years' imprisonment on the grounds of seditious behaviour and unlawful assembly; and by the time that the four survivors came out of Millbank prison in July 1850, the working class, perhaps mindful of the pitfalls of violence so often associated with the Chartist movement, had begun to apply itself to the less adventurous task of making progress strictly within the existing social and political framework. The Great Exhibition, held in Hyde Park the following year and visited by thousands on cheap railway excursions, was symbol of this self-proclaimed era of industrious harmony. Class conflict did not suddenly become a thing of the past, but undoubtedly there took place during the third quarter of the century a change of atmosphere so fundamental that it gave the British labour movement a reformist character of apparent permanence. The Second Reform Act of 1867, enfranchising about a million of the urban working class, provided formal admission for a large part of this movement into the body politic. Yet it is sometimes forgotten, in emphasising the skilful absorption and tactical nuances of Disraeli's legislation, that 1867 did represent, and was seen to represent at the time, a substantial victory for what one may call the disinherited of the Industrial Revolution. The behaviour of the railwaymen is instructive in this respect. In 1848 many of them had been sworn in as special constables to defend London against the Chartists. Then during the next two decades, under the iron control of the companies, barely more than a fortnight of strikes occurred on the railway system of the entire country. But in the Reform crisis itself, many enginemen and various traffic grades, all in uniform, gave their support to the Reform League's impressive demonstration held on 11 February 1867. They were permitted to do so because their employers, while perceiving the men's determination to make this stand, were also aware that the redress of a specific grievance, and not revolution, was the motive involved. Reformism yes, but an insistent reformism: such was the controlling theme of the years which followed the sudden Chartist collapse.

The economic background to this new frame of mind was, of course, the prosperity which resulted from the meridian period (roughly 1850–75) of British capitalism. Gladstone in his 1863 Budget proudly announced that the national income had increased by 20 per cent between 1853 and 1861. Moreover, he added, the real wealth of the working class had grown during these years to an extent unparalleled in Britain or abroad. Obviously there were intermittent checks, and one may doubt how far down in society this bounty was always distributed, yet the basic trend, the material amelioration of the worker's lot, surely remains true. The political effects were manifest: in Cobbett's famous words, 'I defy you to agitate a fellow with a full stomach.' It would be false, however, to apply a simplistic analysis of relative wealth breeding an 'I'm all right Jack' attitude towards political questions during these years. The process was much more unconscious. It was one of men at last being able to afford to practise the virtue of providence and having done so then to discover that the benefits thereby accrued, whether in the form of the Co-operative or the Friendly Society or whatever, in effect involved a personal stake in the continuing well-functioning of capitalist society. In other words, the Owenite or the fully-fledged Chartist did not so much relinquish his ideals in the 1850s and 1860s as instead find them increasingly less applicable to his personal situation. An important role in this transitional phase was played by the employers, who were able to adopt rather more humane attitudes in the wake of limited liability legislation in 1855 and the general increase in prices during the period. Moreover, the Ten Hours Act of 1847 for textile workers, coming a year after the Repeal of the Corn Laws, undoubtedly helped to renew popular confidence in the integrity of the existing system of government. Perhaps even more important in determining the ideological climate of the period was, however, the way in which the occupational structure of the country remained relatively constant. The possibility of a monolithic factory-based proletariat was still remote; and the skilled artisan in a workshop setting, often hoping to become a small master himself, remained for a long time the dominant working-man figure. The classic example of such an economy was mid-Victorian Birmingham, a hive of small-time producers. The sub-contracting tradition, overhands farming out work to underhands, was particularly strong there, as it was also in the thriving cutlery trade in Sheffield. Such conditions of work do not lend themselves to mass movements united in the cause of radical social change; matters of self-respect, the achievement of a certain status in the world, are far more important. And it is in this context, one of a still supple economy, that one should consider the self-made man, archetype of the mid-Victorian social compact.

It is a truism that the only new thing in the 1850s about such a man was the systematic way in which Samuel Smiles and others began to glorify him as an exemplary figure. The story was often told, for instance, of how Thomas Cooper, a Chartist-turned-lecturer, had in his youth defied his lowly origins by committing to memory the first four books of *Paradise Lost* before his health gave way. Now another generation of self-made men was emerging, men such as Ben Brierley and J. B. Leno, born in 1825 and 1826 respectively. Brierley, the son of a Lancashire handloom weaver, subsequently became an established poet and storyteller, writing sketches with titles like *A Daisy Nook Wedding*, *A Bit o' Mint Cake* and *Little Dody's Christmas*. Towards the end of his life he recalled the local Mutual Improvement Society to which he had once belonged: 'The too common frivolities of youth we avoided. From the seeds sown at this time harvests have been gathered. The Crossley Brothers, manufacturers and machinists, sprang from amongst us. Others are successful farmers in America . . .' [2] Brierley was also anxious to insist that writing involved its own equally sober responsibilities: 'Throughout my public career I have endeavoured to conduct myself as a moderately good member of society, avoiding those traits of Bohemianism which are supposed to be the attributes of men who assume an exceptional position in the world of letters.' Leno, brought up around Uxbridge, pursued a roughly similar course (although much more variegated), in the best tradition of the thinking artisan. As he wrote in his autobiography: 'I was born in the P season and, strangely enough, have been Pieman, Pastrycook, Printer, Publisher, Politician and Poetaster.' [3] His most successful literary work was *King Labour's Song Book* (1861), which included numbers like 'Toil On, Toil On!' as well as 'King Labour' itself. The collection received approving notices, including this from the mass-circulation *Lloyd's Newspaper*: 'He appears to have with Carlyle, a hearty admiration of every man who can do something. . . . In these days, when the struggle of life is to escape labour, and to make money without work, the songster who recalls working men to their dignity of downright exertion, performs a most useful service.' Yet Leno himself was a former Chartist who in later years was even to affirm that 'with regard to Socialism, I feel persuaded there is justice at the bottom of it'. Clearly there was a tension, often hidden but certainly present, between the inner aspirations of the self-made man and the role which society expected him to play. To perceive this tension is to appreciate also the rough edges to the apparently smooth and familiar process of Smilesian absorption.

Elements of this paradox are apparent in the person of George Howell, the son of a Somerset builder who in 1865 became Secretary of the Reform League and subsequently attempted to pursue an orthodox political career. When he arrived in London in 1855 he had three ambitions: to make a speech at Exeter Hall in the Strand; to have a book published; and to enter the House of Commons. Some years later, after several frustrated applications, he received a British Museum Reading Room ticket, which he regarded as a privilege not to be abused by reading fiction or any other unworthy subject matter. In a sense this dedication gained for Howell what he desired. Besides his steady emergence as a public figure, he was finally able to record in his diary on 1 January 1868: 'This is my very first year of real comfort, when I felt able to buy a few things and not really pinch for it. Yet I have not lived extravagantly but very moderately and carefully. Never felt that I should live fast, or spend in gaiety.' [4] And: 'I must now try to get a little house through the Building Society.' Yet for all his manifest earnestness and sobriety, Howell was never openly welcomed by those middle ranks of society whose acceptance he so cherished. As early as his first night in London, he had been rejected by the Aldersgate YMCA on account of his corduroy trousers, which had denoted him to be a 'mechanic'; a decade later, during the Reform struggle, he never enjoyed an easy rapport with his predominantly middle-class colleagues. And in 1868 the Liberal Party managers effectively pulled the wool over his eyes by playing adroitly on his inferiority complex. Howell himself never consciously expressed this social unease, but the crotchety nature of many of his communications during these testing years seems to indicate a man caught between opposing backgrounds and interests. More perceptive, but undergoing a roughly similar experience, was Robert Applegarth, the self-made Secretary of the Amalgamated Society of Carpenters and Joiners. He listed his recreations in *Who's Who* as 'work, more work, and still more again',[5] and was always willing, as one would expect, to speak to well-meaning middle-class bodies like the Social Science Association. Yet at the same time he hated the working man to be patronised and turned by the leisured class into a kind of two-dimensional dummy. As he once exclaimed: 'For this model man they are prepared to legislate, talk, write goody-goody style of books for his edification, tell him what he ought and ought not to do, in fact to do everything for him except one, to treat him as a rational thinking being.' It is this conflict of needs, and its partial resolution, which demands exploration, especially in the fields of mid-Victorian popular culture in general and adult education in particular.

The relationship between the middle and working classes had been a difficult one during the 1830s and 1840s, full of ambivalence and tortuous negotiations about the price of a political alliance. In the event, the Anti-Corn Law League went its exclusively middle-class way, with its members refusing to support the Chartist demand for universal suffrage. Once, however, the free traders had begun to achieve their own aims, a process of reconciliation was widely initiated, tending to bypass politics and assume more social, unexceptionable forms. Mutual benefits for all to enjoy, like Manchester's first public parks (1846) and free library (1852), were created within this context. However, one should not think at this stage in terms of wealthy manufacturers, now politically as well as economically powerful, embarking on a methodical policy of buying-off working-class scruples. Instead, they placed their faith in the notion of self-help as a more satisfactory way of promoting industrial discipline and moral rectitude. Herein lay the crucial role of Smiles, who, between the mid-1840s and 1859 when *Self-Help* was published, managed to change the connotations of the term from ones of commonsensical mutualism to almost doctrinal individualism. His influence was profound. Selected almost at random, the edition of the *Todmorden and Hebden-Bridge Weekly Advertiser* for 3 May 1862 included these observations by the Rev. W. M. Hunter on the benefits to be derived from 'self-education': 'The false notions of labour, which nothing could be more absurd, would be done away. And it would be seen, and felt, and acknowledged, that honest labour elevated and degraded not. Evils and errors, the offsprings of ignorance . . . would vanish before the spread of sound culture.' This heavy-handedness was symptomatic of the middle-class approach during these years to the question of the working man's moral and mental advancement. Only when it was leavened by a measure of humanity did the 'message' really get home. Hence the significance of the countless publications founded by John Cassell.

Cassell, previously a general provisions merchant, concentrated heavily on the relatively new phenomenon of the 'family paper'. In particular, he established in 1853 *Cassell's Illustrated Family Paper*, which quickly built up a massive circulation. Prizes were awarded to readers who contributed a 'moral tale', defined by Cassell as 'illustrative of the triumph of religion, temperance, morality, industry, energy, and self-control over idleness, apathy, intemperance, and habitual self-indulgence'.[6] But while maintaining this attitude, and insisting that no foul language should soil his pages, Cassell also included large chunks of serialised fiction, in contrast to most of his respectabilising rivals. This fiction was wholesome, of course, but also satisfyingly escapist, in a sentimental, optimistic sort of way. A similar lack of cant, relatively speaking, also lay behind the appeal of Cassell's other great success, *The Popular Educator*, founded in 1852. Besides containing lessons in French, Mathematics and English Grammar, the first issue instructed its readers in Ancient History, through which 'the wholesome and warning lesson is taught, that, in all ages of the world, and under every variety of circumstance . . . the maxim holds good, that "vice is its own punisher, and virtue its own rewarder" '. And: 'How great, then, is the advantage of the man who is well versed in history, over those of his fellows who are not!' Such candour, very different from the Rev. Hunter's cloud of piety, found its response in 1854 when, upon completion of the original courses of instruction, a new volume was begun because of swelling demand. Meanwhile, other agencies of adult education were achieving much more varied results, being unwilling to admit the reason why the poor and unprivileged should desire learning.

It is a striking fact that the Mechanics' Institutes possessed over 200,000 members by 1860. Nevertheless, even their apologists accept that not only did they fail entirely to win the allegiance of unskilled workers, but also that clerks, small shopkeepers and petty bourgeoisie in general comprised at least half their overall membership. The main reason for this diluting of the Institutes' original aim surely lay in the nature of the continuing middle-class control which was exercised over them. This led to the systematic dissemination of orthodox political economy, the vetoing of any discussion about more controversial political questions like the suffrage issue, and a perspective on the Institutes which saw them as part of a more general breaking-in process. As the 1859 Annual Report of the Yorkshire Union of Mechanics' Institutes put it: 'No more convincing proof of the value of the Institutions could be afforded, than during the recent monetary crisis, when, notwithstanding that many thousands were deprived of employment, not the slightest breach of the peace occurred, nor was any apprehension entertained of such a calamity.' But what the working class wanted from the Institutes were not lessons in character-building, but instead either relief from life's daily grind or the straightforward instruction in the three Rs which the State would not yet provide. James Hole, Honorary Secretary of the Yorkshire Union, commenting on the main Institute at Leeds, wrote: 'it must be confessed that it is the lighter and more amusing departments which have succeeded best; and in its most important department – the classes – it has not achieved a proportionate degree of success.' [7] Moreover, Hole noted with regret that fiction taken out of the library had risen from 25 per cent of all books in 1846 to 46 per cent by 1859, with theology languishing at around 3 per cent. In terms of the basic desire for literacy, the other great levity in middle-class eyes as far as the 'purpose' of adult education was concerned, the story of the Working Men's College is illuminating. It was founded in London in 1854 by F. D. Maurice with the aim of bettering the Mechanics' Institutes which, in Maurice's view, tended merely to 'graze the surface of men's minds than penetrate into them'.[8] Yet in practice the social composition proved to be the usual admixture of artisans and struggling lower-middle class, while as also in the Institutes the keenness to learn how to read, to write and to count revealed itself as virtually the equivalent of trying to throw a six in order to climb up the first ladder. Or to put it more bluntly, the pursuit of a liberal, non-functional education was as yet a luxury which few members of the working class could afford, even if they had desired it.

Of the many manifestations of the social psychology bred by notions of self-help, one of the most fascinating is a bill which is still extant for a 'Grand Astronomical Night' held on 2 January 1867 at the Theatre Royal in Stanley-Cum-Wrenthorpe, Yorkshire. The entertainment featured a play entitled *High Life Below Stairs*, designed 'to illustrate the familiar social phenomenon of the zenith changing place with the nadir'. The hero is called Lovel – 'a shooting star, with an eye to business' – and other characters include a servant named Robert – 'a fiery star, who will make his transit' – and the Cook, 'a fixed star of the first magnitude'. This kind of mythology was obviously important, especially to the younger and less fatalistic sort of skilled artisan, threatened by sweated labour from below, but inspired from above by what one might call the spirit of the Crystal Palace. It may be significant, therefore, that in 1851 the members of the Leeds Mutual Improvement Society consisted on the whole of machine-makers, silk dressers, joiners, coach-makers, and shopkeepers, with an average age of about 23. These were men near enough to the abyss to have peered into it, but also young enough to feel that by dint of their own energies they could pull themselves away. The gulf was absolute between these few and the many others resigned to their station in life. As Hole observed about the rowdy beer-houses of his home city: 'one place of the kind in Leeds has a larger nightly attendance than the Evening classes of all its 17 Mechanics' Institutes put together!' [9] And it was this disparity, involving very different everyday criteria, which was at the root of the working-class failure in this period to achieve more than an extremely occasional and threadbare unity of purpose.

Central to this fragmentation was the emergence of the 'New Model' unions, as the Webbs [10] later called them. The first one came together in 1850, when London members of the Journeymen Steam Engine Makers' Society persuaded skilled fitters, turners and millwrights from Lancashire to unite with them to form the Amalgamated Society of Engineers. Two years later, the need for organisation was confirmed

when the still fledgling Society unsuccessfully resisted the imposition
by employers of piecework and systematic overtime. From this point,
the ASE steadily grew in strength – to such an extent that by the winter
of 1859–60, when London builders struck for a nine-hour day and
employers countered by disavowing the principle of unionism itself,
the Society was in a position to donate £3,000 to the strike fund. The
builders won half their battle, for the Central Master Builders'
Association withdrew its infamous 'Document' which all striking
employees were going to have to sign before they could get their jobs
back; and soon afterwards the builders formed the Amalgamated
Society of Carpenters and Joiners along organisational lines proposed
by William Allan, Secretary of the ASE. In 1860 the London Trades
Council was initiated, from which there emerged during the next few
years the so-called 'Junta', the name given by the Webbs to Allan of
the ASE, Applegarth of the ASCJ, Daniel Guile of the Ironfounders,
Edwin Coulson of the Bricklayers, and George Odger, a shoemaker
and Secretary of the LTC itself. By the end of the decade this group came
to represent in the official mind the national leadership of the trade
union movement. What exactly the New Model unions stood for (as
personified by the Junta), and how representative they were of trade
unionism as a whole, are thus clearly important questions.

Characteristic of these amalgamated societies was their stress upon
financial solidity and centralised control. Neither of these emphases
were exactly novel to craft societies, but between them they had the
deliberate effect of ensuring the exclusion of the great bulk of the
working class. This thorough-paced sectionalism was the inevitable
result of a relatively affluent unionism which demanded high contributions from skilled workers, earning around 30 shillings a week,
so they could pay them back substantial benefits if their livelihoods
were threatened. Not surprisingly, the consequence was a mentality
which abhorred the thought of squandering these resources, whether
it meant sharing them with less able workmen or permitting unnecessary
and expensive strike action. Applegarth in particular was often prepared to intervene personally in order to prevent local societies from
striking, as in the case of the 1864–5 dispute between Birmingham
carpenters and local master-builders. Moreover, any branch of the
ASCJ which wanted to strike had to fill in a rigorous application form
that included the following question: 'What is the state of trade at
present, and what reasons have you for anticipating that at the time
when the notice expires the state of trade will be such as to induce
your employers to concede the advance asked for?' [11] This attitude of
watchful moderation from the centre was at times even broadened to
include a measure of ethical paternalism. The text established in 1857
for the President of the Boilermakers' Society to use when addressing

candidates contained saws like 'We are united not to set class against class but to teach one another that all are brothers' and 'I would enjoin you to be a loving husband, a tender father, a good neighbour and a strict observer of every moral and social duty'.[12] Prince Albert himself could not have expressed these sentiments more faithfully.

Yet there is another and perhaps more important side to the picture. It is one which shows the so-called 'labour aristocrat' permanently worried by pressures from below as well as from above and prepared at the pinch (as in 1852 and 1859–60) to fight with extreme tenacity if he felt the employment of his superior skills to be threatened. The cause of this anxiety was the continuing existence of a large pool of underpaid and often redundant labour, an imbalance summed up in Mayhew's haunting phrase about '100,000 weavers doing the work of 150,000'.[13] The skilled artisan feared these men from the 'dishonourable' trades, and throughout the century campaigned against piecework, overtime and the laxity of apprenticeship regulations. The struggle was always a fraught one, especially with the steady proliferation of the semi-skilled worker, possessing a limited but definite mechanical aptitude. At Birkenhead in the autumn of 1865, aware that they could tap an alternative source of labour if necessary, certain employers tried to get their riveters to place 25 extra rivets into position daily without any additional payment. The riveters duly struck and were supported by the Executive Council of the Boilermakers' Society, which declared soon afterwards: 'When the dark and ominous clouds of depression lower around us and threaten almost the very existence of our Society; when capitalists, like prowling wolves, snatch eagerly at every chance, or every shadow of a chance to grind us to the earth . . . it is time not only to think but also to act.' [14] Given this kind of desperation, it may seem a moot point whether the phrase 'aristocracy of labour' had any relevance even during the 'prosperous' third quarter of the century.

Moreover, a fundamental long-term shift in economic power away from the traditionally élitist craftsman figure and towards the skilled practitioner in the new metal industries was taking place within this 'aristocracy'. Ironworking, engineering and shipbuilding were all specialised occupations which roughly trebled in size between 1851 and 1881; and increasingly, the versatile artisan found himself having to specialise in order not to disappear altogether. The proof of this trend was the rapid decline during the middle decades of the century of 'tramping' round the country in search of varied, often seasonal employment. The ASCJ, with an entrance age limit of 40 and impatient of the older, vagabond type of artisan, hastened the decline when it introduced in 1860 a system of static as opposed to tramp relief for its out-of-work members. Three years later its old-fashioned rival, the General Union of Carpenters, with more members, an age limit of 50, and a much looser organisation, reluctantly followed suit. Many of the lodges protested, forcing the Union's secretary, Robert Last, to defend static relief as being 'sure to benefit a deserving class, who would despise the tramp card'.[15] At the same time Last introduced friendly benefits in order to keep up with the ASCJ. The effect of such developments was inevitably to nurture still further a narrow, sectional mentality. But equally, when the skilled artisan did want something external from society, his awareness of a generally eroding position made him determined to achieve it.

Before the mid-1860s, however, it was usually left to associations of unskilled men to seek reforms which were not solely concerned with maintaining status within a vertical craft structure. In particular, the miners and the cotton operatives took up questions which demanded legislation, such as working conditions, safety in general, and the problem of unscrupulous employers who refused to pay wages on a regular weekly basis. But even over these very specific issues, the non-craft associations failed to muster the collective strength and cohesion necessary to press their case vigorously. Since wages were not high enough to permit adequate contributions and benefits, that respect-abilising process so characteristic of the New Model unions and perhaps politically necessary in mid-Victorian Britain failed to take place. Both the Weavers' First Amalgamation (1858) and the National Miners' Association (1863) were federal in character, coming together at all only at times of a particular agitation. Nevertheless, one cannot simply assign these unions to a pre-1850 tradition of fitful militancy. During the Lancashire Cotton Famine of the early 1860s, for example, the local societies of skilled spinners failed to unite because of bitter internal conflicts between the declining hand-mule and prospering self-actor spinners, whereas the hand-loom weavers revealed a much greater sense of mutuality, doubtless derived from a strong tradition of shared hardship. In other words, the policy and objectives of the skilled New Model unions by no means held the only key to the necessary long-term development of trade unionism as a whole, even if their organisation did. Confirmation of this comes from the power-loom weavers, a first generation of horizontally structured factory operatives, who in 1853 secured from a large group of Lancashire employers the so-called 'Blackburn List', which was a wages agreement on lines suggesting independence from the previously omnipotent laws of supply and demand. As such, it was a clear antecedent of the more proletarian 'new unionism' of 1889–90. Yet it is doubtful whether even the New Model unions were completely bound during their period of high ascendancy to the *laissez-faire* precepts of classical political economy.

The issue centred on the ongoing debate as to whether flourishing trade in general was beneficial for the working class in particular.

Certainly the free market as such was not blindly accepted. The attempts to enforce a strict apprenticeship system are evidence enough. Moreover, even Allan, the most moderate member of the Junta, felt moved in front of the Trade Union Commission of 1867 to repudiate the suggestion of a natural alliance existing between employers and workers: 'There I differ. Every day of the week I hear that the interests are identical. I scarcely see how that can be. . . . It is their interest to get the labour at as low a rate as they possibly can, and it is ours to get as high a rate of wages as possible, and you never can reconcile these two things.' [16] Nevertheless, inherent in the favourite New Model slogan 'A fair day's wage for a fair day's work' was a failure to question the crucial underlying concept of industrial capital. The landed aristocrat remained a much more potent figure of envy than the tight-fisted manufacturer, who was often respected for his doughty rise from lowly origins. Hence the considerable working-class following bestowed upon John Bright, the self-proclaimed 'terror of the squires' and himself an industrialist. Three reasons help to explain this absence of a penetrating economic critique: the inadequate analyses of the middle-class intellectuals; the continuing strength of a fragmented, subcontracting economy which persuaded 'men' to believe that they might one day become 'masters'; and related to this, the way in which these small paternalist firms helped to maintain a certain unquestioning social psychology. This last point was exemplified by the *Leeds Mercury* of 3 June 1856 in a story headed 'Peace Rejoicing at Hunslet': 'Mr Thomas Greaves, file manufacturer, and the workmen in his employ, sat down, on Thursday-last, at the Vincent-place Academy, Sayner-road, Hunslet, to a substantial supper of the good old English fare. After the cloth was removed and the usual loyal toasts had been honoured, the Railway Foundry Drum and Fife Band played a selection of popular music, and the evening was spent with great festivity.' It is in language like this that one senses the social roots not only of the Reform alliance ten years later, but also of the Liberal Party as it was to prosper until almost the end of the century.

Granted this relative absence of a consciously working-class inter-pretation of society, it was hardly surprising that Karl Marx's First International Workingmen's Association made only a slight impact in Britain, appealing almost solely to certain declining societies who clutched at it as a passing straw. Allan expressed the typical sectionalist response when, on being asked by the Royal Commission if his union had been present at the 1866 Geneva Congress of the International, he replied that he and his colleagues had not and that 'they believed the best thing the foreigners could do would be to organise themselves into trade societies similar to ours, and then we could begin to discuss questions with them'.[17] But because the Junta and their associates were not revolutionaries, this did not mean that in political terms they remained out-and-out quietists. This was clearly shown by Ernest Jones's early misjudgements and gradual change of front during the period. He began by scorning class collaboration, writing in 1852 that 'there is aristocratic privilege of the vilest die among the high-paid trades' [18] and simultaneously denouncing the engineers' strike as a negation of the labour movement's need for an explicitly political policy. But slowly, as other Chartists turned increasingly to more mundane, gradualist activities, Jones came to accept that political gains were now going to have to be achieved in a more piecemeal way, through a mixture of unity, organisation and prudence. Even as early as 1857 he declared himself in favour of 'allying with the middle classes if they offer such a measure of reform as we can be justified in accepting'.[19] By this Jones meant manhood suffrage, but in 1865, while not losing sight of this goal, he became a vice-president of the Reform League and knuckled down with a variety of middle-class Radicals to campaign for household suffrage. Nevertheless, trade union support had taken a long time coming for even this very limited purpose. As Howell regretfully told the General Neapolitan Society of Working Men in December 1861, 'our trade societies are not constituted on a political basis', but instead possessed 'more of a social character, their objects being to promote the well-being of their members in all matters appertaining to their daily toil'. It was in this atmosphere of little political commitment until the mid-1860s that the Co-operative societies flourished as an alternative focus of activity, revealing much about the working-class priorities and preoccupations that had come to the fore since the passing of Chartism.

Jones himself, in his more intolerant phase, described the Co-operative movement as 'an attempt of a small knot among the aristocracy of labour to creep on to the platform of the middle class'.[20] This was too cynical a verdict, and ignored the genuinely independent working-class influence which prevailed. Nevertheless, in that the Co-operative societies certainly did move away from the communitarian ideals associated with the Rochdale Pioneers of 1844 and became a flourishing group of dividend-paying store-owners some two decades later, Jones's sense of grievance was justified. This tendency towards a curtailing of Owenite ambitions was already apparent by about 1850, after the tell-tale signs from the early years that the successful stores were those which resolutely refused to give credit. Subsequent local societies inevitably took a similar line, with the result that the 'residuum', moving from job to job and frequently in debt, were effectively excluded from the movement. Once again, however, it would be wrong to assume a simple 'turncoat idealists' explanation for this change of approach. In the autumn of 1861, the proposition put forward in the *Co-operator* that 'co-operation and socialism . . . are founded on principles not merely alien to each other, but repugnant and contradictory' was met with a sharp and hostile response. Yet within a year the Rochdale Co-operative Manufacturing Society abandoned its principle of profit-sharing among members (the celebrated 'bounty to labour') in order to become what was virtually a straighforward joint-stock company concerned primarily with a profitable balance-sheet for its own reinvesting sake. To some extent, of course, one can see this transition in terms of younger members coming to the fore who conceived of self-help solely within the framework of the ethic of 'getting on'. It would be just as reasonable, however, to stress not so much ideals being shed as economic strength and self-sufficiency being emphasised as a precondition for the achieving of anything else. Such an interpretation allows one to view the Co-operative movement as a formative cultural and educative experience, a regular participatory affirmation of working-class independence. This sense of achievement comes shining through in the diary of John Ward, a weaver from Clitheroe, especially in his entry for 15 June 1861, which in a way captures this whole period:

'Another very warm day, and as this was the day for laying the foundation stone of the co-operative cotton mill, I cleaned myself up and got there in time. There was a large procession headed by the band of the Clitheroe Rifle Corps. The stone was laid by Mr Trappes the Town Clerk, with the usual ceremonies. There was a bottle enclosed in the stone containing specimens of the coins of the Queen's reign and all the local newspapers of the date and several memoranda of Clitheroe. After the stone was laid we went back in procession to the Wesleyan school-room, where a large tea-party was held to celebrate the auspicious event. There was a great deal of speech-making and singing and everything passed off in great style. It was near eleven o'clock when we broke up so I came right off home.' [21]

It is evident from his diary that Ward followed closely the progress of the American Civil War and was a committed supporter of Abraham Lincoln and the Federals in the North. In this he was typical of the weaving community as a whole, despite the famine conditions imposed on them by the North's blockade on cotton leaving the South. This was the noble 'silence' of Lancashire, a myth actually grounded in fact, and encouraged by the middle-class Radicals under Bright's leadership in opposition to the pro-South Whigs and Tories. At the outset, however, the working class had shown a much more ambivalent attitude towards the war. In particular, a cohesive group of non-Junta trade unionists, tending to be of Chartist background and headed by Thomas Dunning of the London Consolidated Bookbinders, distrusted the 'democratic' tag attached to the North and doubted if there was much difference in practice between the manufacturers there and the slave-owners in the South. The question was debated especially keenly in the pages of the *Bee-Hive*, the only working-class newspaper which concerned itself consistently with political matters and also had a substantial circulation. But gradually, hastened by Lincoln's emancipation of the slaves in January 1863, almost total working-class solidarity built up in support of the North. The accompanying alliance over the issue with middle-class Radicals had important domestic implications. As Howell was to write gratefully to Bright in October 1867: 'Your presence with us on the American question . . . gave a great impetus to the political tendencies of the Unions, and aided us in our endeavours to bring them into the political arena.' Characteristically, Howell played down the significance of the 'freedom' movement from abroad which had followed the American Civil War. This was the Polish attempt to resist Russian domination, a cause which won enthusiastic working-class support in England (with the Junta no exception), but a strictly non-interventionist stance from Bright and his associates. Again we must turn to Ward, who wrote on 17 April 1864 that 'there is very little news from Poland, and at home there is not much doing but squabbling in Parliament about things that is of no use to us'. It was an entry which suggested a thoroughly independent, if jaundiced, approach to contemporary politics. Less than four weeks later, Gladstone's famous statement – that 'every man who is not presumably incapacitated by some consideration of personal unfitness or of political danger is morally entitled to come within the pale of the constitution' [22] – gave men of Ward's stamp the chance to try to make Parliament into a forum of some relevance.

It is unlikely, however, that the improving workmen who subsequently gave their support to the Junta's specific political aspirations would have done so without the powerful intervention of middle-class Radicals on the side of suffrage reform. Gladstone remained the great symbol of hope after his momentous pronouncement; at the insurgent Hyde Park demonstration of July 1866, a banner with his portrait and a motto reading 'Gladstone and Liberty: An Honest Man's the Noblest Work of God' [23] featured prominently. In these years of the Parliamentary Liberal Party beginning to extend its influence outwards, the Reform agitation was obviously an important coalescing experience. Nevertheless, a much more immediate figure than Gladstone was Bright, whose own exclusively middle-class Reform Union moved perceptibly in policy towards the more working-class Reform League in an attempt to maintain overall control over the Reform movement after the Hyde Park demonstration. During these months Bright pursued his basic anti-aristocracy theme and insisted that the better sort of working man was now deserving of the vote. It proved enough. Despite his indifference towards the notion of independent working-class MPs and his insistence upon household rather than manhood suffrage, Bright was welcomed by the Reform League as a necessary ally in the cause of advancement. This was perhaps inevitable since the League was financially dependent upon wealthy manufacturers; and its leaders, a high proportion of whom were middle class anyway, masked their theoretical attachment to the principle of manhood suffrage by insisting on the additional qualification of 'registered and residential'. By so doing they not only satisfied their Liberal masters, whose cautious Reform Bill they had accepted in March 1866, but also reassured their predominantly artisan membership that the political ambitions of the drifting residuum were no concern of the League's. This moderation was very much the setting for what has been called the 'Rochdale' argument,[24] as summed up by Graham, a colleague of Gladstone's, when addressing the Commons in favour of reform in April 1866: 'Look at the co-operative building and manufacturing societies. Are they ignorant of the value of property? Are they dishonest more than ourselves that they should wish to seize what they know is not theirs?' All this was clearly important, representing as it did a major part of the general mid-Victorian respectabilising process. Yet one should also recall Cobden's words of 1861: 'So long as five millions of men are silent under their disability, it is quite impossible for a few middle-class members of Parliament to give them liberty.'[25] And after the defeat of Gladstone's Reform Bill in June 1866, and the tearing down of rails at Hyde Park the following month, social peace in Rochdale became uneasily juxtaposed in the minds of the nation's guardians with the awareness of another, altogether more demagogic popular tradition.

The question of whether or not extra-parliamentary agitation decisively influenced the making and passing of the Second Reform Bill has had more than its share of historical controversy. Objective comment is therefore difficult. But it does seem that although the leaders of the Reform movement continued to exercise a policy of restraint during the winter of 1866–7, there did come a point, about March or April 1867, when the swelling rank-and-file began to show signs of losing patience with strictly constitutional procedures. It is easy to see why. On 3 December, about 25,000 people, angered by the new Conservative ministry's apparent shelving of the Reform issue, had peacefully attended a demonstration in the grounds of Beaufort House organised by the London Working Men's Association. This was the body founded in 1866 by George Potter of the *Bee-Hive* to provide a rival to the Junta-identified Reform League, although politically its views were little more radical. Then, on 11 February 1867, the Reform League itself had countered by holding its own demonstration, likewise decorous and well-attended. Now, in the spring, Disraeli's recent Reform Bill seemed no advance on Gladstone's of a year earlier, again falling far short of even household suffrage. This was especially disappointing to the many trade unionists who, feeling generally threatened, had stomached their doubts about political action and had joined the ranks of the Reform League during the winter. The upshot was a split within the League between the moderates and the activists, culminating in the decision, vainly opposed by Howell, to hold a mass demonstration in Hyde Park on 6 May. The Home Secretary tried to prevent it from taking place, but on the day over 100,000 people attended. Two weeks later Disraeli accepted Hodgkinson's Amendment, which, by abolishing the distinction in the boroughs between compound householders and personal rate-payers, effectively introduced household suffrage. Was there a causal connection? The evidence that exists is confusing and certainly inadequate. More relevant perhaps was the actual *fact* of the demonstration of 6 May, impressive enough to suggest the possibility of an independent and politically coherent working-class movement. That this did not yet materialise was a measure of, how deep the underlying spirit of reformism had bitten since the much less successful mass gathering on Kennington Common.

Meanwhile, and concurrently with the Reform crisis, there was taking place an important internal conflict over the question of trade union militancy. The rift became apparent in the spring of 1865, when Potter and the *Bee-Hive*, supported by the General Union of Carpenters and several small societies in London, came out in favour of striking North Staffordshire puddlers, thus opposing the Junta's policy of cautious control from the centre. The disagreement was not political as such. Potter simply maintained, in the context of worsening trade conditions from about 1864, that local strikes should be supported *per se*, since they almost always involved great personal hardship. This notion of a broader-based unionism was confirmed by the LWMA's deliberately low subscription of one shilling a year; and Potter received during 1866 valuable support from Dunning, who argued in February in the *Bee-Hive* that the ASE had become 'simply a benefit society' and so had lost its cutting edge. Over the next eighteen months, the conflict intensified and acquired a new dimension. The general determining context was fourfold: the continuing need to show that the working man was deserving of the vote; the public outrage after strong-arm men from a Sheffield saw-grinding union blew up the house of a non-unionist workman in October 1866; the subsequent appointment of a Royal Commission to examine the whole question of trade unionism; and the decision by the Court of Queen's Bench in January 1867 that a union's funds could not be protected by the Friendly Societies Act of 1855 and that even strike action was potentially illegal. In this darkening situation, when an appearance of moderation and respectability assumed paramount importance, the Junta took upon itself the title of the Conference of Amalgamated Trades, consisting largely of engineers, bricklayers, ironfounders and carpenters. Two months later, in March 1867, this group boycotted the St Martin's Hall Conference called by Potter and the LWMA to discuss the pressing subject of 'The Law and Trade Unions'. This absence apart, Potter's conference came close to being representative of British trade unionism as a whole and was by definition somewhat northern-dominated. It adopted a resolution criticising the sectional assumptions of the Conference of Amalgamated Trades and also set up a committee chaired by Connolly of the Stonemasons that was designed to put the broader union view before the Royal Commission. In pursuit of this last strategem, however, the non-amalgamated societies lost not just the battle, but practically the campaign. Connolly, on an unfortunate appearance before the Commission, allowed himself to be squeezed out of the proceedings; while Potter, coming forward as a witness on behalf of his small Union of Progressive Carpenters, was edgy and defensive in manner, leaving a poor impression. The members of the Junta, on the other hand, shone almost continuously. Applegarth in particular answered confidently and responsibly no less than 633 questions, many of them put to him by his middle-class Radical friends, Thomas Hughes and Frederic Harrison, who were sitting on the Commission. The result was to save trade unionism – but very much on Applegarth's terms, which were those of someone far more concerned about protecting funds and status than sanctioning strikes and pickets. And subsequently even Applegarth was to concede that the Junta had paid a high price for showing the acceptable face of unionism.

The year 1868 provided a suitable tail-piece to these events. The legacy from the St Martin's Hall Conference was still sufficiently strong for the Manchester and Salford Trades Council to propose in February the first of an annual series of national trades' congresses. This, the first Trades Union Congress, duly met from 2–6 June at the Mechanics' Institute, David Street, Manchester. Thirty-four delegates attended, representing 118,367 members, but the Junta stayed aloof. These tactics of abstention carried the day, for the Congress, perhaps influenced by the *Bee-Hive's* declining circulation, passed a vote of confidence in the policies of the Conference of Amalgamated Trades. Potter himself was present, but now a somewhat changed man. During the winter he had persistently stressed the need to field independent working-class candidates at the next election, the first to be fought under the new franchise. May 1868, however, found him in touch with Samuel Morley, the Liberal manufacturing philanthropist and leading patron of the Reform League. Morley in turn arranged with a Nonconformist publishing friend of his, Daniel Pratt, to bale the *Bee-Hive* out of its financial troubles in return for the paper's non-enmity towards the Liberal Party. It may have comforted Potter to know that Howell also was the (presumably much more willing) object of similar sort of persuasion. Likewise, the context was the Reform League's desperate shortage of funds, which prompted Howell to come increasingly into contact at the beginning of 1868 with C. G. Glyn, the banker and Liberal Chief Whip. Glyn then put him on to an affluent Radical friend, James Stansfeld, as Howell's diary for 28 January recorded: 'To Stansfelds to lunch. Talked with him on Politics and Political Economy for four hours. Applegarth was also present. We were both much pleased.' Stansfeld not only placed £500 at Howell's disposal, but also converted him to the idea of founding a club that would be housed together with the Reform League and seek to bring together Liberals and the better sort of working man. The club itself, the Adelphi, proved a failure, but was nevertheless an essential social prelude to Stansfeld's and Glyn's major political ploy. This was the secret electoral pact concluded in the summer, costing the Liberal Party £1,900 in return for the Reform League agreeing to abstain from putting up rival candidates and also promising to provide the Liberals with necessary information about the new electorate. The pact was fulfilled almost to the letter. As Glyn wrote contentedly to Gladstone shortly before the election about the League's helpers in the constituencies: 'They are so sound and so sensible & in most places their great object is to unite the two sections of the party *for you* & not to put up their own or any extreme men.' [26] Such services were indeed cheap at the price.

One is tempted to add somewhat wistfully: it need not have been so. As early as the summer of 1867, a correspondence of much significance had taken place in the pages of the *Bradford Review*. S. C. Kell, a local manufacturing Liberal in the Bright and Cobden mould, wrote on 31 August about how the unions must learn to foreswear all kinds of coercion. He concluded: 'There are also amongst the by-laws of many trades unions vexatious restrictions and regulations (apart from those regarding wages and times of labour) which answer no useful end, which irritate among employers, and often hinder an industrious workman from doing himself a good turn; and this tyranny must also be done away with.' And he went on: 'Until trades unions have been thus reduced to their proper and lawful objects, they will not be thoroughly liked by the best friends of the working classes, not will they be heartily supported even by the best men of their own order.' The Positivist J. H. Bridges a week later forcefully attacked this attitude of Kell's, stressing that 'the leaders of this party are capitalists and large employers of labour, and . . . have not fully emancipated themselves (and no wonder) from the prejudices natural to their class'. Not perhaps surprisingly, then, Kell and like-minded industrialists in the Bradford area declined to give Howell any money when he came up to petition them in February the following year. As Howell himself noted in his diary, while failing entirely to see the bargaining implications of his conclusion, 'my private impression is that the Manufacturing class are rather afraid of the power the People now have'. Nor was this fear *wholly* unjustified. At the time of the actual 1868 Election, a vocal minority actively opposed the Reform League's alliance with middle-class Radicalism. In Glasgow, for example, a local Liberal of some means called George Anderson was only sanctioned as a candidate by fifty-three votes to forty-nine at a trades' delegates' meeting sponsored by the Scottish Reform League. And it is in this context, one of a minority feeling let down, that one can understand the indifference shown by most trade unionists towards the outcome of the election and the perceptible pro-Tory vote of the labouring element, probably as much as anything for the sake of opposing those skilled artisans who now formed almost the backbone of the Liberal support. As Mill had wryly observed in the Commons in April 1866 in response to Robert Lowe's claim that the working class were now the 'masters', 'they may be able to decide whether a Whig or a Tory shall be elected, they may be masters of so small a situation as that'.[27] Nevertheless, in 1868 itself, that was by and large all that they wanted for the time being. For as the *Bradford Review* had unwittingly summed up the prevailing social and political climate by including this short notice at the foot of the column containing Bridges's reply: 'We learn that it is proposed to give a banquet to Mr Bright in Brimingham, the tickets to be fixed at a price which will allow the working classes to take part in the demonstration.'

Chapter 2

IDEAS

'Get Mill on Liberty and Political Economy. There are many other works, but go to the fountain head at once. Mill, Gladstone and Bright are great authorities on politics, taxation and government.'

Such was the unadventurous advice offered by Howell in May 1868 to a working man who had asked him what he should read. In the light of Howell's contribution to the election later that year, it is clearly relevant to examine the relation between the influence exercised by the various 'great authorities' of the mid-Victorian period and the thorough-going reformism which simultaneously began to characterise the British labour movement. The theoretician suggestive of this line of inquiry is the Italian Antonio Gramsci,[1] imprisoned under Mussolini's régime and a proponent of the fundamental distinction between a ruling group's 'direct domination' and its more informal 'hegemony'. This 'hegemony' comprises 'the "spontaneous" consent given by the great masses of the population to the general direction imposed on social life by the dominant fundamental group'. Which part of the group is most responsible for maintaining this informal 'hegemony'? Gramsci's answer is clear: the 'traditional' intellectuals, who stood some distance apart from the practitioners of the nineteenth-century industrial process and were respected by them on that account, but failed almost entirely to utilise the radical potential of that social detachment. The methodological implications of this perception are considerable. In the formative words of one of Howell's 'great authorities', J. S. Mill: 'Ideas are not always the mere signs and effects of social circumstances, they are themselves a power in history.' [2]

The connection is especially fruitful when applied to the mid-Victorian period, for in cultural terms there existed then a far more responsive relationship between aristocrats, manufacturers, intellectuals and thinking working men than later in the century. Thomas Hughes, for example, successfully stood in 1865 as a working-man's candidate, only a few years after writing the definitive public school novel; while about the same time, both Mill and Matthew Arnold ignored the advice of their hidebound publishers and brought out cheap popular editions of their works. Nevertheless, for all this relative cerebral homogeneity, real class interests were still at stake.

Bertrand Russell's grandfather, on his death-bed in 1869, suddenly
heard a loud noise from the street and thought that the revolution had
come. Nor did the intellectuals themselves always give satisfaction.
Dickens in *Hard Times* brought the word 'gradgrindery' into the
English language, prompting Macaulay to condemn the novel as
'sullen socialism'.[3] Macaulay himself stayed firmly within the prevailing
Victorian doctrine of improvement and amelioration, sometimes perceiving symptoms but never causes. Most of his fellow-intellectuals
did likewise. At the doctrine's most severe, Andrew Ure put forward
the adage, in his extremely influential *The Philosophy of Manufactures*
(1835), that 'there is, in fact, no case to which the Gospel truth,
"Godliness is great gain", is more applicable than to the administration
of an extensive factory.' At its most clinical, the National Association
for the Promotion of Social Science heard a paper in 1867 entitled
'Suggestions for Checking the Hurtful Use of Alcoholic Beverages
by the Working Classes'. And at its most woolly-headed, Henry
Mayhew, author of the well-informed and very moving *London Labour
and the London Poor*, still felt justified in writing fiction like *The Good
Genius*, a Christian parable in which the good fairy personifies the
'spirit of industry'. All three types of propaganda assumed that society
existed to achieve common ends and took care to praise the 'industrious
classes' for learning to acquire the peaceable virtues of thrift and
application. 'Better fifty years of Europe than a cycle of Cathay' wrote
Tennyson in 1842, with the materialist confidence born of a consensus
of opinion behind him. Here, however, we are concerned with that
small minority who, like Dickens, did offer a sustained critique of
society – however inadequate and thus conducive to the maintenance
of the existing social 'hegemony'.

Yet should one really expect otherwise? Perhaps not. There is the
well-known story of Coleridge walking in the Quantocks in 1797 with
the Jacobin Thelwall and discovering an enchanting 'secret' dell.
'Citizen John', Coleridge remarked, 'this is a fine place to talk treason
in.' Thelwall replied: 'Nay, Citizen Samuel, it is rather a place to make
a man forget that there is any necessity for treason.' [4] So likewise by
the middle of the nineteenth century, with industrialisation an increasing reality and democracy apparently advancing inexorably, the
desire amongst sensitive spirits to preserve against all change the
beautiful, the noble, and the civilised became almost obsessive. As
the author of *Culture and Anarchy* saw tremblingly at the end of a
famous poem:

> 'We are here as on a darkling plain
> Swept with confused alarms of struggle and flight,
> Where ignorant armies clash by night.' [5]

Such a mentality could not envisage, could not allow itself to envisage, the equally stern reality of a through socio-economic analysis necessarily resulting in perhaps violent class conflict. For a man like Arnold, the mainspring of this fear was ultimately psychological, producing not only a governing criterion, the peaceful pursuit of social harmony whatever the faults of the particular society, but also a deeply equivocal attitude to political action itself. As he once wrote: 'Treatment of politics with one's thought, or with one's imagination, or with one's soul, in place of the common treatment of them with one's Philistinism and with one's passions, is the only thing which can reconcile . . . any serious person to politics.' [6] Yet for all that, these neurotic mid-Victorian prophets did offer their critiques of society and sometimes even tried to put their proposed remedies into practice; and in so doing they provided the labour movement with intellectual nourishment during what was to be the germinal period of the century.

'What means this bitter discontent of the Working Classes ? Whence comes it, whither goes it ? Above all, at what price, on what terms, will it probably consent to depart from us and die into rest ? These are questions.' So asked Thomas Carlyle, in typically trenchant prose, in his pamphlet *Chartism*, published in 1840 and famous for the coining of the phrase 'the condition-of-England question'. His enormously influential answer to the last and most urgent problem was essentially that of moral regeneration. In particular, he attacked, and demanded a change of heart from, those *laissez-faire* manufacturers who had made such killings since the beginning of the century. In his central tract, *Past and Present* (1843), statements like 'God's Laws are become a Greatest-Happiness Principle, a Parliamentary Expediency' and 'Good Heavens, "Laissez-faire, Do ye nothing, eat your wages and sleep", is everywhere the passionate half-wise cry of this time' gave a memorable colouring to Carlyle's view of the world as a place demanding mutual dependence rather than atomistic individual endeavour. He believed that men should be bound together by volunary obligations of love and duty, not by what he characterised as the 'cash nexus'. An important part of these obligations comprised the 'organisation of labour', including such revolutionary concepts (to the industrial world of the early 1840s) as a just and regulated wage, permanence of contract, and factory and sanitary legislation. In a phrase, 'Deep, far deeper than Supply-and-demand, are Laws, Obligations sacred as Man's Life itself.' Yet even the early Carlyle (pre-1850) is often regarded as a reactionary figure. It is not difficult to see why. He made fun of Plugson of Undershot, his fictitious cotton manufacturer, but felt in awe of the industrial process itself and was even capable of exalting what he called its 'Captains'. He professed to despise the backwoodsmen on their estates while still regarding the landed aristocracy as the guardians of the nation's wisdom. He maintained that 'Labour must become a seeing rational giant, with a *soul* in the body of him, and take his place on the throne of things', yet denied the working man a politically educative experience through Parliament, Chartism, the trade unions, or whatever. He believed in the emancipation of the human condition, but defined a man's liberty as being 'to learn, or to be taught, what work he actually was able for; and then by permission, persuasion, and even compulsion, to set about doing of the same!' This final paradox, implying despotism and repudiating democracy, was perhaps the most damaging of all to the coherence of Carlyle's thought and anticipated his notorious (if sometimes exaggerated) hero-worship of later years.

Yet for all its potential dangers, Carlyle's ultimately aesthetic vision of a morally ordered society was the clear forerunner of the much more consistent paternalist critique by Ruskin and the socialist critique by Morris that were offered later in the century. An aphorism like 'Man has lost his soul, and vainly seeks antiseptic salt' can be seen as either very limiting or very inspiring. Unfortunately, thinking working men for too long received this belief in such a socially blunted form that, within the all-consuming *Realpolitik* of industrialised existence, they could only see it, and all notions to do with changes of heart, as manifestly transparent and, therefore, in the last analysis, meaningless.

The crux of this inadequacy was ultimately Carlyle's nervousness, his lack of trust in the capacity and good faith of the working class acting autonomously. This defensiveness was inherited by the 'industrial' novelists who wrote under Carlyle's inspiration during the 1840s and early 1850s. As early as 1841, Charlotte Elizabeth (Mrs Tonna) wrote *Helen Fleetwood*, in which she both gave a sympathetic account of factory conditions and described socialism as 'the moral Gorgon upon which whomsoever can be compelled to look must wither away'. Four years later, Benjamin Disraeli coined the phrase 'The Two Nations', using it as the sub-title for his novel *Sybil*, and wrote that between these two peoples, the rich and the poor, 'there is no intercourse and no sympathy'. But for all its occasional vivid glimpses of the inhumanities of industrialisation, the greater part of *Sybil* remained traditionally 'silver fork', both in treatment and in message. As the landed Charles Egremont tells the heroine, daughter of a Chartist leader: 'The aristocracy of England are not tyrants, not oppressors, Sybil, as you persist in believing. . . . Enough that their sympathies are awakened; time and thought will bring the rest. They are the natural leaders of the People, Sybil, believe me, they are the only ones.' Disraeli's contribution to the ongoing 'condition-of-England' debate was certainly not negligible, but more penetrating analyses of everyday suffering followed from Elizabeth Gaskell in *Mary Barton* (1848) and *North and South* (1855), from Charles Kingsley in *Alton Locke* (1850), and from Charles Dickens in *Hard Times* (1854). Ultimately, though, all three writers, like Carlyle and Disraeli, were concerned to preserve the existing social order. Mrs Gaskell was criticised for favouring the operatives in *Mary Barton*, but she herself emphasised that 'No one can feel more deeply than I how *wicked* it is to do anything to excite class against class'; [7] Kingsley stressed, in a pamphlet called *Who are the Friends of Order?* that was published in 1852 after establishment criticism, that he and his fellow Christian Socialists were 'most eminently conservative of order, property, and all else which makes human life pleasant to its possessor, or useful to the state'; and Dickens categorically wrote to a friend in 1855 that 'The people will not bear for any length of time what they bear now. . . . I want to interpose something between them and their wrath. For this reason solely, I am a Reformer heart and soul.' [8]

All three statements help one to understand why these writers were strong on descriptive details and poetic images about the suffering of the poor, but weak on appropriate suggestions for remedial change. They were unable to overcome their middle-class prejudice against State intervention and instead put forward variations on the 'Lady Bountiful' theme. Or as Kingsley put it after an especially powerful description of street squalor, 'Go, scented Belgravian! and see what London is!' Such ostensible but confused social purpose inevitably tended in practice to reduce the working-class characters of these novels to two-dimensional, cardboard proportions, objects to be alternately commiserated with and feared. This not only rendered unconvincing these working-men archetypes, but also emphasised to a significant extent the already fraught and contradictory position on the social question that the authors had taken up.

The most central of these novels was Dickens's *Hard Times*, in which he showed many of the same virtues and defects as Mrs Gaskell: authentic compassion, hostility towards organised labour, an ultimately static social vision. In dealing with the question of industrial England, Dickens was on unfamiliar terrain, a deficiency he tried to compensate for early in 1854 by going up to Preston, where the strike of some 20,000 weavers had already been in progress for several months. He found the situation disappointingly quiet in terms of gathering material, but about the actual fact of the strike he wrote in *Household Words* on 11 February that 'In its waste of wealth that seeks to be employed, in its encroachment on the means of many thousands who are labouring from day to day, in the gulf of separation it hourly deepens between those whose interests must be understood to be identical or must be destroyed, it is a great national affliction.' And Dickens in *Hard Times* itself depicted trade unionism as a despotic force creating situations in which 'private feelings must yield to the common cause'. But whereas in the *Household Words* article he had emphasised the lack of forceful compulsion applied by unions upon working men, in the novel he has the peace-loving Stephen Blackpool sent to Coventry for declining to participate in an unstated union policy. The villain of this episode is the demagogic Slackbridge ('an ill-made high-shouldered man'), based on Mortimer Grimshaw, one of the strike leaders whom Dickens had seen in Preston. But Grimshaw was in fact an entirely untypical figure, far less influential than the more moderate George Cowell, who is entirely absent from the novel.

If this treatment of the labour question is unsatisfactory, so also is Dickens's apparently scathing critique of *laissez-faire* capitalism as it operated in Coketown. Although his own approach to specific social problems tended to be Benthamite, the removal of ugly lumps from the surface of society, Dickens realised that in practice the utilitarian doctrine also sanctioned a wealth of mechanistic, profit-making in-humanities. As Carlyle (to whom *Hard Times* was dedicated) had observed about the infamous and Benthamite New Poor Law: 'If paupers are made miserable, paupers will needs decline in multitude. It is a secret known to all rat-catchers.' [9] So what was Dickens's answer? Inevitably, humanise the Benthamites. Thus Gradgrind, happily sitting at home proving that 'the Good Samaritan was a Bad Economist', is abruptly taught the values of love and compassion by his distraught daughter. But the greatness of Dickens is that he manifestly doubts in the effectuality of such a simple solution, even while putting it forward for want of anything else. Bounderby, the bullying manu-facturer and friend of Gradgrind, does not have a change of heart; Gradgrind himself finishes up abjectly dependent on circus folk who transcend all industrial questions; and pious Stephen Blackpool con-tinues to believe that everything is 'aw a muddle', but leaves a dying prayer that 'aw th' world may on'y coom toogether more, an get a better unnerstan'in o'one another, than when I were in't my own weak seln.' It is a faint hope near the end of a deeply pessimistic book. Dickens saw industrialised society on the rack, but was unable to perceive any realistic way out. 'His hero is essentially the iron-master' [10] Ruskin once said about him. Certainly he neither questioned at a fundamental analytical level the industrialising process as such nor accepted the right of the oppressed class to adjust for itself the im-balances which that process was causing. Yet Dickens did possess a unique descriptive sensibility – and it was one which encouraged generations of working-class readers to evaluate their own condition in a way which no iron-master, however humane, could by definition have done.

Less profound is Kingsley's *Alton Locke*, the story of a self-educated London tailor working in wretched conditions who seeks to rise in society. He is repudiated, associates with violent men, and takes part in the Chartist demonstration of 10 April 1848. The events of that day are grossly distorted in the novel, which ends with the hero politically disenchanted and pliant in the hands of good Lady Ellerton, who teaches him the Christian response to society's ills. She stresses that 'there is no real rank, no real power, but worth; and worth consists not in property, but in the grace of God'. Such an apolitical approach was very different from both the fading ideology of Chartism and the increasingly thrustful artisan and lower-middle class desire for self-advancement. As Kingsley put it more explicitly in a letter written in 1852: 'the real battle of the time is . . . the Church, the gentlemen, and the workman, against the shopkeepers and the Manchester School.' [11] Yet for all his sustained attacks upon the cruel perversities of 'King *laissez-faire*', Kingsley still accepted that doctrine's cardinal tenet that strikes were worse than useless and also put forward a fraternal alternative that was in fact, as with Mrs Gaskell, Tory Paternalism in disguise. Leno, who read *Alton Locke* soon after it was published, mistakenly came to the conclusion that its author 'had genuine sympathy with the working class in their struggle for political independence',[12] and in these terms expressed his gratitude to Kingsley when he met him one day. The result was a rude rebuff. As Leno later wrote: 'His reply was to the effect that I had misunderstood his motives in writing the work in question, and, in a word, that he did not require my thanks.' Leno would not have been as shocked by this as he was if he had read more closely Alton Locke's final deferential message to his fellow-workers: 'Show that you can do justly, love mercy, and walk humbly with your God, as brothers before one Father, subjects of one crucified King – and see then whether the spirit of self-sacrifice is dead among the rich!' Lady Ellerton for her part tells Alton that the working class, in order to receive the clergy's support, must abandon the pursuit of political change and seek instead more social and improving goals. As for the Charter itself, she calmly observes that 'you made a self-willed idol of it'. This tone of mildness and reconciliation had its effect. Leno soon forgave Kingsley and subsequently wrote in his autobiography: 'I have found my satisfaction since in reading the whole of his wonderful works, and shown my gratitude by a very wearisome pilgrimage of a score of miles on a terribly hot day to his shrine and dearly loved home at Eversley.' Not even Lady Ellerton could command that much devotion.

Alton Locke was of course one part of the wider programme of propaganda issued by the Christian Socialists, who came together on the evening of 10 April 1848 and formed a coherent, active group for about six years. Its key figure in a general inspirational sense was F. D. Maurice, who, like Kingsley, was ordained in the Church of England and in 1848 held a professorship at King's College, London. His attitude towards the working class was summed up in his response to Carlyle's *Chartism*: 'They need to be directed, to be treated as *subjects*, it is true, but they also need to be sympathised with, to be treated as *brethren*.' [13] From this position – encourage, befriend, educate, but ultimately never invest – Maurice was not to veer. Nor, despite some disagreements, did J. M. Ludlow, the 'ideas' man of the group. Ludlow came back from Paris in 1848 full of French notions of co-operation, but failed to develop them to the point where productive association would be the mainspring of the State's economy rather than a voluntary, isolated activity sponsored by a minority of thinkers like himself. However, for all his theoretical advocacy of household suffrage (in opposition to Maurice), Ludlow was equally insistent that the prospective voters first show themselves worthy of the privilege. Here he was at one with Kingsley, who two days after the Kennington demonstration had placards posted up over London which concluded with the message: 'Workers of England, be wise, and then you *must* be free, for you will be *fit* to be free.' [14] This attempt to hive off the masses from direct political action was amplified during the next few years, as the Christian Socialists advanced a theory of co-operation with as much a social as an economic rationale. In the words of Maurice, from a lecture delivered in December 1850 entitled 'Reasons for Co-operation': 'Our Association-shops are schools, and very practical schools for learning obedience and government . . . for showing how a human relationship may be substituted for the mere animal connection between Driver and Slave.' [15] The inadequacy of this paternalistic replacement for the cash nexus of *laissez-faire* subsequently manifested itself both in the failure of the various associative experiments and the rapid dissolution which followed of the Christian Socialist group itself. Maurice in particular turned, perhaps with relief, to adult education proper and its many improving values. As Frederic Harrison later wrote shrewdly about the Working Men's College which was founded in 1854: 'The College has thriven and increased on the basis of the Christian Socialism of Maurice and the muscular Christianity of Tom Hughes, as a useful and well-conducted school of secondary education on the established and moderate lines, with some Christianity, a little arm-chair Socialism, and a mild infusion of real working men.' [16] But to the men of 1854 at least half the battle seemed won: the ghost of Kennington was laid and what remained, within a prosperous economic climate, was the continuing piecemeal task of moral re-generation and thus social reconciliation.

However, mention of what was to turn into the 'Rochdale argument' recalls the Pioneers of 1844 and prompts one to wonder whether perhaps a great chance to implement their ideals was lost in the early 1850s. In an obvious sense, of course, the socially conservative assumptions of the Christian Socialists precluded at the outset their bringing into being anything genuinely self-creating. Thus Ernest Jones's hostile reaction to their Society for Promoting Working Men's Associations, which was founded in June 1850 and eventually guided the erratic fortunes of twelve small productive societies, consisting of tailors, shoe-makers, builders, piano-makers, smiths and bakers. Jones strongly criticised these societies as apolitical, profit-seeking, and isolated from the rest of the working class. As he wrote with typical incisiveness in the *Northern Star* in August 1850, 'the experience of eighteen centuries' had shown clearly that 'co-operation, however salutary and successful, that abstinence, mortality and toil, that all the efforts of united industry and intelligence are ineffectual to remove the dead weight of misery, so long as the sharp sword of monopoly power is wielded by one dominating class'. But as we have seen, this total approach, demanding a basic change in property relations, was becoming increasingly less influential. Moreover, it seemed early in 1852 that a major breakthrough in co-operative consciousness had been achieved, when the Christian Socialists, in the process of supporting (albeit reluctantly) the ASE's strike action, apparently managed to wean that Society away from the blinkered sectionalism under which it had been conceived. In April, after the defeat of the strike, the Executive of the Engineers added these observations to various specific resolutions: 'We have learned that it is not sufficient to accumulate funds, that it is necessary also to use them reproductively; and if this lesson does not fail in its effects, a few years will see the land studded with workshops belonging to the workers.' [17]

Yet the lesson did 'fail in its effects' – miserably. The prime cause, predictably enough, was the unwavering paternalism of the Christian Socialists, who first inspired these workshop idylls, but then insisted not only that the projects should be financially dependent upon rich philanthropists like Edward Neale, but also that part of this dependence should involve the confinement of union activities to the maintenance of welfare benefits and nothing else. The Executive of the ASE accepted these terms in April 1852 and explicitly condemned the use of strikes at the same time as they pledged themselves to associative workshops. By so doing they jettisoned that great majority of workmen for whom the need to be able to strike was a fundamental imperative in the struggle to stay alive. And soon afterwards, the rank-and-file of the ASE flatly declined to support the notion of co-operative engineering workshops. The result was to strand middle-class idealists like Neale and Ludlow, who were forced increasingly to participate in schemes for consumers' rather than producers' co-operation. As Neale complained years later, in 1870: 'the noble idea conceived by the Rochdale Pioneers of regenerating society from top to bottom . . . has given place to the desire to obtain good articles at the cheapest possible price.' [18] Neale's grievance was understandable, but barely justified, for there was never any chance of transcending the competitive ethic of society without first genuinely appreciating the needs of the men who suffered under it. And Kingsley showed this awareness when in 1856 he sent to Hughes a bitter-sweet obituary notice of the Christian Socialist movement: 'If I'd had £100,000, I'd have, and should have, staked and lost it all in 1848–50. I should, Tom, for my heart was and is in it, and you'll see it will beat yet; but we ain't the boys. We don't see but half the bull's eye yet. . . . Still, *some* somedever, it's in the fates, that Association is the pure caseine, and must be eaten by the human race if it would save its soul alive.' [19]

About this time, the middle part of the 1850s, the intellectual focus of the period tended to move away from the trauma of 1848 and industrial soul-searching towards the dilemma of 1867 and cultural bolstering. The Christian Socialists were, as an active group, eventually succeeded by the Positivists, the English followers of the French philosopher Auguste Comte, who died in 1857. Three in particular stood out: E. S. Beesly, a Professor at University College, London; Frederic Harrison, lawyer and writer; and J. H. Bridges, an active sanitary reformer in the Bradford area. All exiles from Wadham College, Oxford, they now reassembled in the early 1860s as a direct response to the questions of social conflict raised by the strike of London builders. Following Comte, they preached the gospel of humanity and sociological reform, scornful of revealed religion, co-operative panaceas, or recourse to the 'squires and rectors', as Beesly called them in 1862 in an attack on Kingsley. It was an accommodating and commonsensical doctrine that made a special appeal to the self-advancing sort of working man; and it appeared to place the Positivists firmly within the developing political consciousness of the New Model unions. Thus it was Beesly who, addressing the working-class audience at an impressive pro-Federal meeting in London in March 1863, hailed the gathering 'as proof that you will no longer, in the absorbing interests of industrial questions, lose sight of those political questions which concern your class most vitally, though they may not seem to come home so palpably to each one of you'. [20] Furthermore, after that respectabilising political ambition was achieved, the household suffrage of 1867, it was Harrison who stemmed the threat of the Sheffield outrages by sitting on the subsequent Royal Commission. There, after making the best possible use of Applegarth's evident moderation as a witness, he then produced the influential minority report which was soon to legalise the position of trade unions. It would be wrong, however, to think of the Positivists solely as skilled practitioners of the absorptive parliamentary process. For example, the striking letter by Bridges in 1867 to the *Bradford Review*, emphasising the need for the working class's political independence, was merely one reiteration of what Beesly had been saying for a long time. But as we have seen, the message failed to bear any immediate fruit. The reason for this suggests similarities with the Christian Socialist failure in 1852: namely, the lack of a tough economic or industrial policy that took into account the perennially demoralising realities faced by the hundreds of thousands of unimproving workers who formed the major part of their class. The Positivists were too partial to arbitration as a means of ending strikes, too inclined to believe in the omnipotence of education, and too prone to accept the nineteenth-century materialist progressive myth. As Harrison noted in his diary in 1861 during a tour of the industrial North: 'Wonderful, indeed, is that skill of brain and of hand of the workman! How enduring, how dextrous, how docile he is. What a world of energy and combination it is. What an opening for improvement – what a boundless career before them, employers and employed.' [21] Smoke got in Harrison's eyes and the clear-sightedness of his vision suffered accordingly.

Less influential, but indicative of the crucial failure of the intellectuals to come to constructive terms with the gathering forces of democracy, were the reactions of three guardians of culture – George Eliot, the late Carlyle, and Matthew Arnold – to the 1865–7 Reform crisis. George Eliot, a Positivist in sympathy but unable to accept that philosophy's penchant for uniform solutions, brought out in June 1866 her 'political' novel, *Felix Holt, The Radical*. Her position in the book is essentially paternalistic and assumes the existence of a slowly changing but intricately ordered society. As the artisan hero asserts after being involved in an unprepossessing riot: 'If there's anything our people want convincing of, it is, that there's some dignity and happiness for a man other than changing his station.' Moreover, in a peculiarly unconvincing scene in which he speaks against a trade unionist possessed of 'mere acuteness and rather hard-lipped antagonism', Felix repudiates the pursuit of political power by the working class as being certain to lead to corruption and debasement. This unhelpful attitude, falling back on education and social improvement, was confirmed in January 1868 when John Blackwood issued Felix Holt's imaginary *Address to the Working Men*, which he had commissioned from George Eliot soon after the passing of the Second Reform Act. In it,[22] there is the usual emphses on the complexity of the organism called society, a warning about the disastrous consequences

of attacking 'the classes who hold the treasures of knowledge', a call
to the working men to turn 'Class Interests into Class Functions or
duties', and an underlying lack of faith in their ability to act both
independently and honourably. Blackwood himself said it all when,
on receiving the proofs of the address, he expressed the wish that 'the
poor fellows were capable of appreciating it' and added that 'if they
were we should be all right'.[23]

If George Eliot only at an unrealistic price kept her nerve about the
apparent coming of mass democracy, then both Carlyle and Arnold
seemed to lose theirs entirely. Carlyle's famous article, 'Shooting
Niagara: and After?', appeared in *Macmillan's Magazine* in August
1867. One extract is sufficient to convey its febrile tone: 'Inexpressibly
delirious seems to me, at present in my solitude, the puddle of Parliament and Public upon what it calls the "Reform Measure"; that is
to say, the calling in of new supplies of blockheadism, gullibility,
bribeability, amenability to beer and balderdash.' And even more
sternly: 'The intellect of a man who believes in the possibility of
"improvement" by such a method is to me a finished off and shut up
intellect, with which I would not argue: mere waste of wind between
us to exchange words on that class of topics.' A similar narrowing of
horizons, seeking vainly to retrench, was also manifested at this time
by Matthew Arnold. His response to the Hyde Park demonstration of
July 1866 was tremulous, leading him in the first edition of *Culture and
Anarchy* (1869) to cite approvingly the Roman way of dealing with
riots – namely, 'flog the rank and file, and fling the ring-leaders from
the Tarpeian rock!' Moreover, in the book as a whole, Arnold adopts
a generally prejudicial attitude towards the working class, stressing
its susceptibility to violent demagogues and the likelihood that it will
arrive 'at the banquet of the future without having on a wedding
garment'. This weakness is mitigated, however, by the overall quality
of Arnold's analysis of society and his ringing advice to the working
class to stay clear of insensate middle-class leaders like Bright who
were seeking to shape a democracy based on quantitative, manufacturing values. Nor is Arnold a quasi-feudal paternalist in the
Kingsley mould. Instead, he believes in the State as the guardian of
culture, being the truest expression of man's 'best self', which is, in
Arnold's Rousseau-like words, 'not manifold, and vulgar, and unstable,
and contentious, and ever-varying, but one, and noble, and secure,
and peaceful, and the same for all mankind'. It is an exciting but
inadequate vision, for Arnold set his mind obstinately against the
notion of a pluralistic, self-renewing society. Moreover, his analysis
entirely lacks the economic depth which was clearly indispensable if
his monolithic ideal was to be achieved. But above all, his dream of the
State embodying in some mysterious way the values of high culture

('sweetness and light') conceived not at all of the broader, more indigenous cultural traditions that needed to be sustained if an industrialised population was to remain generate. These deficiencies make Arnold pale by comparison with J. S. Mill, the other major social thinker of the 1860s vitally concerned with the outcome of the Reform crisis.

It is easy to underestimate Mill, son of the Benthamite James Mill and maker of such Ure-like pronouncements as 'it is the common error of Socialists to overlook the natural indolence of mankind' and 'to be protected against competition is to be protected in idleness, in mental dullness'. Moreover, in the same book, *The Principles of Political Economy* (first published in 1848 and thereafter constantly revised and reissued), Mill cites as justified the description by a Swiss manufacturer of the English working class as 'the most disorderly, debauched, and unruly, and least respectable and trustworthy of any nation whatsoever whom we have employed'. Yet Mill simultaneously insisted, which most of his Benthamite contemporaries did not, that such a condition was understandable, demanding education and above all mutuality if it was to be changed. As he wrote in a memorable and revealing passage, which saw him rise far above the predominating Manchester liberalism of his day, he was by no means convinced 'that the trampling, crushing, elbowing, and treading on each other's heels, which form the existing type of social life, are the most desirable lot of human kind, or anything but the disagreeable symptoms of one of the phases of industrial progress'. Moreover, he defined 'social improvement' as being 'a state of society combining the greatest personal freedom with that just distribution of the fruits of labour, which the present laws of property do not profess to aim at'. At roughly this point began Mill's long and tortuous relationship with the coming of political democracy, which he saw as in itself desirable, but yet potentially incompatible with individual liberty, the primacy of the best, and his own peculiarly charged, atomistic background. His was the hopeless task of a man trying, in Marx's words, 'to reconcile irreconcilables' and in the end forced to concentrate on practicalities. Thus from an article published posthumously [24] in which he sought ostensibly to decide whether the existing economic system or Socialism offered 'the greatest resources for overcoming the inevitable difficulties of life', Mill concluded in a thoroughly limiting way that 'the intellectual and moral grounds of Socialism deserve the most attentive study, as affording in many cases the guiding principles of the improvements necessary to give the present economic system of society its best chance'. Such an evolutionary view, assuming the gradual humanising of capitalism, was critically at odds with his own awareness of the human evils caused by the free play of market forces, let alone Marx's perceptions about the inevitable

spread of large and impersonal financial groupings. This absence of
the apocalyptic on Mill's part was confirmed in July 1866 in dramatic,
culminating circumstances. As Radical MP for Westminster and a good
friend to the self-improving figures in the labour movement, he was
asked to address the crowd that was threatening to re-enter Hyde Park.
He proceeded to put to them two chillingly formal questions: did they
want revolution? and could they carry it through if they so desired?
This raising of the stakes was not dissimilar, though in a different vein,
to the military protection of the capital on 10 April 1848. Moreover,
the tactic worked again, for a mass meeting was instead subsequently
held at the Agricultural Hall, Islington. And as Mill noted a few years
later in his *Autobiography*, with a disappointing illiberality towards
open-ended change, 'at this crisis I really believe that I was the means
of preventing much mischief'.

From completely different intellectual origins came John Ruskin, the
greatest of the mid-Victorian prophets, who began his autobiography,
Praeterita, with the words: 'I am, and my father was before me, a
violent Tory of the old school.' Another time he maintained it as a
cardinal principle that 'all forms of government are good just so far as
they attain this one vital necessity of policy – *that the wise and kind,
few or many, shall govern the unwise and unkind*'.[25] Perhaps inevitably,
then, Ruskin saw the working class in an essentially dependent role
and tended to concentrate, until eventual disenchantment took over,
on morally regenerating the natural aristocracy of the country. He
was indifferent towards the labour movement's attempt to acquire
strength on its own account and scornful of those who looked ex-
pectantly to the vote. As he put it in *Time and Tide* (a series of public
letters written during 1867 itself and addressed to Thomas Dixon, an
infinitely deferential corkcutter living in Sunderland): 'Your voices
are not worth a rat's squeak, either in Parliament or out of it, till you
have some ideas to utter with them; and when you have the thoughts,
you will not want to utter them, for you will see that your way to the
fulfilling of them does not lie through speech.' Yet the fact remains
that a questionnaire sent in 1906 to that year's Labour and Lib.-Lab.
MPs revealed that the single book which had done most to shape their
beliefs was Ruskin's *Unto this Last*. In this work, originally serialised
in 1860 in the *Cornhill Magazine*, but dropped because of middle-class
outrage, he went beyond Carlyle (second in the poll) by arguing with
great lucidity the inhumane *and* unnecessary value system of *laissez-
faire* economics. Here, and in a torrent of subsequent publications,
letters and speeches, Ruskin put forward and demonstrated his propositions: production and consumption are inextricably related, supply
and demand do not exist as autonomous iron laws, 'there is no wealth

but Life'. Or in the words of his celebrated question: 'If the whole of England were turned into a mine, would it be richer or poorer ?' [26] Furthermore, Ruskin substituted in place of individualism an embryonic Welfare State, including State education, old age pensions, and a greater number of public works. Nor was this a soft-sell to keep the workers politically quiescent, for Ruskin during the latter part of his active life strenuously sought to emancipate the condition of the industrialised individual. Even in his days as an art critic, he had written the remarkable 'On the Nature of Gothic' chapter in *The Stones of Venice* which included the seminal utterance that 'all human work is dependent for its beauty on the happy life of the workman . . . you must either make a tool of the creature or a man of him . . . you cannot do both'. Then in the 1870s Ruskin tried to put his vision of an organic community into practice in a series of experiments, most prominently the St George's Guild near Sheffield. They all failed, but as Ruskin insisted, he could only hope to achieve 'mere raft-making in the midst of irrevocable wreck'.[27] Yet this was perhaps the point: by the time that Ruskin's greatest disciple, William Morris, began his practical political endeavours, the forms of industrial society, and the burrowing working-class response towards them, were shaped in too deep a mould to be changed. G. B. Shaw in later years expressed himself grateful towards his fellow-Fabian Sidney Webb, without whom he felt [28] he would have turned into 'a mere literary wisecracker like Carlyle or Ruskin'. This they were not, but the fact that Shaw believed them to be so and turned against them was indicative of the failure of the mid-Victorian intellectuals. All had criticised in one way or another the ethical assumptions of middle-class capitalism, yet out of the halcyon years of that capitalism there emerged the makings of a reformist tradition, devoted to status, efficiency and infiltration, against which Morris's stringently Socialist morality was to come too late to tell.

Chapter 3

TRANSITION

1868 — 1880

'*I had a challenge last Monday night*
Billy Gladstone wanted me to fight;
The challenge was brought by Jackey Bright
To poor old Benjamin Dizzy.' [1]

This verse from a contemporary broadside entitled *Dizzy's Lament*, seems in a political sense to have been fairly typical of middle-to-late Victorian street literature: part hero-worshipping, part irreverent, ultimately deferential. As such, the tone accords with the traditional view which sees this period, the 1870s especially, as above all the age of Gladstone and Disraeli. So perhaps it was. Certainly between 1868 and 1880 each man enjoyed in turn a period of six years as Prime Minister and during that time cultivated a popular-based, polarising image unique up till then in British politics. 'Everywhere the proletariat is the tag, rag and bobtail of the official parties' [2] wrote Engels in disgust after the 1868 Election. The charisma of the two leaders, still far more important than the growing party organisations, deepened this political dependence during the next decade. And significantly, Engels added in 1868 that 'if any party has gained strength from the new voters, it is the Tories'. The key area in this respect was Lancashire, which in 1865 returned three more Liberals than Conservatives, but in 1868 eleven less. This new Conservative tended to be strongly Protestant, worked as a manufacturing operative, and was distinctly cynical of the Manchester brand of Radicalism epitomised by industrialists like Bright. He has been well described as 'the man for whom Blackpool was soon to be built' and 'strangely unlike the Yorkshireman'.[3] Yet it is the electorally less volatile Yorkshireman who remains a more central figure in the history of the late nineteenth-century labour movement. Instinctively a Gladstonian Liberal, as befitted his generally more skilled occupation and thus vested social position, he yet formed the active nucleus of the independent third party which evolved at the end of the century. The primary cause of this was to be the increasing conflict of interests (rather than ideologies) between himself and his employer, which in the end the Liberal Party was unable to reconcile. As early as the 1870s, however, there existed an *awareness* of independence on the part of this Liberal working man. He voted steadfastly for Gladstone but preferred to participate in politics through his chapel, his union, his co-operative society or whatever rather than through the invariably middle-class local Liberal association. Sturdy deference of this sort inclines one to treat the 1870s (still a very under-researched decade) in terms of paradox and transition. Many situations were apparently on the turn. The mass of vertical craft structures remained dominant in a still essentially fluid, homogeneous society, but were beginning to yield just somewhat to a more monolithic, horizontally based industrial proletariat. Trade union leaders continued to maintain Junta-type tactics, but found themselves increasingly at odds with local rank-and-file militancy. And radical dissent from Liberal orthodoxies existed, but tended to be more populist in character than Socialist. In other words, at an often more obscure level than that of high politics there were taking place during the 1870s protean developments whose muted resolution act almost as an epitome for the entire half-century.

The end of the Reform League came swiftly after its secret electoral pact of 1868 with the Liberals. The Radical secularist Charles Bradlaugh unequivocally attacked Howell for his treacherous complicity and, in a state of confusion and recrimination, the League dissolved early in 1869. Its successor was the Labour Representation League, an amalgam of metropolitan labour groups brought together in August 1869 by Robert Latham, a Radical lawyer practising in London. Its specific determining context was the way in which, earlier in 1869, both Odger and Potter had been forced by rival Liberal candidates to retire from by-elections at Stafford and Nottingham respectively. From these rather narrow origins the League never really recovered. At heart, its leaders were more than happy to be accommodated into the mainstream of British political life, but occasionally, when the local Liberal associations proved more than usually non-compliant, they ventured to assume a quixotic, unconvincing independence. After the publication of a discreet manifesto in August 1869 and pending the official inauguration, Bradlaugh did try to persuade the League to adopt a more aggressive programme, but was defeated on 4 November when Odger, backed by Allan as Treasurer and also Applegarth, successfully moved a resolution that 'the state of the country proves the faults of class legislation'.[4] Latham as President then sealed the move towards moderation when he stated that the purpose of the League was 'the harmonising of working men's interests with those of the general community in order that the growth of the nation in prosperity and intelligence shall embrace all classes'. Not surprisingly, given such flaccid premises, the bulk of provincial trade union leaders virtually boycotted the League and preferred instead to apply themselves to safeguarding the position of their own movement. As early as 1869 the Positivists had held a meeting to secure unionist support for Harrison's Minority Report, which was in disagreement with the majority of the Royal Commission in its conclusion that the unions should receive protection by coming under common rather than criminal law. At this meeting, Beesly defied the presence of Samuel Morley in the chair and spoke strongly in favour of class conflict, even referring at one stage to 1848 and the 'Days of June'. Of this moment, Harrison subsequently wrote to Beesly: 'Your speech was excellent – Something quite startling – How Karl Marx grinned a ghastly grin – and S. Morley a sickly smile.' [5] Morley's apprehension was not unjustified: as the campaign against the anti-union legislation gathered momentum in the early 1870s, the general acquiescence which had permitted Howell's pact of 1868 became transformed into a mood momentarily far tougher and uncompromising.

For some time, however, the entrenched labour leaders successfully conducted a holding operation against the popular tide. During 1870, with the Liberal government failing to produce its promised labour legislation, the London Trades Council bitterly disappointed those delegates of the second TUC (held at Birmingham in August 1869) who had entrusted it with the task of convening the next Congress in London. No Congress was in fact held in 1870. The LTC itself, virtually the body of the Junta, further maintained its position during this year by means of the *Bee-Hive*, already under a Liberal owner and now edited less by Potter than by the Rev. Henry Solly, a veteran founder of working-men's clubs and institutes. The Solly philosophy was summed up in the edition of 19 February 1870, when he declared that the newspaper sought 'to make England's Beehive resound with the voices of the working bees rejoicing in cheerful labour and well-earned reward, true to their brother bees of every class, and to the Queen Bee on her honoured throne'. Regular series under Solly included 'Men who have Risen', 'Extracts from *Punch*', and the ultra-submissive 'Letters to Statesmen'. On New Year's Eve 1870 there even appeared a laudatory article under the heading 'The Origin of Prussian Greatness'. Early in 1871, however, things changed. Pratt as publisher ran into financial difficulties, Solly departed from the paper, and Potter, albeit in a more sober guise, returned as editor. Still more significantly, the government in February brought out its proposed Bill which, although protecting union funds, in effect made picketing a criminal offence. Suddenly the Junta tradition of cautious moderation lost its relevance. At the ensuing TUC, held in London at the beginning of March, the presence of a record forty-nine unions, aggrieved and now thoroughly impatient of negative delaying tactics, proved decisive. The Junta passed away as a cohesive group (the Conference of Amalgamated Trades dissolving itself a few months later), while at this Congress a Parliamentary Committee was established to further union interests at Westminster. Soon afterwards this resolve was justified and hardened when Parliament passed the Criminal Law Amendment Act, duly outlawing picketing and so providing the battlefield for the next four years of labour politics.

Confirmation of a new post-Junta era came when the TUC met again at Nottingham in January 1872. Northern delegates dominated the proceedings, showing a grittiness and determination which permanently alienated one middle-class observer, Thomas Hughes, from the trade union movement. Furthermore, when the question arose of choosing the year's Parliamentary Committee, the Congress identified the unlucky Potter, who had been Chairman, with the Junta in London and firmly rejected his candidature; while the more fortunate Howell, Secretary of the 1871 Committee, just managed to scrape sufficient votes. The dominant figure at the Congress, and elected overwhelmingly to the Committee, was Alexander MacDonald, founder of the National Miners' Association and pledged by the assembly to secure total repeal of the recent Act. In practice, however, the suspect Howell and favoured MacDonald formed a close working partnership during the spring and early summer of 1872. With their colleagues almost all northern-based and generally absent from the lobbies in London, each man found in the other a penchant for social climbing and artful politicking. The upshot, after lengthy negotiations with the Liberal MP for Oxford, W. V. Harcourt, came in May with a proposed compromise Bill, removing certain prejudicial clauses from the Criminal Law Amendment Act, but failing entirely to provide for the specific legislation of peaceful picketing. The scheme met a deserved fate. Beesly at once attacked the amendment for discharging the Liberals far too lightly from their obligations; the government took advantage of the ensuing row to drop the Bill altogether; and in January 1873, at the TUC held in Leeds, Howell especially received heavy criticism. He managed to weather this storm, but it was indicative that when Congress chose the year's Parliamentary Committee, the group of moderate candidates from 'New Model' craft societies put forward by the LTC – men like Henry Broadhurst, George Shipton and J. D. Prior – all finished nowhere in the voting. In the spring of 1873, A. J. Mundella, Liberal MP for Sheffield and one of the working man's most prominent patrons, recognised the swelling desire for legal redress when he changed from his non-committal attitude of a year earlier and agreed to sponsor a Bill repealing the Act. The government then proceeded to hive off the new Bill – with the result than on Whit Monday there took place in Hyde

Park a mass demonstration of protest attended, according to the *Daily Telegraph*, by over 100,000 people. At this point, with the unions apparently enlarging their bargaining power all the time on the peak of a rapidly expanding market following the economic trough of the late 1860s, an 'explosion' of popular consciousness actually seemed not impossible. That this is not an entirely idle suggestion is shown by various other militant tendencies which had been manifesting themselves at the same time as the campaign against the anti-union legislation.

A distinctive phase of relatively subterranean history began in September 1869 when, in the general context of high unemployment in England and Gladstone's proposed land legislation for Ireland, J. S. Mill founded the Land Tenure Reform Association. It had a largely middle-class membership and sought to implement Mill's vision of small-scale peasant proprietorships. Altogether different was the Land and Labour League, which began a month later, aimed to nationalise the land, and enjoyed a much more federal, popular basis. It soon came under the active influence of Marx, and indeed its leading figures – John Weston, Martin J. Boon and George Eccarius – were all members of the General Council of the International. The attitude of the established trade union leaders and their associates was changeable, but tended to favour the more moderate body founded by Mill. The difference between them was illustrated early in 1870 when both Potter and Applegarth proposed in the *Bee-Hive* that the best way to cope with the problem of the jobless was for unskilled labour to emigrate in large numbers. Boon criticised these suggestions vigorously and stressed they were merely another example of the aristocratic craft societies attempting to suppress the sweated threat from below. He further insisted that emigration was in general the panacea put forward by the idle rich to solve the question of over-population. Or in the flamboyant, home colonising words of the Land and Labour League's Inaugural Address of 1869: 'If green fields and kitchen gardens are incompatible with the noble sport of hunting, let the hunters emigrate.' This sort of language, evoking the familiar mixture of a lost rural paradise and anti-aristocratic animus, had particular appeal for the many thousands in the East End made almost destitute by the sudden collapse of the London shipbuilding industry. The wave of bitterness this produced was generally Republican in tone, brought to a head by Queen Victoria's refusal to subscribe to the relief fund for those affected. As a result of all this, a great part of the politically conscious working class was activating during 1870 almost entirely at cross purposes with its nominal leadership. Mill realised this earlier than most when, in the spring of 1870, he tried to broaden the basis of his

Association by formally repudiating the 'unearned increment' of the land-owning class. The gambit proved a failure: Mill's Association never acquired a popular following and indeed was not to hold its first (and only) public meeting until May of the following year. But before then, while the moderate reformers waited patiently in the wings, the rival Land and Labour League, paradigm of the 1870s, rose and fell like a rocket in the sky.

Events in France held the key. On 4 September 1870, after the Prussian victory at Sedan and Louis Napoleon's abdication as Emperor, the French Republic was proclaimed in Paris. Less than a week later, a large working-class meeting held in London gave it full support. Other demonstrations followed, all demanding that Gladstone formally recognise the Republic. Also in September, Daniel Chatterton provided the Land and Labour League with an effective organ by founding the *Republican*, which began monthly but was before long coming out each week. This new paper, hostile to the whole accommodating tradition once epitomised by the Reform League and now by the Labour Representation League, helped to stimulate a period of remarkable growth on the part of the working-class Republican movement. During the autumn three new clubs were begun in London, while in the early part of 1871 a body of provincial support built up, especially in the South and West. For a short time, phrases like 'that knavery called liberalism' (one of the *Republican*'s) actually seemed to carry some substantive weight. There is recorded an episode which caught exactly the flavour of the movement at its height. It came early in 1871 when Howell, bravely addressing a Land and Labour League meeting in the East End, asked the rhetorical question: 'Would Englishmen have surrendered at Metz?' To which a powerful voice boomed out from the audience: 'Yus, if they had been led by the Duke o' Cambridge.' [6]

Soon, however, the League passed into dissension and oblivion. The turning-point came in February 1871 with the formation of the revolutionary Paris Commune. Support for a radical social recon-struction represented a very different type of cause from attacking aristocratic privilege or upholding the freedom of a people from Prussian oppression. Working-class response to the Commune was not so much hostile as incomprehending. Dunning, for example, observed in April that the Communards must be insane since they were actually contemplating the abolition of rent; and there was a significant contrast between the absence of trade union contributions to the International's Relief Fund for refugees from the Commune and the £600 which was raised about the same time for Antwerp cigar-makers on strike. Moreover, there was little coherent advice offered by the leaders of the Republican movement, who differed acutely over the question of military intervention on behalf of the Commune. In this

situation, with a chasm opening between the socialist International and
the pro-French but inexorably respectabilising labour movement,
Odger, a disenchanted member of Mill's Association, attempted to hold
the ring. But fierce personal attacks by the *Republican* drove him back in
June 1871 to his former allegiance. Soon afterwards there drained away
almost the last vestiges of active working-class support for Marx's
International. As Howell wrote complacently several years later in an
article about that body: 'The attempt to engraft continental notions on
English ideas is absurd and certain of failure – the talk about "pro-
letarians" and "solidarity" is confusing to the English mind, they are
big words which do not convey a single idea to British workmen.' [7]
In terms of men like himself, this diagnosis was certainly true. One
has only to read of Applegarth carrying a resolution through the LRL
in 1871, condemning certain remarks hostile to the Royal Family made
by a 'spokesman' of the working class, to appreciate the residual
strength of loyalty, moderation and ideological insularity. The villain
was Bradlaugh, author that year of *The Impeachment of the House of
Brunswick*. However, the sudden collapse of the Republican movement
should not be attributed solely to the inability of the labouring ranks
to harness their relatively mundane concerns to the more free-ranging
mandates of certain middle-class Radicals. Bradlaugh in fact not only
disassociated himself in 1871 from the Land and Labour League
because of the unacceptable extremism of the Paris Commune, but
also throughout his career repudiated as too narrow all doctrines of
class conflict and preferred to call himself, in Wilkesian phrase, a 'man
of the people'. In this sense he merely exemplified the transitional
aspect of the 1870s, an era of sporadically impressive vigour but
ultimately handicapped by an inability to see beyond the pawns on the
other side of the board. The pattern of this activity was uneven, but on
the whole upwards until the economic depression which began in 1873
and set in hard during the latter part of the decade. Therein lay the
significance of the 'new unionism' of 1871–2, embryonic forerunner of
the much better-known adult version of 1889–90. Although succumbing
to many of the sectional and psychological weaknesses of longer-
established trade unionism, it nevertheless in patches pointed the way
ahead to a potentially more thorough-going proletarian future.

The long struggle for a nine-hour day undertaken by Newcastle
engineering workers in 1871 provided the spur for this wave of activity
on the part of hitherto unorganised labour. The strike on Tyneside was
a wholly organic one, arising very much from discontent inside the
engineering workshops and sustained thereafter by largely non-union
men. Its leaders tended to draw on a wide-based popular appeal,
typified by John Burnett, a cricketer and chorister of local standing as
well as a union official and founder of the Nine Hours League. Sig-

nificantly, when men from the London headquarters of the ASE tried to assume control of the strike, they met with nothing but hostility. Results justified this attitude, for by the end of the year the employers had given way; and this notable success then triggered off an astonishing response throughout the country. Between that year, 1871, and the conclusive end of the short economic boom, 1875, unions were established by agricultural labourers, dockers, gas-stokers, car-men, cab and omnibus drivers, railwaymen, sailors, firemen, brick- and tile-makers, box-makers, builders' labourers and coal trimmers. All were to evaporate or be severely emaciated with the onset of the depression. Nevertheless, important personal as well as economic causes explain this sudden collapse and subsequent virtual disappearance for the next decade-and-a-half. The problem was essentially one of method: namely, how suitable was the New Model technique, operating on closed, vertical principles, for the great mass of unskilled and therefore potentially undifferentiated labour? The 1870s gave the answer. Whereas the skilled aristocrats sought exclusiveness, with all its trimmings of high dues and benefits, administrative centralisation, and a cautious industrial policy, the best hope for the numerous unskilled, who were generally under-employed, lay in exploiting the labour shortage at times of flourishing trade. This in practice meant militancy, which in temporarily propitious economic circumstances was capable of forcing employers to conciliate the sweated millions as well as the better-ensconsed skilled thousands. Too often in the early 1870s, however, the implications of this crucial difference of approach remained hidden. And to reiterate a familiar theme, the primary reason for this was the way in which these new unions were compelled to rely on largely irrelevant advice and leadership.

Three specific examples illustrate this millstone. The first concerned that traditionally deferential group, the railwaymen. In 1871 the Amalgamated Society of Railway Servants was founded under the auspices of M. T. Bass, the brewer and Liberal MP for Derby. It was a horizontal 'all grades' union and within a year had a membership of over 17,000. From that point, however, it fell away and by 1882 was down to less than 6,000. The explanation is clear. Bass only envisaged the Society in terms of paying out friendly benefits and applying pressure on Parliament to reduce working hours because of the danger of accidents. Not surprisingly, the rank-and-file soon lost interest in such a narrow perspective and, after several unofficial strikes, forsook the disciplines of organised unionism. Similar misguidance was the fate of the General Amalgamated Labourers' Union, founded by Patrick Kenney in 1872 after unskilled London builders had managed to secure, after a lock-out, a pay increase of $\frac{1}{2}$d an hour. Membership quickly rose to 5,000, but again there took place the steep and sudden decline. This time the figure chiefly responsible was Applegarth of the Carpenters, who, when asked to help, imposed 'amalgamated' principles on the new union, with disastrous consequences. In 1873 some fourteen out of a total of twenty lodges refused to hand over money when Kenney came to centralise the union's funds; and that was that. The third example, more complex, centres in Liverpool, traditionally a hive of rough, almost feudalised Protestant Toryism. In 1872, however, a myriad of deprived groups, including dockers, street sweepers and needlewomen, all pressed hard for wage increases. Some ephemeral successes were scored, but in the end there emerged no lasting organisation to carry these workers through the harder times ahead. One of the reasons for this was the as yet unresolved sectionalism within the groups themselves. To take the dockers alone, it is a striking fact that in 1872 three types of porters (cotton, provision, and grain warehouse) militated separately and in an entirely uncoordinated way for higher wages. The more important cause of long-term failure, however, was the excessive dependence upon two inadequate leaders. One was James Samuelson, a seed-crushing industrialist who sought to encourage New Model unionism among unskilled workers in order to further peaceful relations. The other was William Simpson, a self-made confectioner who, in the Tory populist tradition, encouraged the poor man to defend his rights, but at the same time deplored strikes and took no interest in organised unionism. Together these two men spoke up for the oppressed of Liverpool and, provided the oppressed did not resort to strike action (as the carters and omnibus men boldly did), represented them not unskilfully at negotiations with employers. But it was hardly enough – as is shown by a comparison with the sort of leadership which was being provided at the same time for the unskilled of London's East End.

The Labour Protection League was formed late in 1871 after an initiative taken by Patrick Hennessey, first President of the Land and Labour League. It sought to better the pay of London's waterfront workers and was so successful that by October of the following year it had 30,000 members, some of whom were affiliated builders' and engineers' labourers. In economic conditions ideal for rapid and effective strike action, the League began by dealing with the miserably low wages paid on the wharfs and then moved on during the summer of 1872 to the docks proper. For several months progress was almost miraculously unchecked. The leaders of the League, unlike most of their trade union contemporaries, did not mince words about the intensity of the struggle that was taking place. For example, Thomas Venner, a colleague of Hennessey's at the outset, described the Wharfingers Association in June 1872 as 'a society to keep down the price of labour' and one which 'did not seem to value their human

commodity as they did their merchandise'.[8] This rigorous approach
was confirmed soon afterwards when Charles Keen, a leading figure in
the British remnant of the International as well as Secretary of the
League, severely turned on the more moderate Rev. Hansard, Rector
of Bethnal Green and another of the League's founding fathers.
Hansard's innocent crime was that of presenting the Prince of Wales
with an address of loyalty on behalf of the League at the opening of the
Bethnal Green Branch of the South Kensington Museum. Then in
November 1872 Keen assembled spokesmen from a variety of London's
unskilled labour groups, including delegates from the League itself, to
form one Amalgamated Labour Union. But these powerful ambitions
came to nothing, almost certainly because of the ensuing depression.
Unlike the Liverpool instance, it is reasonable in this case to treat
economic circumstances as a fairly blanket explanation for the collapse
of organised unskilled labour. Certainly the Labour Protection League
had experienced difficulties throughout – fragmented interests, local
job-preserving, 'aristocratic' stevedores – but on the whole its leaders
had merged extremely skilfully wider political goals with prevailing
and often very individual short-term sectional concerns. Now in 1873,
however, with trade in decline and employers of unskilled labour back
in control, there was needed more than ever independent political
leadership and a strong, unilaterally-motivated trade union movement.
Why these blessings in sore times were not available is to a considerable
extent explained by seeing how, and with what fateful consequences,
other more established unions had responded to the favourable climate
of the early 1870s.

It has only quite recently been realised what adroit use employers
made in the 1870s of the concept of arbitration. Working at its smoothest
it meant talking instead of striking; wages being held steady while the
process of settlement took place; and the establishment of the principle
that wages were dependent on the varying price of the commodity
produced, which was very different from the notion of a minimum
standard wage autonomous of supply-and-demand considerations. It
is easy to see the sort of appeal which arbitration made to improving
labour leaders. Odger expressed well the sense of an achieved inter-
dependence, when in 1869 at the TUC, he preceded the passing of a
resolution in favour of Courts of Arbitration and Conciliation by
comparing capital and labour to a shopkeeper and his customer. Again,
an LRL pamphlet of July 1870, disavowing the dynastic Franco-Prussian
war, included this smug passage: 'Working men desire to settle their
quarrels with their employers by arbitration. They have come to
understand that reason is a higher, a nobler, a more equitable in-
strumentality for the settlement of misunderstandings than brute

force.' [9] Indeed, there had already been in existence from March 1869 the Board of Arbitration and Conciliation for the Manufactured Iron Trade of the North of England. This mechanism, operating in a rapidly expanding industry, killed off any effective ironworking trade unionism for many years. The key figures were David Dale, a Quaker ironmaster from Darlington, and John Kane, Secretary of the National Amalgamated Association of Ironworkers. They came together, the Board was established, and within two years a sliding scale was introduced to regulate wages – something that the ironworkers had once resisted, but which now with mathematical implacability bore out the formative words of Rupert Kettle, a Wolverhampton judge and first Arbitrator to the Board, that price was 'the only legitimate fund out of which wages can be paid'.[10] Kane's services proved invaluable. At the meeting in Darlington which established the Board, there had been an atmosphere of great anxiety in the context of the ironworkers threatening strike action, with one master observing that he 'had great difficulty to quell the men in the Middlesbrough district' and another that 'they were all in an agitation at Hartlepool to get a rise of wages'.[11] Things soon changed. Kane's union formally outlawed strikes on account of its role in the Board of Arbitration; and over the next decade, as the union's autonomous function became ever more nebulous, only rarely was its membership greater than the number of ironworkers who paid a penny a month to be represented on the Board. But as Kane had stressed in the Preface to his *Rules of 1869* about rebels against the union: 'I shall prefer their censure so long as I act according to our rules in preference to their applause, which too many have sought to earn by pandering to ignorance, prejudice and disorder.'

The foremost public figure associated with the method of arbitration was Mundella, himself a hosiery manufacturer. After some early local successes in the Midlands in the 1860s, he made its propagation the main part of his life's work and took great pains to establish harmonious relations with the more receptive trade union leaders. In October 1871 he was able to tell a friend about Applegarth that 'I am working him as a settler among the working men in forming Boards of Conciliation. . . . He will be true to me.' [12] Applegarth for his part wrote to Mundella a few weeks later from Lancashire asking him 'to write a circular for a board of arbitration in the cotton trade', adding that 'you can write such a circular better than anyone I know' and 'if issued promptly, this will have an important bearing on several disputes in the Burnley district'. [13] Yet at heart Mundella's attitude towards the working class was precisely that one of patronising contempt which Applegarth on another occasion rebuked so bitterly. For example, he wrote this, again to his friend Robert Leader, shortly before the TUC of January 1873: 'I am sorry not to be at Leeds. I have so little confidence in the wisdom

of these men. They are deplorably deficient in tact and knowledge.' [14]
The key text, however, in an historical explanation of how the widespread
acceptance of Mundella's method of arbitration contributed to the
general decline of organised trade unionism in the 1870s, undoubtedly
comes from a letter he wrote to Leader in 1869: 'My only desire is that
employers will have the sense to adopt what is good in my plan and to
seize the present state of trade as a favourable opportunity of doing it;
otherwise I fear, when trade revives . . . Normansell and all his societies
. . . will not be in so tractable a frame of mind as at present.' [15] In the
event, the failure by other employers to take up at once Mundella's
plan of buying off the unions cheaply proved irrelevant – for when trade
did revive in the early 1870s, miners' leaders like John Normansell did
prove 'tractable' and accepted the half loaf of arbitration at a time when,
à la the Labour Protection League, the whole one was there for the
taking. Why did they acquiesce so tamely? Possibly because of
the procedure's innate respectability, consummated in 1874 when the
Bishop of Manchester summoned the parties to his palace in order to
settle a local building dispute. Ultimately, though, one must examine
the mining unions themselves and see how their internal states determined the different, decisive responses to Mundella's method.

The 'aristocrats' of the industry were the miners in Northumberland
and, to a lesser extent, Durham. In this period they shared with the
cotton-spinners and shipbuilders a distinct sense of exclusiveness, a
certain conjunction with their employers, derived from their leading
role in maintaining the nation's exports. The dominant figures were
the respective secretaries, Thomas Burt of Northumberland and William
Crawford of Durham. Burt rose steadily from pit to Parliament, while
Crawford emerged in 1872 from the Blythe Co-operative store because
it was felt that, in the words of the historian of the Durham Miners'
Association, 'a man with some financial training would be a better
agent than a simple pitman'.[16] Both relied heavily on friendly benefits
to create disciplined control from the centre, and they infinitely preferred arbitration to strike action. For the time being this seemed
enough as wages rose steadily along with coal prices. In June 1872 a
large miners' demonstration was held at Durham. Forty thousand
well-behaved men attended, carrying a host of placards, many of which
showed pictures of arbitration boards and underneath, such welcoming
messages to the mine-owners as 'In the past we have been enemies; in
the future let us be friends.' Similar sentiments were voiced in August
1873 when Normansell's South Yorkshire Miners' Association, almost
a branch of the unions in the North-East, held its own gala in Chester-
field. J. Stores Smith, managing director of a local mine, addressed
the assembled company and spoke warmly of the 'friendly relationship
which exists between employers and employed'. But he went on: 'If . . .

you should allow rash counsel and passionate selfishness to rise up to the top of your demands . . . you will find that . . . the God of right and truth will be against you and in the end you will be discomfited.'[17] Despite the far from consensual tone of these words, all three Associations – Northumberland, Durham and South Yorkshire – continued to comprise the major part of MacDonald's moderate and accommodating National Miners' Association. MacDonald's lack of militancy was epitomised when he told a Select Committee on Coal in 1873 that 'If I felt that the strike would injuriously affect the trade, I would recommend them not; and I have done so frequently.'[18] This appeasing attitude had already prompted Thomas Halliday of Lancashire to form in 1869 the rival Amalgamated Association of Miners, which was mostly centred in less powerful unionist areas like Halliday's own county, the Midlands, and South Wales. By 1873 it had a total membership of about 99,000, not far short of MacDonald's Association. But within two years that rivalry was over, and Halliday's organisation in abject abeyance. As prices fell, so did wages, in which cycle only the strongest could afford arbitration, while the weakest went to the wall.

A series of disputes broke the Amalgamated Association. In 1874 a great deal of money was lost trying to prevent blacklegs breaking up a major strike in Lancashire. The Association then tried to moderate its policy because of a shortage of funds, but in 1875, following severe 'arbitrated' wage cuts, the miners in South Wales struck for the third time in four years. Whereupon Halliday sounded the death-knell of his Association through being unable to offer assistance. The miners themselves, in a hopeless situation, thereupon accepted the need for an automatically regulated sliding scale of wages; and trade unionism in South Wales, bereft of a purpose, went into virtual extinction for the next twenty years. A similar pattern was enacted on all other coalfields outside the North-East. The resultant bitterness was particularly acute in South Yorkshire, where the rank-and-file of the union discovered in 1875 that as a consequence of their leaders investing over £30,000 in a disastrous 'co-operative' colliery – the Shirland Colliery Company, with Mundella as chairman – there was no money left to subsidise a strike to resist wage cuts. Even in the North-East, where Burt and Crawford pleaded resignation and fortitude, considerable popular resentment was aroused against them. Crawford himself came to share the prevailing disenchantment after being told by the owners in 1874, following a series of wage cuts, that the notion 'that wages should follow profits' was 'a proposition opposed to every law of political economy'.[19] As he put it late in 1875: 'If the workman was to be stripped naked by the laws of political economy, he might some day be forced to seek his protection outside those laws.' But that day was not yet, for in practice as opposed to rhetoric Crawford simply resorted to the sliding scale, which in effect meant substituting a succession of small pills to swallow in place of several large ones. The Durham miners reluctantly accepted the procedure in 1877 and wage cuts went on anew. Meanwhile, in Northumberland in the same year, Burt was coming under severe criticism in the light of proposed 25 per cent wage reductions. The result was an eight-week strike, disavowed by Burt and costing the union almost £60,000. It failed – and the men returned to the cold comfort of trusting in Burt's conciliating Joint Committee with the owners. Even the 'aristocrats' were paying a heavy price for survival in the late 1870s.

Throughout all these events, Mundella seems to have felt few qualms. When, for example, he received at the 1874 TUC held in Sheffield a vote of thanks because 300,000 ironworkers had peacefully accepted through arbitration a substantial wage cut, he was able with largesse to decline the vote and ask Congress to pass it on to its more deserving Parliamentary Committee. Yet even the best-known member of that Committee was in the end to feel doubts about the rightness of his policy. As MacDonald observed in November 1879, defending his actions with ill-disguised unease: '. . . had the trade expanded since 1874 as it did for twenty-five years previously, they would be well employed now'. [20] MacDonald was justified in expressing regret. The mining interest, great white hope, as it were, of a powerful, monolithic unionism, had squandered its potential badly during the 1870s. Instead, the skilled New Model societies, invulnerable in their highly fragmented, multi-layered way to the guiles of arbitration, still retained much of their old strength and predominance within the trade union movement. As Broadhurst, Secretary of the Parliamentary Committee from 1875 to 1890, was able to remark with satisfaction in his autobiography, *From a Stonemason's Bench to the Treasury Bench* (1901), following a long panegyric on the material progress made during his lifetime: 'The status of Labour has advanced with equal strides, for where now the employee may meet his employer on equal terms at the Arbitration or Conciliation Board, in my early years Labour had practically no rights and no recognition.'

The collapse of collective bargaining power was accentuated during the second half of the 1870s by the increasing ineffectuality of working-class political leadership. In 1873, as we have seen, the mood of the TUC was one apparently susceptible to the creation of an independent third party. No one, however, made the decisive initial move. Harrison the Positivist toyed during the autumn with a formal break from the Liberals, but first decided [21] that a solely unionist party would be 'too classy' in its outlook and then discovered, during informal negotiations with Joseph Chamberlain, that there were too many incompatibilities involved in an alliance between labour and largely middle-class Nonconformist interests. The TUC for its part, meeting in January 1874 in the context of not only the anti-labour legislation but also a succession of local vetoes on working-class Liberal candidates, heard bold pronouncements about the need for autonomous political activity, but finally left it up to individual delegates to question candidates about their labour policy and then vote accordingly. So the Liberals were let off lightly, losing in the election later that month only about ten to fifteen seats on account of working-class estrangement. Two 'indpendent' MPs were in fact elected, Burt at Morpeth and MacDonald at Stafford, but both on orthodox programmes unexceptionable to middle-class Radicalism. The new Prime Minister was Disraeli, who with his Home Secretary, R. A. Cross, made a bid in June 1875 to woo labour away from the Liberal middle ground by repealing the Criminal Law Amendment Act. It was not in the end enough. Disraeli was ultimately unwilling to jettison middle-class allegiance, with the result that in 1877 John Gorst, the Party's Principal Agent, resigned because of his leader's refusal to sanction at an organisational level genuine working-class Conservatism. Moreover, the new generation of trade union leaders – generally crafts-based figures like Broadhurst, Shipton of the LTC, and Prior of the ASCJ – had now just about got what they wanted, freedom to retrench, and they returned contentedly to the Liberals, their natural political affiliation. It was in vain that Edith Simcox, a pioneer organiser of sweated female labour, expressed the hope to the TUC held at Glasgow in October 1875 that 'now the working classes were possessed of political power they would use that power in future with more consideration for the interest of the governed, and with less devotion to the interest of the ruling classes'. [22] Indeed, the TUC became for some years an increasingly irrelevant annual event. 'Moderate in tone, and altogether free from anything like bitterness or invective against society' was the kindly pat on the head which *The Times* [23] gave to the 1877 proceedings at Leicester. Broadhurst maintained a firm guiding hand throughout, and in 1880 was rewarded when he joined Burt and MacDonald by becoming, in effect, Liberal MP for Stoke-on-Trent. The achievement subsequently earned a characteristic chapter heading in his autobiography: 'Within the Precincts'.

At another level, however, there were throughout the 1870s certain manifestations that looked back to a more sceptical past and ahead to a more independent future. One example, barely documented, was the agitation on behalf of Roger Tichborne, the unsuccessful and in fact fraudulent claimant to the Tichborne estates. He was seen as a man cheated of his rights, a victim of establishment corruption. When he appeared at Spitalfields in the East End in August 1872, a mass demonstration of support greeted him along with great cries of 'fair play for the oppressed'.[24] Two years later, with the case finally lost, an attempt was made to disbar Tichborne's counsel, Dr Kenealy, who, according to *Reynolds' Newspaper* of 22 November 1874, was 'summoned to appear before the benches of Gray's Inn'. The mass-circulation Sunday paper went on: 'The public will certainly view with suspicion and distrust the proceedings of a hole-and-corner, irresponsible tribunal, members of which may . . . be mere toadies and tuft-hunters to the bench.' The editorial concluded: 'Even if the tribunal pronounces a sentence of disbarment on the doctor, there still will be tens of thousands of "fools and fanatics" who will believe every word he has written or spoken.' Trading on language like that, almost reminiscent of the 1630s, Kenealy was able to run for some time a flourishing, popular-based Magna Charta Association proclaiming the hallowed theme of 'the rights of the free-born Englishman'. Moreover, at a more sustained pitch than this substratum of populist anti-aristocratic feeling, there were taking place significant political developments in working-men's clubs in the metropolis, especially in Soho and in the East End. These met on Sunday evenings, were generally attended by men from crafts like tailoring and boot-making which were not yet organised on New Model lines, and tended in practice to be powerfully free-thinking debating chambers. Such clubs formed the backbone of the Manhood Suffrage League, founded in 1875 under the impetus of William Morgan, a shoe-maker and active friend of the Labour Protection League. This new league met weekly at 'The Queen's Head' in Little Pulteney Street and was influenced doctrinally by a mixture of Bronterre O'Brien, Karl Marx and Robert Owen. Its strength steadily increased, to the point where in 1880 it was able virtually to take over the ameliorating Social and Political Education League founded four years earlier by the incorrigible Solly. Also in 1880, after sustained pressure on Bradlaugh's National Secular Society to become more overtly political, the Stratford branch broke away and formed the Stratford Dialectical and Political Club. This London evidence remains fragmentary,[25] but what at least is clear is that the Socialism of the 1880s did not so much appear out of the blue as from certain streaks of scarlet apparent on the horizon some years earlier.

Nevertheless, it is still difficult to determine what exactly was the ideological bearing of working-class activity as a whole during these ambivalent 1870s. One has only to read the memoirs of a retired Lancashire election agent, *Twenty-Five Years' Fight with the Tories* by Joseph Howes, to realise the extent to which crude thuggery continued to lie near the surface of popular politics. When Odger, for example, preached Republicanism in the early 1870s, he was 'very badly treated by his opponents and subjected to great brutality in some of the towns he visited'. And this is surely the interest of the popular agitation over

the Eastern Question in the latter part of the decade: it apparently
showed the working class on a moral tight-rope between fine-minded
selflessness and bullying imperialism. The basic narrative of that
agitation is well known. In May 1876 about 12,000 Bulgarians were
massacred after rebelling against the Sultan of Turkey. On 6 September,
Gladstone fanned the mood of widespread indignation when he brought
out his pamphlet, *The Bulgarian Horrors and the Question of the East*.
It called on the Turks to clear out of the province 'bag and baggage',
and by the end of the month 200,000 copies had been sold. On 9
September, Gladstone reiterated the theme to 20,000 people standing
in pouring rain at Blackheath. Two months later, however, Disraeli at
the Guildhall made a major attack on Russia, the ostensible protector
of the Bulgarian Christians, and in so doing inspired the music hall
refrain which the 'Great' Macdermott proceeded to make famous:

> 'We don't want to fight,
> But, by jingo, if we do,
> We've got the ships, we've got the men,
> We've got the money too.'

During most of 1877, however, matters stayed in abeyance pending
Russia's delayed resolution of the question. But in December the
government assumed a more aggressive stance and a wave of peace and
counter-peace agitation was resumed. Between January and March
1878 a series of peace meetings in London, Sheffield and the Midlands
(all areas of particularly high unemployment) were stormed and taken
over by gangs of rowdy pro-government mobs, usually led by either
Tory medical students or ex-military men. War seemed imminent, but
partly because Disraeli never really intended it, and partly because the
pro-peace labour leaders held firm (in contrast to most of their middle-
class Liberal associates), diplomacy continued and in July 1878 Disraeli
returned from the Congress of Berlin proclaiming 'peace with honour'.
It proved a hollow triumph in all senses. The underlying imperialism
of his position soon led to a superfluous war in Afghanistan, which
Gladstone brilliantly exploited in his stumping popularising Midlothian campaigns of 1879 and 1880. Calling on his listeners to
'remember that the sanctity of life in the hill villages of Afghanistan
among the winter snows is as inviolable in the eye of Almighty God
as can be your own',[26] he seemed to capture the imagination of a whole
generation of sturdy and self-reliant artisans. Disraeli could offer
nothing in return and in 1880 the Liberals won the election comfortably.

As a broad outline, all of that remains substantially true, but several
points need elaboration. On the Liberal side there were some early
doubts on the part of the labour leaders about how wholeheartedly to

support Gladstone. Beesly, writing in the *Bee-Hive* in September 1876, stressed 'the necessity of not allowing the leaders of the so-called Liberal Party to trade upon this cry of horror and to use it as a means of wriggling themselves back to office'. Even Howell for a time maintained a sceptical attitude, and in October helped the TUC to set up a 'vigilance' committee on the Eastern Question. Moreover, it is an interesting rider on Gladstone's celebrated Blackheath speech that an eye-witness, describing the meeting soon afterwards, wrote of a 'large and respectable' gathering and 'not Rags but people in Cloth Coats & Top Hats'.[27] On the Tory side, the xenophobic 'jingo' tag so often applied in an all-purpose way to the agitation has perhaps been exaggerated. The buoyant festive atmosphere was probably just as important a motivation. The *Wolverhampton Chronicle*, describing the events of 31 January 1878, reported that 'Cheers and counter-cheers, and music, both vocal and instrumental, "God save the Queen" and "Rule, Britannia!" predominating, were indulged in without stint, and speech-making was out of the question.' Moreover, Gladstone himself seems to have been just as popular a target of abuse as the symbolic Russian bear. That evening in Wolverhampton, for example, at a subsequent torch-light procession accompanied by a brass band playing 'Macdermott's war song', the cry went up 'Three groans for Gladstone' and the request was 'complied with without loss of time, and with great vehemence'. In sum, then, one is left with the image of a fragmented working-class response: to a considerable extent indifferent, but with many improving working men supporting Gladstone's moral stance and a large part of the residuum finding in aggressive chants a vicarious relieving outlet. Significantly, two Radical MPs for populous constituencies, Joseph Cowen of Newcastle and Jacob Bright of Manchester, proved by February 1878 to be conspicuously absent from the pro-peace ranks. And, in general, the impression is confirmed of a paternalist Tory-residuum alliance sundered by the middle ground of Liberal-voting shopkeepers and artisans. The 1870s had in this sense shown little advance on the politics of 1868.

But the larger imponderable remains: did the 'moral' Gladstone, as a result of the Bulgarian agitation, in some way prevent the Liberal Party and its self-improving affiliates from following their 'true' course behind the more 'materialist' Chamberlain? It is a question that can only really be answered within the context of the changing electoral politics of the 1880s and beyond. But what one can say is that in the late 1870s Gladstone evoked a far more profound working-class response by appealing from a lofty height to moral and intellectual status than the earthbound Chamberlain did by promising municipal happiness on the Birmingham model. It is an important distinction. William Morris,

Treasurer of the pro-peace Eastern Question Association, was soon to become a Socialist and attempt to convert the working class wholesale to Gladstonian morality without the *laissez-faire* whitewash. He failed – perhaps because in a general sense the earthbound vision was beginning by the 1880s to come into ascendancy even after it had passed out of Chamberlain's specific orbit.

Chapter 4

CLASS

'For my part I have never under-rated the power of the middle classes, whom, in spite of their individual good nature and banality, I look upon as a most terrible and impacable force.' [1]

Although few of his contemporary intellectuals possessed the same Marxist rigour as Morris, here writing in a letter in 1883, the year of his conversion to Socialism, nevertheless roughly between then and the end of the century there was established a reasonably authentic class grid and a distinctive class way of looking at social and political questions. The milestones on the 'Magnificent Journey' are familiar enough: in 1881 the formation of Hyndman's Democratic Federation, soon afterwards called the Social Democratic Federation; in 1884 Morris splitting to form his own Socialist League; in 1886–7 sustained unemployment inspiring bloody riots in Trafalgar Square and elsewhere; in 1889–90 the 'explosion' of new unionism; in 1892 the election of three independent Labour MPs; in 1893 the foundation of the Independent Labour Party; and in 1899 the decision by the TUC to encourage the election of independent working-class MPs, leading to the setting-up in the following February of the Labour Representation Committee. Not that it was really as magnificent as that. A mixture of sectionalist economism and what one might call the Bulgarian mentality – that is, a Gladstonian-type inability to perceive beyond certain surface symptoms of the late-Victorian 'grab and brag', in this case the Boer War – did much to mitigate the LRC's temporary virtue of political independence. Put schematically, a re-made and far more durable working-class consciousness co-existed by the end of the century with the continuing post-Chartist phenomenon of 'false' consciousness, involving a misapprehension of the economic factor, a working class divided within itself, and a still socially aspiring élite. The paradox is profound. To understand it, one must consider not only the specific motive forces that over a period of some twenty years forged the LRC, but also the general socio-economic, political, religious and cultural context that in large part has given the twentieth-century Labour Party its particular quality.

In the light of the mid-Victorian tradesman–small master–skilled workman nexus of popular Radicalism, the subsequent trend towards more rigid occupational stratification was inevitably of considerable significance. From both above and below, that stratum of society, generally temperate and Nonconformist, now found itself under increasingly severe pressure as it sought to sustain 'the People's William' whom it had elevated in the late 1870s. Categorical statements are difficult, but the last quarter of the century definitely did see a growing tendency towards the concentration of capital and the factory system of production, both of them developments antithetical to the more intimate workshop organism of the Birmingham type. In that city, indeed, even a traditional button-producing firm was deploying over a thousand workers by about 1900. Similarly, the small tradesman was tending to become an anachronism, especially in burgeoning suburban areas. With the spread of such names as Lipton, Boots, Home and Colonial, and W. H. Smith, the total of multiple stores proliferated from about 1,500 in 1880 to 11,645 by 1900. Scale and mechanisation were the key themes, thorough distribution through an advanced railway system of standard consumer goods the symbol of a new and even more unilateral phase of the Industrial Revolution. Against this general background, the strain on the Liberal nexus is clear: employers became increasingly impersonal objects, a sense of alienation deepened by the stress on productivity in response to far more pressing international manufacturing competition; while work itself, steadily more sub-divided and machine-dominated, began to pass beyond the pale of even Smilesian exaltation. Indeed, sadly for those of the labour aristocracy who had taken Smiles seriously, the gradual disintegration of the sub-contracting framework meant that the chances of the sub-contractor becoming a small master faded also. In big firms, moreover, what recruitment that did take place from below tended to draw less on the aspiring journeyman-type figure than on the incipient white-collar class, which was at least guaranteed to be competent at bookwork. Politically conservative and socially deferential, this new stratum flourished as a result of increasingly complex production processes (complex in a supervisory sense) and concentrated joint-stock companies. 'The children of small shopkeepers and better class artisans, who have been consumed by an ambition to wear black coats and be a "gentleman"'[2] was how in 1886 one exceptionally dispassionate clerk in Liverpool described his colleagues who now provided the most direct and galling check from above on the old labour aristocracy.

Perhaps even more serious to the artisan élite, if for the time being less conclusive, was the threat from below. In particular, the quickening rise of the versatile semi-skilled operative, able to work modern machinery after only a short period of training, offered a direct challenge to the craft control of the labour market through zealously maintained apprenticeship restrictions. In Sheffield, for example, renowned for its light trades, the skilled worker's supremacy was undermined by the team master, a new type of large-scale sub-contractor who deliberately exploited technological advances, especially in the cutlery trade, to employ semi-skilled youths at low wages to fulfil virtually mindless tasks. Similar changes were taking place also in the sphere of boot-and-shoe production, another traditional stronghold of craftsmanship. Indeed, the list is endless: coach-builders, wheelwrights, saddlers, plumbers, cabinet-makers, watch-makers – all tended to succumb to inexorable division-of-labour pressures. The result was in many places the creation of a new generation of sweated labour, as in the notorious, immigrant-based cheap clothing industry of East London. This sense of being swamped was caught by F. W. Galton, the editor of an 1895 anthology, *Workers on their Industries*, in which he wrote in his introduction of 'the steady divorce of the worker from anything like a complete knowledge of a trade' and the way that the skilled workman was increasingly replaced by 'boys or other subordinate labourers', who in turn 'find themselves, on arriving at man's estate, with no other means of gaining a livelihood than the already overflowing unskilled [i.e. semi-skilled] labour market, or the ranks of that great army of casual labourers whose existence is a reproach to our methods of industrial organisation'. The gloom was evident and the Applegarth era a halcyon memory, soon to attain the mythic status of a golden age.

One should not exaggerate the late-century trend towards occupational proletarianisation. In all sorts of ways, despite also the numerical growth of horizontally structured though localised transport workers and coal-miners, the working class remained riddled by differences of status within itself. Quite apart from the general sweated context, the specific emergence of a non-domestic-outworking female labour force made it extraordinarily difficult for non-aristocratic labour as a whole to organise and, as it were, to rise mechanically above the perennial surplus-of-labour problem. Nor did the decline of the old-time craftsman result by any means in the blanket cessation of highly skilled workers maintaining wide wage differentials. Engineers, iron- and steel-workers, and shipbuilders all rose to the top of the labour pole with the general growth of the metal industries during the second half of the century, accompanying and then to some extent replacing the aristocratic spinners in the declining textile industry. These new aristocrats, earning by the end of the century over 40 shillings a week, tended to be politically quiescent, in marked contrast to the worried bookbinders, boot and shoe operatives, and fancy-leather workers who comprised an important part of the LRC's early trade union backing. Moreover, in general terms, this transmuted strengthening of the labour aristocracy was further hardened by the continuing psychological polarity between the untouchably skilled worker and the rest. As Thomas Wright put it starkly in 1873: 'Between the artisan and the unskilled labourer a gulf is fixed.' [3] Gradually, however, both employers and semi-skilled organised labour came to realise that in market terms the fixity of this gulf was contrary to the logic of mechanised development. Wright himself had added presciently that 'with the labour market habitually overstocked, there is fast arising a sectional difference of mode of life and feeling between the regularly and irregularly employed classes'. Such words help make sense of the steady shift during the 1890s of the new unionists towards the narrowly based sectionalism of their older forerunners. In other words, the axes of internal working-class occupational status were changing: the skilled/unskilled dichotomy was being replaced by a chasm between the more-or-less skilled and the more-or-less unemployable, the residuum, together with the almost unorganisable sweated. Nevertheless, over and above the fact of this strengthened if admittedly more broad-based labour élite lay a transcending awareness of the social caesura directly above. Rising and declining occupations and wage differentials lend themselves to relatively concrete analysis, a sense of apartness does not. 'The clerks who are sustained in their long hours of unhealthy toil by the one triumphant thought that they have not fallen back into the abyss below' [4] wrote C. F. G. Masterman in 1901: it hardly needs the modern sociological stress on the centrality of the workplace in defining social status to confirm the authenticity of these penetrating words. And once you are told you live in, or on the brink of, an abyss, as the working class in general ceaselessly was, it must have been difficult, looking round, to do otherwise than burrow further inwards and conclusively apart from the social forms of liberal civilisation.

A similar exclusiveness, almost a freezing of society at a certain entry-point, is also apparent in the late-Victorian patterns of educational and residential stratification. The long-term background was the phenomenal expansion of the professional middle class, from 272,000 such men in 1851 to 684,000 recorded in the census twenty years later. In ideological terms, moreover, middle-class utilitarianism, no longer needing to thrust for democratic rights, found itself increasingly in harmony with the socially far more acceptable upper-class evangelical tradition. Bright himself admitted as much when he told Edinburgh working men in November 1868: 'There is no longer a contrast between us and the House of Lords; we need no longer bring charges against a selfish oligarchy; we no longer dread the power of the territorial magnates; we no longer feel ourselves domineered over by a class.' [5] Middle-class Radicalism, bankrupt of ideas about a more total social reconstruction, continued for some time, and with significant effect, to act as if the old time-honoured early- and mid-Victorian 'charges' were still valid, but in the end socio-economic logic worked inexorably to substantiate Bright's words. The formal solidifying began as early as the year he uttered them. The Public Schools Act of 1868 nicely balanced upper- and middle-class wishes by maintaining the traditional primacy of Classics while at the same time replacing already increasingly expensive 'free' places for the local poor with a system of 'open' competitive examination, necessarily involving costly pre-examination preparation. A year later the Endowed Schools Act, following the Taunton Commission's explicitly class-conceived report, took away the 'deserving poor' from the higher grade grammar schools and created instead exhibitions to these preferentially treated fee-charging schools that again were in practice extremely difficult to obtain without private coaching. The blocking of opportunity at the secondary level was thus almost total; and the chances of a child from a poor family getting to one of the new university colleges, let alone Oxford or Cambridge, were never so slim as in this latter half of the century.

Nor did even a remotely homogeneous social ideal inform the primary education specifically provided for the working class. H. G. Wells was not being unduly emotive when in his autobiography he described Forster's Education Act of 1870 (not in fact made compulsory until 1880, free until 1891) as 'not an Act for a common universal education', but 'an Act to educate the lower classes for employment on lower-class lines'. Rigid teaching of the three Rs by drill methods was at the core of this conscious attempt to build up a not unable disciplined industrial work-force in the face of especially threatening Prussian competition. As Charles Booth was to observe poignantly about one of the new board schools, 'ragged little *gamins* run quietly in harness, obedient to a look, a gesture of the teacher in command'. Perhaps inevitably, narrowing of the educational vision was also affirmed within the adult sphere. In particular, government-aided technical instruction increasingly tended to replace the study of pure science for its own sake. Inspired by the recent Royal Commission on Technical Instruction, the Birmingham and Midland Institute was typical in welcoming with open arms the financial support of local manufacturers to start in 1885 a School of Metallurgy. Sir Owen Roberts, Secretary to the Clothworkers' Company, put the whole in perspective when he warned the Keighley Technical Institute in 1888 that 'all efforts to develop and improve the technical education of the people must fail of their purpose and legitimate development until the teaching in elementary schools was made more practical in its character as a preparation for the technical institution'. And even more categorically: 'Elementary education must have in view the factory and the workshop, rather than the counter and the office, as the normal and ordinary destinations in life of the children with whom it was dealing.' [6]

Residential patterns followed similarly detached guidelines. Even in the 1840s, Engels had noted how the new generation of Manchester businessmen were able to shuttle back and forth between inner city and suburb in such a way that the existence of the submerged masses lodged somewhere in between barely impinged upon their consciousness. The social implications of this stratification went deep. Whereas in Leeds and Bradford at the beginning of the century mill-owners, professional men and mill-workers all lived in their respective city centres, by the 1880s at the latest affluent suburban areas like Headingley and Heaton had grown up in sharp juxtaposition to the slummy courts and declining terrace houses of central areas like Leeds Bridge and Goitside. This residential pattern was national, but perhaps most pertinently played out in London: there the working class remained predominantly concentrated on low ground near the river, while the middle class as a whole moved north and south in search of healthier parts. The determining influence was the rapid development of efficient but quite expensive urban transport. From the 1860s suburban interstices on the main railway lines proliferated fast (and with them the W. H. Smith bookstall empire); in 1863 the underground began; and a few years later the old horse buses were replaced by the far more capacious, but for the time being no cheaper, horse-drawn tramways. This last mode of transport was originally conceived of in terms of ease of movement between terminus and place of work; and when the horse tramway did become less expensive from about 1880 and threatened to extend its scope, then already established middle-class suburban areas like Harrow and Stanmore at once started effective opposition groups designed to prevent the coming of such an insidiously egalitarian device. The same exclusiveness permeated the suburban middle-class approach towards cheap workmen's fares on the railways. An area like Ongar kept its gladed charm by resisting any such reforming proposals, whereas what has been called the 'working-class agglomeration of Edmonton–Tottenham–Walthamstow' [7] was created precisely as a result of the Great Eastern Railway reluctantly agreeing to run cheap workmen's trains there. William Birt, General Manager of the company, was frank enough to tell the 1884–5 Royal Commission on the Housing of the Working Classes that 'the selection of the workmen's escape routes to the suburbs should be strictly limited' not only because of railway economics, but also because 'from the Edmonton district, and from the Walthamstow and Stratford districts, we issue tickets to Liverpool Street, and these districts are spoilt for ordinary residential purposes'. Therefore: 'Other districts which are not spoilt should not be thrown open to the working classes,

otherwise these districts will become spoilt too.' And in 1898 Henry
Partington of the London and North Western was even blunter about
the ill-received parliamentary legislation of 1883: 'The Cheap Trains
Act presumes that certain districts where the landowners and others
are notoriously averse to the introduction of the working-class element
would become reconciled to it.' [8] And clearly they would not.

Ironically enough, some of the very worst late-Victorian slums in
the central areas of London were those where the merchants and
professional men had remained in residence as late as the 1850s. Much
of North Kensington was a case in point, full of large family houses
perforce turned into squalid, crumbling tenements for the pockets of
labourers and laundry workers left behind from about 1860. As the
century went on, so the situation steadily worsened for central London's
inhabitants, whose sense of being stranded was exacerbated by a
significant decline of rural immigrants. Above all, the omnipresent
material condition was that of acute overcrowding. An entire population, wedded as casual labour to an East End economy that was
losing its viability even in Mayhew's time, literally lived out Booth's
dictum that 'trades leave, people stay'. [9] At first sight the fact that the
population of the City proper fell from 113,387 in 1861 to 51,439 in
1881 might suggest more living space for those who remained. In fact
the opposite happened. In a not untypical City ward, Cripplegate,
housing per acre declined during these same twenty years from $32 \cdot 83$
to $12 \cdot 27$, while in already densely populated nearby working-class
areas, like Bethnal Green, Lambeth, Southwark and St Pancras,
numbers went on increasing almost right to the end of the century.
The key phenomenon was that of displacement. Offices and warehouses (in themselves drastically pushing up the price of land and
cost of ground rent), street development, and railway lines and terminii
all proceeded apace, in effect driving the local population out of overcrowded areas into even more overcrowded areas adjacent. The construction of Farringdon Street alone displaced no less than 40,000
people; and Dyos has estimated that, even on the most stringently
minimalist calculations, the railways were responsible between 1853
and 1901 (with 1860–80 the most destructive period) for the displacement of 76,000 people at the very least. The Rev. William Denton,
citing waterfront workers, tailors and shoe-makers, summed up the
worsening situation in a pamphlet written in 1861: 'The poor are
displaced, but they are not removed. . . . It is a mockery to speak of
the suburbs to them. They are chained by imperative necessity to the
same spot, and the distance of a few hundred yards is of the greatest
moment to them.' At the beck and call of the overstocked and fluctu-
ating casual labour market, this population would hardly have been
able to move out even if the railway companies had been more

effectively compelled to run cheap trains. The GER, pressurised into doing so after wreaking havoc in Bishopsgate through the building of Liverpool Street station, were very much the irrelevant exception in this respect. As one contemporary sardonically informed a reporter from *The Working Man* in 1866: 'Where all they all gone, sir? Why, some's gone down Whitechapel way; some's gone in the Dials; some's gone to Kentish Town; and some's gone to the Workus.' [10] But the actual readers of *The Working Man* itself probably knew a different experience. For as Denton had added later in his pamphlet, the evidence was that 'with very few exceptions, no skilled labourers and superior artisans reside in the City'.

Instead they tended to move to the Tottenham complex jerry-built specially for them. Really they had little choice, such was the absence until at least the 1890s of a significant government or municipal cheap-housing policy, further compounded by the inextinguishably capitalist norms of the supposedly philanthropic Model Dwelling Companies. The need to get the 'clear 5 per cent' return, together with the decision not to allow families to occupy one room only, between them ensured that often not even skilled workers could afford rooms. Very different were the mores of the unashamedly speculative builders, who in the 1860s and 1870s made use of the still cheap land in the less attractive suburbs to build houses fast and nasty. West Ham's population went up from 19,000 in 1851 to 267,000 by 1891; and Morris in 1883 re-membered his birthplace, Walthamstow, as 'once a pleasant place enough, but now terribly cocknified and choked up by the jerry-builder'.[11] But if this was the broad pattern – new working-class suburbs turning into quasi-slums themselves – there was not quite the chronological inevitability about the exodus of the more-or-less skilled that one might expect. Two decades of expansion were followed in the 1880s by recession. As a Metropolitan Board surveyor told an 1882 Select Committee: 'I never remember so many empty houses in the suburbs of London as there are now, especially for working-class people. There are an enormous number of houses empty at Tottenham, Stamford Hill, Peckham, Battersea and Wandsworth.' [12] The problem, and not only in London, was specifically one of cheap transport, without which all affirmations about the healthiness of suburban life remained liberal platitudes. 'I fear the desire of many to live as near to their works as possible, and the absence of facilities of cheap conveyance from the outlying portions of the Borough militate against any changes in this direction' [13] was the comment of Sheffield's Medical Officer of Health in his 1892 Report on the absence of working-class suburban emigration. Even in Glasgow and Manchester, the best cities for cheap transport, never more than 2 per cent of the population used workmen's tickets; while in London, the usage only started to become at all widespread in the 1890s after positive government action had at last begun to implement the Cheap Trains Act. As a result, many of the emigrants of the 1870s returned for a decade or so to the central city areas before finally moving out again towards the end of the century. It must have been a harrowing experience while it lasted. Nevertheless, when the final shift did come it was surely a conclusive one. Ostracised by the railway companies on behalf of the Ongarians, but equally alienated from the horrors of Cripplegate, such men, the more-or-less skilled in regular employment, could only hope to retrench in watchful isolation.

Shortly before his death in 1884, Mark Pattison of Oxford was asked what he thought was the most signal fact in contemporary history. 'The fact that 5,000,000 of our population possess nothing but their weekly wages' [14] is reputed to have been his unhesitating reply. And certainly, the notion of a self-respecting property-owning democracy – at the heart of the Rochdale argument – seemed especially distant during the dangerous 1880s. Several key documents both reflected and stimulated the decade's rapidly changing intellectual atmosphere. In 1881 Henry George's widely-read *Progress and Poverty* proposed a radical single tax on land. In 1883 the Rev. Andrew Mearns exposed London's slum-housing standards in *The Bitter Cry of Outcast London*. In 1889 *How the Poor Live and Horrible London* by G. R. Sims made an almost equal sensation, read as it was in conjunction with Charles Booth's first published findings. The effect of these works, especially *The Bitter Cry*, was to inspire fear, as well as a less personal sense of shared guilt, on the part of the propertied class. The way in which the Lord Mayor's Relief Fund for the unemployed shot up in forty-eight hours from £3,000 to £80,000 after the rioting in Trafalgar Square on 8 February 1886 was clear evidence of this. Moreover, Gladstone two years earlier had only been politic when he had actively propagated the cheap circulation of Robert Giffen's disingenuous *The Progress of the Working Classes in the Last Half-Century*. Nevertheless, neither old-fashioned largesse nor rosewater encouragement were by themselves enough – as was apparent to the increasingly vocal Radical section of the Liberal Party. Oxford's Cobden prize essayist for 1880 set the tone for the next few years when he asserted that 'we have had too much *laissez-faire* . . . we need a great deal more paternal government – that bugbear of the old economists'. [15] But the question was: how much and how drastic? All sorts of snares beset the path of the nascent New Liberalism. On the one hand, vigorous tackling of the unemployment question, the great social cry from the mid-1880s and apparently a straightforward enough good cause, was in fact always going to offend industrial interests if only because of its loaded side-issues of poverty and conditions of work, especially hours; while on the other hand, old-style Gladstonian Liberalism, offering the Bulgarian variety of emancipation, still had a certain mileage with the skilled workers who after 1886 represented even more than before the backbone of the Liberal vote. Radicalism and the 'economic factor': [16] the problem is one of timing, Ireland a substantive symbol as well as an extraneous causal episode.

At first, despite considerable disenchantment expressed in the early 1880s towards Gladstone's Irish coercion and general foreign policy, it seemed that within Liberalism the material axis would be the all-important one. As a groundswell of counter-opinion built up around the tracts of George, Mearns, and even the early Socialists, Gladstone vacillated, seemingly played out in a constructive sense after the sustained round of reforms enacted by his earlier ministry. Ten years later Harcourt would announce that 'we are all Socialists now', but in 1879 he anticipated the directive emptiness of what was still mainstream Liberalism when he admitted to Dilke that 'I never felt it so difficult to mix a prescription good for the present feeling of the constituencies.' [17] The way was clearly open for Chamberlain to recapture that Radical initiative within the party which he had temporarily lost to Gladstone over the Eastern Question. In December 1882 he was confidently told by John Morley that 'the workmen are full of the ideas of Henry George' and that 'in London "Nationalisation of the land" is the one subject that would furnish a basis for agitation'. [18] Chamberlain himself wrote the same month with friendly menace to a Tory hostess: 'The Whigs as a party are played out, and the next great fight will be between the Tory democrats and the democratic Radicals. It will never do for the latter to be outbidden, so you must prepare for something very drastic.' [19] And a year later, he made his first call with the serialisation of his Radical Programme in the *Fortnightly Review*. It caused a stir, of course, and was equated in some hysterical minds with Socialism, but it was certainly not authentically 'drastic'. Over housing, most notably, bold and squire-terrorising proposals for taxation of large properties were combined with an almost positive antipathy towards government-subsidised building. As he told the 1884–5 Royal Commission, 'the reconstruction and rehousing of the poor can be safely left to private enterprise'. [20] The explanation for this major retreat from the vaunted municipal ideal of the 1870s perhaps lies in Birmingham itself, where not only were the middle-class ratepayers now less inclined to foot the bill for gas-and-water Socialism, but also the working-class recipients were finding increasingly less to be grateful for. Again, it was housing which showed the cracks. One correspondent, presumably middle-class, said it all when, writing to the *Birmingham Daily Post* in November 1883 about the non-construction of artisans' dwellings, he complained that 'ground rents are now so increasingly heavy that it is almost a matter of impossibility for the general speculator to build property of this class that will pay him his "clear 5 per cent" '. Chamberlain seemed, in Birmingham at least, caught in an impasse. For all his growing reputation as a Radical protagonist, the working-class Liberal vote at local elections declined steadily there during the early 1880s, while in the richer wards of the city, like Edgbaston, the business vote was likewise drifting away, towards the security of the Conservatives, defenders of the established order. It did not take Chamberlain long to realise what was happening and resolve his dilemma. In a speech at Ipswich in January 1885 he explicitly asserted: 'I am putting the rights of property on the only firm and defensible basis. I believe that the danger to property lies in its abuse.' [21] At the same time he began to use the famous 'ransom' image – the money (in the coinage of social reforms) that the propertied order would have to pay to sleep safely at night. But during the course of 1885, it became steadily clearer that the Liberal middle class was not yet prepared to pay for a costly social programme. By 1886, after the working-class rejection of what little ransom money had been offered, Chamberlain admitted defeat, joining the hardened-into-Conservative propertied order and leaving Gladstone to reinterpret Liberalism in terms of a quite different currency.

It is in this perspective that one must put the mythology surrounding the fact that the Liberals won eighty-six seats more than the Conservatives in the election of November 1885. There is no doubt of Chamberlain's desire to score a Radical triumph. He wrote to Mundella on 7 October that 'we shall sweep the country with free education and allotments, and the Tories will be smashed and the Whigs extinguished'.[22] It seemed plausible: following the Third Reform Act of 1884, enfranchising about 2 million miners and agricultural labourers, and the Redistribution Act the following year creating popular-based single-member constituencies, the chances were that Chamberlain's celebrated cry, 'three acres and a cow', would prove irresistible. In fact, however, the Liberals fared poorly in the towns; while in the rural areas, among the new voters, the Liberal bias was caused much more by fears of the Conservatives reimposing protectionism than by the seductive quality of Chamberlain's allotments gambit. But as Labouchère justly remarked, it was the absence of an urban cow that really mattered. Chamberlain keenly desired this working-class vote, but was unable to put forward any far-reaching social and economic proposals precisely for fear of alienating manufacturers like himself. Instead, he plumped for the 'three acres' slogan, which barely went beyond Mill's 'unearned increment' land solution and was in itself little more than an attempt, inspired by Henry George, to revive the old manufacturing–populace alliance against the idle landlord. Chamberlain recognised the built-in urban limitations of this, but was thwarted when he tried to transcend the issue by propagating the issue of free education. Mundella's warning on 11 October was categorical: 'The ratepayers in the large towns are so poor just now, that they are frightened out of their wits at the prospect of increased demands for education.' [23] Additional Nonconformist sectarian grumbles followed, and as a result Chamberlain was forced to emaciate this major part of his programme in the last few weeks of the campaign. Moreover, the very fact of an apparently wide-ranging programme was viewed by many Liberals, even Radicals, with considerable distrust; and defeat at the polls for Chamberlain's 'new-fangled propositions',[24] as Bright had called them in October, confirmed these misgivings. Chamberlain himself accepted the situation honestly enough. He told Harcourt on 6 December: 'The boroughs do not care for our present programme, and I confess I do not know what substitute to offer them.' [25] Gladstone, however, did, as he prepared to lead the Liberals back to the non-programmatic, single-question, and above all ethical path from which they had been led astray.

Gladstone's espousal of Irish Home Rule, and Chamberlain's subsequent estrangement from the ensuing Bill, was undoubtedly a watershed in British politics. Whereas Gladstone retained the support of the bulk of the organisational, Radical, and working-class elements in the Liberal Party, Chamberlain joined the general middle-class rejection of Irish independence at the July 1886 Election. Defence of property and national pride between them created a massive Conservative majority in which for the first time suburban clerkdom played its full deferential part. In this apparently unpromising situation, Gladstone for the next few years sought to transcend the clear trend towards class-defined political alignment. His chosen weapon remained the apparently supra-economic ethical issue of Ireland, around which he sought to rebuild the Liberals as the party which stood for 'the masses against the classes'. In practice, this revival of individualism, the concentration on a people struggling for self-determination, together with the hastened passing of the Whigs, had the important effect of accentuating the position of the chapel element (including from about this time the Wesleyans) in the Liberal Party despite the secession of Chamberlain, the one-time champion of the Nonconformists. What the concentration on the Irish issue did not do was to lead to a strengthening of the working-class Radical element in terms of Liberal policy-making and candidate-selecting. These Radicals had justifiable grounds for complaint: their support for Irish independence had a far more resilient history than that of Gladstone and his middle-class supporters in the party organisation; the party in electoral terms was now more dependent than ever upon its working-class support,

as even it had recognised by plumping almost always for the new
working-class rather than the middle-class divisions during the redistribution bartering of 1885; and late in 1886 Salisbury's ruthless
attitude towards Churchill confirmed that, in the new world of 'villa
Toryism', the dream of a Tory democracy would have to be consigned
to the more fanciful history books. Nevertheless, for the time being
the Irish tactic continued to attract the allegiance of the labour élite to
Gladstonian Liberalism. And when some sort of break at last came,
its relatively non-ideological character was deeply influenced by the
holding action of these few years.

Until about 1889 'Ireland blocks the way' maintained conviction.
Gladstone candidly told Rosebery that year: 'I look back with pleasure
to the times of liberation in which my political life was cast, and with
doubt to the coming times of construction.' [26] That these times were
coming was made evident as three specific elements began to undermine Gladstone's basis of political action. One was the emergence of a
fresh generation of thinkers within the party, epitomised by L. A.
Atherley-Jones, son of Ernest Jones and MP for a working-class Durham
constituency. In an article entitled 'The New Liberalism' in *The
Nineteenth Century* for August 1889, he stressed that 'the masses are
not moved by – are, in fact, wonderfully indifferent to – "the woes of
Ireland" ', and added caustically that 'the Irish constabulary are not
Bashi-Bazouks, nor Irish magistrates Turkish pashas'. A further source
of criticism came from the London-based 'Progressives', especially the
Fabians and the Metropolitan Radical Federation, successful in the 1889
London County Council elections and advocates of major housing
legislation together with thorough municipalisation of urban utilities.
The third element came from beyond the pale of detached political
debate: this was the fairly widespread expectancy of organised labour by
1890 that the Liberal Party would officially back an Eight Hours' Bill.

Gladstone shaped up to the situation equivocally from the start.
In his Limehouse speech of December 1888, he accepted the issues of
artisans' dwellings and free schools as 'ripe for public discussion', but
then carried the metaphor further to insist that they were as fruit on
the other side of that familiar high wall, the Irish question. Three years
later, his famous but often overrated endorsement of the National
Liberal Federation's Newcastle Programme was barely any more
open-handed. Reluctance was apparent throughout: as Ripon had
advised him in December 1890, 'a whole series of labour questions
would come to the front' [27] if the primacy of the Irish issue was not
maintained. In the event, at Newcastle in October 1891, Gladstone
only minimally broadened the Liberal vista. He concentrated his
attention on local option and disestablishment proposals, leaving eight
hours an open question, possibly desirable in itself but cloaked in the

usual Gladstonian array of conditional sub-clauses. Not long afterwards, the LTC met him to talk about eight hours and, as Lansbury
later recalled, 'no beginning even of a comprehension of our wishes
seemed to penetrate to the great man's mind'.[28] Inevitably, ignoring
enhanced social expectations after Newcastle, Gladstone proceeded to
fight the 1892 Election almost entirely on the Irish issue, emerging
with a majority only with the support of the Irish Party and failing to
stop the election of the first independent Labour MPs to Parliament.
Such disloyalty only heightened Gladstone's moral untouchability.
He wrote to Morley in September 1892 about the selfishness of the
working class in asking for social legislation: 'I am disgusted by finding
a portion of them ready to thrust Ireland, which is so far ahead in
claim, entirely into the background. Poor, poor, poor human nature.' [29]
Yet in the period of power left to them after the Lords buried Home
Rule in September 1893, neither Gladstone nor the government as a
whole showed signs of even wanting to come to grips with more
pressing domestic matters, notably the unemployment question so
brilliantly publicised by Keir Hardie in the Commons and so lament-
ably eschewed by Fowler and Shaw-Lefevre at the Local Government
Board. A million unemployed, perhaps, but middle-class Nonconformist Liberalism would hardly have remained moral, let alone frugal,
if it had welcomed the proposal for large-scale public relief works made
early in 1895 by the Select Committee on Unemployment.

Even more, however, the political distancing took place at constituency level. As early as April 1888, Keir Hardie stood as the miners'
candidate at the Mid-Lanark by-election in opposition to the middle-
class Liberal. But the issue was not generalised until somewhat later,
in November 1890, when James Tims, Secretary of the Metropolitan
Radical Federation, requested Francis Schnadhorst, Secretary of the
Liberal Central Association, to withdraw fifty Liberal candidates (not
only in London) so that they could be replaced by fifty Federation-
backed Labour ones. Schnadhorst's response was cool. This negation of
working-class Radical aspirations tends to be attributed solely to
circumstances beyond central party control. Sidney Webb wrote to
Beatrice in September 1891 after a discussion with Schnadhorst: 'He
really seems to have tried all *he* could to put them into seats. But, as I
said at the end, the thing *was not done*; and however virtuous he may
have been, the effect remains.' [30] And some ten years later, the contents
pages of Ostrogorski's classic study [31] spoke eloquently of the local
Liberal Associations who were ultimately responsible for selecting
candidates. Of their social composition: 'The aristocracy hardly represented. The very slight participation of the upper middle class. . . . The
indifference of the working classes. The lower middle class [elsewhere
defined as 'shopkeepers, clerks, and superior artisans'] alone is left to

take an interest in the Caucus. The alacrity with which it does so. Being a victim of social exclusiveness, it finds social and political distinction in the openings afforded by the Caucus.' And: 'The intellectual standard of the Caucus-men. The narrowness of their political horizon. . . . A readiness to submit to the impulse given by leaders, to cultivate an unbending political orthodoxy, and, finally, to exclude spontaneity and independence of action and the spirit of criticism.' It was significant, moreover, that independent working-class candidates tended to emerge in the non-residuum constituencies where lower middle-class Radicalism, strong numerically and still living in close proximity to organised labour, failed to advance beyond traditional Gladstonian precepts. In East London, by contrast, the residual constituencies that did vote Liberal did so precisely because the absence of this Radicalism prompted the candidate to offer a more concrete and attractive social programme to the voters. Indeed, the issue of working-class candidates has been seen too much in non-substantive symbolic terms, the social thwarting of the respectabilising working man, not enough as the specific yardstick measuring relative approaches to direct social action. Above all, this was so in the context of revitalised trade unionism and the party's inextricable identification with industrial interests. And not only at a local small-shopkeepers-keeping-their-noses-clean level: as Schnadhorst admitted to Gladstone in September 1891, in the context of Tillett's challenge at West Bradford to the big local worsted spinning manufacturer, he was very anxious about the existence of 'independent labour candidates whom we cannot adopt as they are being started against long tried Liberals like Illingworth'.[32] The 'cannot' spoke volumes. But it took an alert, budding politician to appreciate fully how deep-rooted the divide had become. In July 1894, after a Liberal employer and ex-mayor had superseded the projected local trades council candidate at the Attercliffe by-election, the young Scottish Radical Ramsay MacDonald wrote to Keir Hardie that 'the time for conciliation has gone by'[33] and pledged his support to the Independent Labour Party at the coming election. It was only a matter of time, or rather industrial circumstances, before organised labour as a whole reluctantly followed suit.

Of course, one can stress too much these tangible causes of discord. One of Vincent's most illuminating statements has been that to emphasise exclusively 'the criterion of welfare' in treating the background to the rise of Labour is 'to foist a modern *Realpolitik* of bread, on men who needed politics chiefly to supply the circuses of their lives'.[34] And it is certainly significant that when the rather élitist, Fabian-dominated 'New Liberalism' of the early 1890s assumed distinctly more ethical, anti-imperialist and participatory forms later in the decade, then it received a much warmer working-class hearing. As L. T. Hobhouse wrote in neo-Gladstonian terms in the *Manchester Guardian* in July 1899, there was 'all the difference between benevolent officialdom setting the world in order from above, and the democratic Collectivism which seeks not to restrict liberty but to fulfil it'.[35] Yet for all the evidence about solid working-class Liberal voting in Edwardian London and Lancashire, it is doubtful whether that experience has the same typicality or long-term significance as the steady, if slow, move from Liberal to Labour in more thoroughly industrial areas like the West Riding, the North-East and South Wales. That major rift had already come, or was showing unmistakable signs of coming, during Queen Victoria's reign. Its specific values will be considered later, but suffice here to emphasise the fact of the break and its materialist basis, an orientation not so much Roman 'bread and circuses' as born of an awareness that the price of Gladstonian Liberalism had become too high, its rewards too doubtful. Moreover, when Gladstone himself retired in 1894, the major part of his party met the challenge pitifully. After disastrous election results in 1895 – signifying the end of an era with a solid anti-Liberal vote registered rather than positively pro-Labour – all that Rosebery had left to offer was the belief that 'the best chance for the Liberal Party lies much more in reaction from the present government than in any gospel of its own'.[36] As early as October 1891, an exchange between Herbert Gladstone, MP for West Leeds, and G. W. Haigh, Secretary of the Colne Valley Division of the Labour Union, had anticipated the implications of this barrenness. After Haigh had complained about a recent speech of his at Leeds, Gladstone wrote coldly on 10 October with regard to the working-class desire for manhood suffrage and the payment of MPs that 'a slight knowledge of parliamentary history shows emphatically that no Gov^t pledged to deal with the IQ & large social matters such as the liquor traffic could attempt a larger programme in the course of a Parl^{nt} of average duration'. Gladstone then went on to stress the need for unity in order to keep the Tories out. A little over a fortnight later came Haigh's considered reply: 'You are not on the question at all. . . . We recognise both political parties as political enemies.' And after contrasting the lack of parliamentary action to the sweet words at Newcastle: 'When speaking of parliamentary history you may think, we are like mushrooms, sprang up yesterday morning and with no knowledge of parliamentary history. But it is this knowledge of parliamentary history which makes us revolt and set out on the course we have, and the able, and more or less wealthy men you speak of withdrawing from the cause of progress will be no obstacle in our way.' Bold words, not altogether sustained during the course of the decade. But the sense of independence remained – and eventually created a new party desirous of taking over 'the cause of progress'.

Since class *is* 'a relationship, and not a thing',[37] it is insufficient to consider only the relatively infrastructural aspects of the period's developing social stratification. A prime example of the working class digging in hard was the Co-operative movement, which, though still remaining politically faithful to Liberalism, increased in membership from 547,000 in 1881 to 1,707,000 by 1900. Shortly afterwards, in July 1903, a series of articles in the *Todmorden and District News* recalled the foremost local co-operator of the nineteenth century, John Hartley, whose achievements included this proud moment: 'On the 28th July, 1887, the present handsome and commodious premises were opened in Crown-street. . . . Without exception they are the most conspicuous buildings in Hebden-bridge.' And the writer also emphasised: 'There was nothing about Mr Hartley's personal appearance, or in his style of language or address that partook in any way of what may be described as "the commercial". . . . He had sprung from the working class and kept in many ways its styles and habits.' At an institutional level alone there are many other examples of a similar and increasing working-class apartness from, or resistance to, middle-class mores. The General Secretary of the Northumberland District Extension Committee wrote in 1884 about the progress of the University Extension movement in his area: 'It is now an established fact that the working classes will not attend lectures which are entirely managed by members of the higher classes. It is also an established fact that they will attend lectures which are managed by members of their own class.'[38] During the same year, the Working Men's Club movement, one of Solly's improving inventions, successfully emancipated itself from financial control from above. But perhaps most striking of all was the fate of 'the People's Palace', a creation of the writer Walter Besant that sought in true mid-Victorian fashion to spread sweetness and light in the East End. The first stage of it, the Queen's Hall, was opened in 1887 and quickly proved a complete flop in the eyes of the local working class. Arthur Morrison in *A Child of the Jago* (1896) sardonically called it 'the East End Elevation Mission and Pansophical Institute', observing that, in the familiar pattern, it was patronised by 'tradesmen's sons, small shopkeepers and their families, and neat clerks, with here and there a smart young artisan of one of the especially respectable trades'. The working man, in other words, even if he was of a culturally improving frame of mind, simply did not want to know about something imposed so loftily from above. A sense of class independence had begun to replace the centrality of the old sober-progress-or-drunken-decline conceptual dichotomy; and religion indubitably, especially Nonconformity, proved the test-case in this solidifying of working-class values.

Chapter 5

RELIGION

'It is not that the Church of God has lost the great towns; it has never had them.'

This famous dictum by A. F. Winnington-Ingram, issued in 1896 in his stirringly titled *Work in Great Cities*, was surely true. Engels half-a-century earlier had made his equally well-known pronouncement,[1] in a broad sense unchallengeable, that 'all the writers of the bourgeoisie are unanimous on this point, that the workers are not religious, and do not attend church'. In 1851 the religious census provided the first statistical confirmation, showing that in the populous industrial areas not only did up to half the inhabitants not attend services, but also that those who did tended to be Nonconformist. But as a leading Wesleyan Methodist commentator, J. B. Dyson, wrote only five years later with regard to the Congleton Circuit in the Potteries: 'We have not taken hold of the poorest – we have not reached the outcast and dregs of society.' [2] Subsequently there were few signs of a reversal of this failure, though until perhaps the late 1890s working-class institutional allegiance to religion seems as a whole to have stayed at roughly its mid-Victorian level. A low level it certainly was, for the series of provincial censuses taken in the early 1880s showed clearly how absenteeism was at its heaviest in large industrial cities like Sheffield and specifically working-class towns like Gateshead; while even in a more old-fashioned city like Bristol, boasting a 35·6 percentage of church-goers, the sense of working-class detachment was barely less pronounced than elsewhere. 'Can they be brought in?' asked Bishop Ryle of Liverpool poignantly in a pamphlet in 1883, but conclusively they could not, to judge by the even lower 1902 Anglican attendance figures. Charles Booth's findings in London were equally stark: 'The general conclusion is that the great masses of the people remain apart from all forms of religious communion.' And soon afterwards, the *Daily News* religious census of 1902–3 revealed in massive detail that in the poor areas of London (using Booth's distinctions) 11·7 per cent of the adult population attended services, in the working-class areas 13·2 per cent, and in the upper working-class ones 16·1 per cent. But perhaps the final evidence should come from an entirely nineteenth-century industrial creation, Middlesbrough, where a few years later Lady Florence Bell estimated attendances of about 22,000 from a population of around 90,000 and stressed the mood of massive working-class indifference: instead Ironopolis (as one of the town's professional football teams had been called) took all.

'Indifference' to organised religion was undoubtedly the central motif. Thomas Wright summed the matter up succinctly and authoritatively in *The Great Unwashed* in 1868: 'To speak of widespread infidelity among the working classes, or of their being *actively* opposed to religion, or religious institutions, is simply to talk nonsense.' Thirty years later, the vicar of a county town in the south of England re-iterated this theme of passive detachment: 'I am afraid I have many working men in my parish who have not even Sunday clothes, and who pay no observance to Sunday, except to stay in bed in the morning and eat more than they do on any other days. . . . It is indifference, not hostility to religion.' [3] To explain this primarily non-doctrinal apart-ness, the notion of thwarted respectability is obviously important, especially in the socially more fluid mid-Victorian period. Edward Miall, a leading Nonconformist, wrote in 1849 of 'the square pew, carpeted perhaps and curtained, the graduated scale of other pews, the free-sittings' as major causes of disharmony, in both the Anglican and Nonconformist world, together with 'the entire absence of coloquialism from the discourse'.[4] There was also the aggravating dress problem. Mostly it proved insuperable, but an indicative exception was in the working-class parish of All Saints in Newcastle, where in 1882 the vicar managed to cajole the women to risk ignominy by attending church with shawls covering their heads, but then over the next few years watched them defy penury by acquiring bonnets as the condition, even the rationale, of their continued attendance. Apartness, however, was not just a question of the working class being unable to afford the price of stepping into the shadow of the middle class. A continuing sense of grievance, the undertug of injustice, meant that the major part of the organised working class felt itself in-stinctively opposed to the rest of society even if at the same time it sought acceptance. 'I did not admire the other boys . . . but, in con-tradiction, I wanted to be one of them' [5] is how Evelyn Waugh (writing about his schooldays at Lancing) once described these compatible levels of consciousness. At its most specific, this oppositional mentality recognised institutional religion as a form of social control, which often it clearly was, as is evident in the mid-century church-building activities of the mill-owners in the not untypical small industrial town of Glossop. In its more common and generalised form, Walsham How was surely correct when he concluded in his 1888 Church Congress Report that there existed 'a terribly deep-rooted notion that the Church was for the rich and comfortable'.[6] And a random issue (12 March 1899) of the populist *Reynolds' Newspaper* contained in one column 'Our

Spiritual Guides', 'Terrible Scandals', and 'Immoral Clergymen' as three successive headings. Or as Easton put it more bluntly still in Robert Tressell's novel, *The Ragged Trousered Philanthropists* (1914): 'all this religious business' was simply 'just a money-making dodge'.

But if this was typical of working-class cynicism about the profession of religion, it certainly did not represent the sum of popular religious sentiment. Other levels of analysis are needed, including those of myth and superstition as well as a vaguer, more general sense of the numinous. *Cassell's Saturday Journal* reported in 1895 the recent death of 'a Taunton oracle' known as 'Billy the Piper' well known in the West country as 'a past master of witchcraft and fortune-telling'. One of many letters, 'mostly from illiterate people', that were found at his house when he died came from a woman living near Exeter: 'Everything is going wrong at my home today. I don't know whose been, or if they caused it without coming. Mother was going to have the chimney sweept, and the man isn't come yet, and I expect he will come after dinner, so as I shan't have a chance to burn the water as you said.' This is obviously an extreme and rural instance, but a similar sense of the pagan is discernible in the fact that according to the *Daily News* survey the two favourite services of the urban poor were the Harvest Thanksgiving one and 'Watch Night' on New Year's Eve. Nor should one ignore the continuing prevalence, despite clerical disapproval, of 'churching' by working-class women after the birth of their last child. At a more orthodox level, apart from the basic birth-marriage-and-death rites of passage, the absence of a deep-rooted doctrinal revolt from religion was shown clearly by the general willingness of the working class to send its children to Sunday School, usually of whichever denomination was geographically nearest. Research work [7] at Rawmarsh, a heavily industrial town near Rotherham in Yorkshire, confirms the drift of Newman's remarks in Tressell's novel. Churchgoing was not for him, but 'the old woman goes sometimes and of course the young 'uns goes; you've got to tell 'em something or other, and they might as well learn what they teaches at the Sunday School as anything else'. In other words, at a certain stage in life, but only then, a certain amount of ethical instruction seemed desirable. As Lansbury put it sardonically in 1897: 'Of course people have a sort of belief: they believe in a God, but it doesn't mean anything in their lives.' [8] Each half of the assertion demands emphasis. Oxford House in the East End was the story of a settlement's uphill struggle to create religiously orientated lives out of what appeared to be a deadweight materialism, yet late in his life Winnington-Ingram, head of it in the 1890s, recalled that whenever he spoke at the nearby Victoria Park on Sundays 'the crowd, few of whom went to church or chapel, were always on my side in answering the secularist's questions'.[9] Or as a small boy gravely informed Mayhew: 'Yes he had heer'd of God who made the world. Couldn't exactly recollec' when he's heer'd on him, but he had, most sarten-ly.'

Despite all this, the 'Methodism or Marxism' debate has rumbled on. And in a dialectical sense rightly so – for the history of nineteenth-century popular religion (not to mention the origins and character of the Labour Party) is as much about the quite substantial minority who did care as about the rest who remained for most of their lives relatively indifferent. In particular, one must consider the far-reaching implications of the fact that the Methodists (including the Calvinistic sect in Wales) rose in number from a little over 100,000 in 1805 to close on three-quarters of a million by 1851. The appeal, as reflected by that year's census, was predominantly to the new industrial population of the North, where the production of coal and textiles was already on a large scale. It is easy to be too simplistic about the nature of this appeal, especially as research is increasingly showing the extent of non-attachment to institutional Christianity in rural England before the Industrial Revolution. Nevertheless, the nineteenth-century industrial experience was still quite different from anything that had gone before: explicitly materialistic, socially increasingly fragmented, and empirical in spirit rather than universal. In a psychologically often desperate situation, Methodism, with its organisational flexibility, was able to make a distinctive mark. Marx's dictum bears repeating: 'Religion is the sob of the oppressed creature, the heart of a heartless world, the spirit of conditions utterly unspiritual. It is the opium of the poor.' The revivalist stress on personal salvation transcending the material condition, the ability to make sense of the new industrialism in terms of regular work rhythms, and the creation of autonomous regulative communities – these were the central motive forces that underlay the validity of Marx's perception. To be too categorical about the specific nature of this regulative control is pointless, for within Nonconformity as a whole it varied from the rigid moral discipline exercised by the middle-class Presbyterian elders of still crafts-based Aberdeen to the self-creating sense of the other that informed the hard lives of single-occupation Durham mining communities. What mattered at a time of fundamental social change was the sense of participation, illusory or otherwise, in the survival and growth of an ordered but emancipatory religious presence on earth. The early Methodists who instructed that they be buried with their class tickets left a world which had in a sense taken away almost everything else.

Inevitably, though, the question of Methodism's popular appeal was also affected by the perennial problem of internal working-class differentiation. Often it was simply a matter of money: the residuum, even the unskilled labouring class, were unable to take part in the maintenance of financially self-supporting Nonconformity. This social cleavage was exacerbated by the 'shopocracy' mentality of the sort of congregation described in *The Autobiography of Mark Rutherford*. Looking back on his early worship in an Independent chapel in a small mid-Victorian provincial town, he recalled wryly that 'these services were not interesting to me for their own sake . . . what I really liked was clanship and the satisfaction of belonging to a society marked off from the great world'. All this mattered in a negative sense, but the crux from a working-class point of view was essentially cultural and behavioural, a question of normative practices. In the simple words of an old man to a missionary of St Giles, London, in the 1860s: 'It is true I have not been what is called a religious sort of chap, but you see I had no time to spare to attend to it and I am not a scholar.' [10] It is in this sort of perspective that one must put the self-respecting aspect of Methodist influence especially; and the recollections of an aged Staffordshire potter of the time around 1850 when he became a Primitive Methodist preacher are in this respect thoroughly representative: 'My connection with the Mutual Improvement Society fostered regular habits of study, as far as possible, and gave me increasing power of expression. These things were noticed, as they usually are in Methodism at large, and it was suggested by friends that I should prepare to take the position of a local preacher.' [11] This is not to say that advance within Nonconformity *necessarily* involved Smilesian values. The tradition of religious radicalism from Bunyan onwards continued to exercise a strong mental pull, together with the more specific subsequent influence of the structure of Methodism on developing trade union organisation. Nevertheless, it was radicalism of a certain and familiar type: liberationist, supra-economic, thoroughly concerned with individual moral standards. Furthermore, within the confines of a society still divided as much by behavioural as specifically economic shibboleths, the effect of Methodist allegiance was often in practice to ostracise certain types of political conduct. As Emanuel Lovekin, a tramping navvy who rose to be a colliery manager and dedicated Primitive Methodist, wrote in the 1890s about his Chartist youth: 'I very probaley learnt a lesson for my after life, For I was more carefull in what Society I mixt up in.' [12]

The nexus of religion, status and cultural norms dominated the Nonconformist onslaught on the drinking, gaming and recreational habits of the labouring and residual class. Attacking the landed aristocracy and this majority of working men with fine impartiality, the various sabbatarian and temperance societies created a sharp divide within the labour élite itself. The Applegarth school accepted the new Puritanism and until about the late 1880s, and in their own minds even longer, seemed to gain enough respect from above to justify to themselves the generally mute disregard from below. This divide was not simply a question of self-improvers and the rest, for a certain part of the working class did desire respectability and its accoutrements (epitomised by chapel weddings) while realising that it could not be for them as a full-blown way of life. The galling experience of a keen sabbatarian doing the rounds in Islington about 1890 reveals this sense of having perforce to construct and justify an alternative code of conduct: '22 Popham Road. Had conversation with person here upon subject of closing business on Sundays. She did not see her way clear to do so she said. Sundays they did more than other days and she thought there was no harm in trying to put by a little for the future. I spoke of the realm of the soul and how unwise to neglect for the sake of earthly gain.' [13] In the light of the famous couplet from *I should like to die, said Willie* – 'But I'll have to tell the angel when I meet him at the door/That he must excuse my papa 'cause he couldn't leave the store' [14] – the irony is considerable. Nevertheless, the distance from the Nonconformist ethic derived even more powerfully from the developing sense of specific oppositional working-class mores. Booth recognised this hardening of the class structure when he argued that since those members of the working class 'who do join any church become almost indistinguishable from the class with which they then mix, the change that has really come about is not so much *of* as *out of* the class to which they have belonged'. Or as a clergyman had observed from a slightly different perspective at the 1881 Church Congress, working people feel 'that they compromise themselves in some way by going to a church'.[15] But for all this creation of a resolutely detached class consciousness, based increasingly firmly on cultural modes, it was Nonconformity itself which proved in the end as responsible as anything for the final breaking (in class terms at least) of the mid-Victorian compact.

The root of the matter was the phenomenon of an increasingly middle-class movement attempting more strenuously than ever before to impose its morality upon the nation as a whole. In 1896 the Free Church Congress even declared its resolve to obtain the Sunday closing of all pubs without the option. Inevitably the chosen political weapon was the Liberal Party, purged of the Whigs after 1886 and now utterly open to ethical infiltration as long as Gladstone maintained his supra-economic resolve. Yet, paradigmatically, the contemporaneous drift of the middle class as a class towards suburbia, Conservatism, and even Anglicanism, was precisely the cause of the failure of this most vocal part of the class to impose overall cultural hegemony. The cryptic phrase 'a carriage never goes to a meeting-house for three generations' said it all: losing numbers steadily to the counter-attraction of moneyed churchiness, the still powerful and financially even more pivotal remains of middle-class Nonconformity – men like the mustard manufacturer Jeremiah Colman, Gladstonian MP for Norwich until 1895 – succumbed because they themselves behaved as a class even while they sought in their political policy and ethical directives to transcend the economic factor. The end of the honest and uncompromising Nonconformist architectural tradition was one symptom, the swallowing-up of the small employer another, the public-school alliance with the landowning aristocracy a third. One has only to read Mark Rutherford to catch exactly this sense of spiritual self-satisfaction on the one hand, cultural control as a form of social and political power on the other. Physical segregation, a flight to the outer suburbs shared on a less ambitious scale by the new white-collar lower middle-class of first-generation chapel deacons, confirmed the impossibility of the duality. The old chapels in the centre of London, let alone the nearby new solidly working-class suburbs, had little chance of maintaining or building up religious vitality in the face of seekers of green pastures like Thomas Scrutton, who was described in his obituary in 1896 as 'a shipowner, a leading Congregationalist layman, and a member of Stepney Meeting, who had now retired to Blackheath'.[16] Scrutton in fact 'had forsaken Liberalism because of the growth of "mad Radicalism" ', but even those who had not, aware of that Radicalism's stunted growth, were tending likewise to become far removed from the working-class support upon which they were numerically dependent. For, undoubtedly, physical distance mattered. As the French religious sociologist Boulard has written about certain parts of France and the Rhineland that are both religious and industrial: 'It is apparently the case that in these *recently* industrialised areas it has been possible to *foresee* the effects of industrialisation on the life of the Church, and thus new immigrants were drawn, as they arrived, into social and religious organisations where they could again take root.'[17] But in nineteenth-century Britain this consciously homogeneous process was at best temporary. The middle class held off for quite a long time the stratifying implications of an *ad hoc* industrial revolution, but finally felt able to depart from the scene of the crime, leaving behind a sense of profound detachment from a formal religious culture and many rows of pews up for hire.

Shaftesbury, however, was as important a figure in Victorian England as Smiles. Nevertheless, it was not until quite late in the century that the Church of England as a whole managed to make even the slightest impact on the social question. As the Rev. Henry Moseley wrote in 1846 about a clergyman's plight in the Midlands: 'There is nothing to fill up the space between him and the industrial masses . . . it is a desolate position.' [18] The loss of influence seemed total, the memory of rural domination another world. All sorts of reasons compounded the basic incomprehension: the rigidity of the parish system, the lack of lay participation, the pitiful value of incumbencies in the poorer districts of the city. Nor did comprehension always dawn when the Anglican leaders formally addressed themselves to the situation. 'It would be a good piece of physical exercise, and give a capital appetite for dinner' [19] was how a speaker at the 1881 Church Congress framed his advice to out-of-touch clergy in mining districts about the desirability of making a weekly trip down the pits. Yet within the context of growing urban social stratification, Anglicanism was inherently more likely than Nonconformity to furnish a positive response. Not only did its aristocratic connections make it far removed culturally from the world of temperance, but also its traditional paternalist strain encouraged, from Oastler and Shaftesbury onwards, a basic anti-industrial animus that at its best led to a hardy social conscience. This emphasis on works as well as faith was apparent in South Wales, where by the 1880s Nonconformity still retained the preponderant allegiance of the miners and ironworkers, but was showing itself much more complacent about their welfare than the rival Llandaff Diocesan Conference. Often, of course, this Anglican concern manifested itself in a primitive form of Tory dole money for the residuum. In Morrison's words: 'Judicious attendance at churches, chapels and prayer-meetings beyond the Jago borders was rewarded by coal-tickets, boots and the like'; and in the Jago itself, Father Sturt was notable for being 'no common milch-cow in the matter of gratuities'. It was a poor basis for allegiance, inevitably involving bitterness and recrimination when the source of charity dried up. But at least in comparison with still primarily self-help Nonconformity, it indicated a sense of social responsibility potentially in tune with the mood of the 1880s.

But how should one see the collective orthodoxy of this decade: simply as the product of guilty heart-stirrings or also the consciously conceived exercise of will-power to calm an apparently rising political temperature? The motives of the university men who instigated the settlement movement – the fullest expression of 'Christianity in action', the great new byword – may have been individually pure, but their action itself has also to be seen within the setting of other new agencies of social guidance like the Church Lads' Brigade and the Boys' Club movement. Recreation and education were as important as religion in these organisations, the whole dressed up in a quasi-military framework as fitting preparation for service to the imperial ideal. The Hon. J. G. Adderley, head of Oxford House, was quite frank in his settlement's first Annual Report (1884): 'Colonisation by the well-to-do seems indeed the true solution to the East End question, for the problem is, how to make the masses realise their spiritual and social solidarity with the rest of the capital and the kingdom: how to revive their sense of citizenship, with its privileges which they have lost, and its responsibilities which they have forgotten.' [20] In this language of apprehension as well as more noble sentiments, one can appreciate why both the leaders of the settlement movement and the second generation of Christian Socialists failed on the whole to advance remedially beyond the ideas of Henry George despite having the advantage (unlike Chamberlain) of not themselves being directly dependent upon industrial capital. Barnett at Toynbee Hall was merely typical in the way he maintained the distinction between the deserving and the non-deserving poor, while at the same time looking hopefully to the immoderate rich for a change of heart and behaviour. Not surprisingly, the settlements only appealed in any substantial measure either to artisans and the lower middle class eager to take part in such self-improving occasions as the Sunday evening 'Tobacco Parliaments' at Toynbee Hall or more generally to games-lovers eager to make use of the settlements' facilities. 'Far too largely given up to billiards' flatly stated the Oxford House Annual Report for 1897. And four years later, Masterman described a movement at the end of its first flush when he wrote of the London settlements that 'the buildings remain and a few energetic toilers, and the memory of a great hope'.[21] Irrelevant politically, diverted materially, the settlements could only hope to return to status-ridden faith after the failure of service.

Nonconformity likewise found itself unable to maintain the pristine values when it sought, much more intermittently, to widen the scope of its appeal. The Quaker adult schools, for example, moved during the last quarter of the century from being religious and educational in character to being increasingly social, typified by the rowing club and drum-and-fife band at Scarborough. Another major concession to the secular was the rise from the mid-1870s onwards of the Pleasant Sunday Afternoon movement. Its qualities were mildly ethical and thoroughly non-revivalist, the services far more diluted than the Love Feasts, which once had been the only form of Methodism without a specifically theological orientation. The appeal of the movement was considerable, as at Scunthorpe in July 1896, when 600 people (over 450 more than the membership of the local Primitive Methodists who were organising the service) waited patiently to be entertained by the Hull Excelsior Minstrels. The response of the Nonconformist establishment was lukewarm. 'It is possible to attempt to brighten the hours of the day of rest at the expense of its sacredness' [22] noted the Wesleyan Conference of 1895; while in the Quaker world, the Sunday Schools and their subsidiary mission churches, full of hymn-singing and premeditated persuasion, tended to be virtually ostracised by the middle-class Friends. Doubtless this was inevitable: new forms of popular appeal were ultimately incompatible with the culture and ideology of orthodox Nonconformity, certainly as mediated by its prosperous subscribers, on their way to becoming socially established. The fate of the Wesleyan mission-halls – 'shabby, dilapidated mission-halls of tin or drab brick' [23] Masterman called them in 1904 – symbolised this detachment. They failed because, although being part of a great attempt by Hugh Price Hughes in the late 1880s to regenerate inner-city vitality, they were run exclusively by a small group of middle-class organisers who insisted on provable religious conviction before they distributed any charity and consequently made little appeal to the authentic have-nots. Yet though it was the only alternative to direct populism, apparent in the pockets of Irish working class loyal to the Catholic priesthood, it is doubtful whether in the long run a more open-handed appreciation of pressing social concerns would have been very much more efficacious. In a sense, organised religion changed horses too late: overtaken by economics, it recognised the danger belatedly and half-heartedly, shedding its indistinct spiritual colours merely to finish a poor blinkered last to the State, the new and apparently neutral 'Leviathan' [24] of social action.

The history of the Salvation Army confirmed the thorniness of the dilemma. William Booth was adamant from the Whitechapel beginnings of the Army in 1865 that the spiritual condition of man was of paramount concern, his material trappings an irrelevance. Nevertheless, this did not prevent him from virtually pioneering modern methods of evangelicalism, including brass bands, simple joyous hymns, and popular pamphlets like William Corbridge's *The Up Line to Heaven and the Down Line to Hell!* Booth was also adamant that, unlike the missionary enterprises run by the Wesleyan Reformers and Methodist New Connexion from which he had disassociated himself, the Salvation Army had to be run by working-class people if it was to hope to shift working-class apathy. Results were mixed. On a Sunday in 1887, about 42,000 people attended Salvationist services in inner London – a substantial enough figure, yet hardly a major dent into the prevailing indifference. Furthermore, the officers themselves were in practice generally from the lower middle class and the Army made little impact during the 1880s on really poor parts of the East End like Bethnal Green. In 1888 Booth showed that he recognised the situation by opening at Limehouse the first shelter for sustenance and lodging. Then, two years later, the publication of his *In Darkest England and the Way Out* showed the full extent of his change of policy. In it he coined the phrase 'the submerged tenth', repudiated the 'deserving' distinction, and put forward a scheme for co-operative, individually regenerative farm colonies in the Essex countryside. Yet Booth's target of attack firmly remained not poverty, but non-belief. As he stated in the Preface: 'In providing for the relief of temporal misery, I reckon that I am only making it easy where it is now difficult . . . for men and women to find their way to the Cross of our Lord Jesus.' A palliative indeed – and when the early shock that the book caused was forgotten, and the scheme itself came to little, Booth drew his spiritual horns in, renamed the new Social Reform Wing the Social Wing, and left the materially ameliorating side of the Army's activities to more junior officers in routine positions. But again, it is unlikely whether the Salvation Army could really have become a pivotal social agency without having at the same time betrayed at the cultural level alone its original, determining spiritual nature. In one particularly unfortunate year, 1882, no less than 669 Salvationists were physically assaulted, an antagonism that culminated in June when Booth bought and occupied the notorious 'Eagle' (of 'Pop goes the Weasel' fame) on the City Road. Great demonstrations resulted and the *Daily Chronicle* referred to 'the murderous temper of the mob, who raged and howled in an appalling manner'. As Booth himself later admitted about the 'roughs' of society: 'Our success among this class has come far short of what it ought to have been.' [25] Working-class culture was becoming, in other words, thoroughly resistant to a counter-culture as strong as the Salvation Army's. What it might, however, accept – and the 'roughs' themselves, increasingly organised, were by no means just the classic residuum – was a certain type of ethic, gritty and independent at base, a little sentimentalised 'after hours', and certainly not too pushily good. In a moment we must return to the North, where this type of ethic was to flourish and where, because the pursuit of religion tended to be socially less divisive, the break with institutionalism in the 1890s proved of particularly critical import.

The decline of working-class Secularism, traditionally but not exclusively associated with independent and Radical craftsmen in the metropolis, accentuated this centrality. A detailed study [26] of predominantly working-class conversions to unbelief during the second half of the century has shown that religion was disavowed less on theological grounds than as an obstacle (presumably deferential) to social progress. These freethinkers tended to be men in poor jobs, but anxious to get on in the world. They also tended to be men apart for one reason or another from hearth and family. Indeed, the sense of an upright and determinedly non-cosy morality comes through strongly in these lines from a typical mid-century freethought hymn:

'Take the spade of perseverance;
Dig the fields of progress wide;
Every rotten root of faction
Hurry out and cast aside.' [27]

The improving tone of Secularism was also reflected in its offspring of the 1850s, the National Sunday League, which sought to replace the religious Sunday not with base pleasures, but instead with a judicious mixture of shop-trading and art-gallery visiting. The key figure in this eminently reformist world was G. J. Holyoake, a keen co-operator whose book, *The History of the Rochdale Pioneers*, included this panegyric to a building erected by one of Manchester's 'Captains of Industry': 'Towering in variegated marble, head and shoulders above all surrounding structures – occupying the site of sixty-three former tenements – it stands the Monarch of Warehouses. The factory worker grows taller by looking up at it.' Even after Bradlaugh became dominant in the movement from the mid-1860s and sharpened its republican and atheistical image, he still failed either to push the membership of the National Secular Society beyond about 6,000 or to transform its essentially individualist Radicalism. A turning-point came in 1885 when, a year after Bradlaugh's public debate with Hyndman on Socialism, Annie Besant left the Society and joined the socially more analytical Fabians. The older generation of leaders clung on, but the Society itself rapidly lost influence and indeed relevance, reaching a nadir in 1896 with its opposition to the proposed introduction of Old Age Pensions. Moreover, at the grass-roots level of Secularism, the Working Men's Clubs, the move there during the 1890s away from serious discussion towards entertainment pure and simple was merely another facet of the general late-century emaciation of improving Radicalism. The Secularism of the minority was giving way to the Secularism of the majority; and the more resistant attitude of the other main strand of working-class political leadership, ethical and Nonconformist, now became the crucial one.

Primitive Methodism, although strongest in the North after its rapid expansion of the 1820s, was certainly not confined to there. A striking report in *The Primitive Methodist* was this in November 1887 by the Teignmouth branch of the Torquay Mission: 'We have just held our harvest thanksgiving services. . . . During the effort the Rev. J. S. Stanwell favoured us with his popular lecture on the Devil.' And quite soon afterwards, Charles Booth quoted the observation of a Congregationalist minister in London that 'the Primitive Methodists are the only ones amongst us who touch the poor at all', with Booth himself adding that 'it is probably the simplicity and directness of their beliefs and the democratic basis of management which attract'. Indeed, the memory of the 1820s – the eschatological fervour and the rebellion against oligarchic middle-class Wesleyanism – seems to have persisted for most of the century as a powerful compelling force. The social divide certainly remained strong: at Rawmarsh, right up to 1914, a 'Wesleyan gate' for the clerks and time-keepers stood side by side at the steel works with a 'Primitive gate' for the steelworkers, furnace men and labourers. Yet these and similar internal stratifying appearances were in a sense deceptive. The Cornish evidence [28] is suggestive: not only did Primitive Methodism there tend to dispense with the early and rather crude 'hell-fire' preaching, but also, after a series of mid-century expulsions of 'dissolute' members, it began to acquire an increasingly solid social ethic. And in general, Primitive Methodism's appeal tended to be increasingly for the improving sort of working man, especially in the single-occupation mining communities where the sect became increasingly concentrated after about 1850. There the Lib.-Lab. tradition took firm and explicit root: Burt and Crawford were only the best-known of the early exponents. The relationship between religious practice and certain qualities of political leadership was perhaps not directly causal, but undoubtedly there were, as has been justly cited [29] in this context, 'elective affinities'. The quality of these affinities was much more complex than simply that of sensible compromise. The fact that at Rawmarsh at the end of the century only the children of Primitive Methodists wore shoes at the steelworkers' school, despite all the parents earning virtually the same wage, was but one side of the self-improving ethic. The other was an authentic moral consciousness based on self-respect and far removed from silent deference. *The Primitive Methodist Magazine* observed in 1886 that the poor child 'should certainly be taught contentment with his lot, but not such contentment as the heartless employer would have him practise, to live and die in the same position as he was when he began life'. In practice, however, active participation in Primitive Methodism did tend, as in Lovekin's case, to preclude forthrightly independent political action, let alone Socialism. The lodges of the Derbyshire Miners' Association, dominated by Primitive Methodist leaders, even imposed fines on their members of 1s for swearing and 2s 6d for anyone 'boasting of his independence towards his employers and managers, on account of being a member of the Association'.[30] Such a leadership, concerned with economic security and personal salvation, remained antithetical to bolder, less respectable political notions. In an industry only relatively slowly succumbing to determinedly lower middle-class colliery managers, the miners proved to be the last major trade union group to affiliate themselves to the Labour Party. Instead, it was elsewhere, in more pluralistic communities, that explicitly middle-class Nonconformity played its major role in the alienating process.

In September 1887 the *Nonconformist* cautioned that 'we are not quite sure that unionists act wisely in determining to give their movement a markedly political character'. Over the next few years, this reserve turned to hostility as Nonconformity practically abandoned its view of trade unionism as a bulwark against wider collectivism. The two key figures in relation to this estrangement from the organised working class were Hugh Price Hughes and Keir Hardie. Hughes definitely believed in broadening the appeal of Wesleyanism, yet his democratic conviction remained firmly Gladstonian. Around 1890 he practically reiterated the GOM's maxim when he asserted that the social crux was not a question of political parties, but that 'the real dividing line will, I think, be increasingly betwixt those who are in sympathy with the masses of the people, and those who are in sympathy with wealth and privilege'. His attitude was similarly lofty towards the economic factor (in this case the piecework system) after he had discovered that the Bricklayers' Union was imposing a maximum number of bricks to be laid per day: 'It is terrible, terrible. If the working men become selfish and lazy, not making the very best of the capacities God has given them, they are simply committing suicide.' [31] Hardie also believed in hard work and the ethical approach to life, but not in institutional Congregationalism, from which he had broken away in 1884. What he found impossible to accept was a morality which could ignore grave social and economic injustices, yet which was prepared, as in 1890, to jettison the Irish cause because Parnell's private life offended 'the Nonconformist conscience'.

This Nonconformist role in the middle-class solidification was reflected by the experience of R. F. Horton, an exceptionally advanced minister who recalled about his time at Hampstead in the 1890s that 'every time I pleaded the cause of the people, the wealthy employers and successful professional men charged me with introducing politics into the pulpit'.[32] Hardie's precise argument was that the pulpit would only become relevant if it did develop a political conscience. But when he asserted this to the 1892 Congregational Union meeting at Bradford, home of Illingworth, he was greeted with considerable hostility. There are many other examples of this antagonism (or more commonly at a local level indifference) towards the pursuing of tangible social questions, certainly justifying Hardie's point in 1910 that 'for every Labour man who has left the Church because of antagonism to his former beliefs, ten have been driven out by the unsympathetic attitude of the Church itself'.[33] Bradford it was that proved the great test case. In June 1892 twelve Nonconformist ministers sat on the platform of a pro-Illingworth meeting chaired by Briggs Priestley, another Liberal

MP, who had recently moved in the Commons the critical negating amendment to a Factory Bill. Fred Jowett, elected that year to the town council on behalf of the Bradford Labour Union, warned the twelve in plain words: 'If you persist in opposing the labour movement, there will soon be more reason than ever to complain of the absence of working men from your chapels. We shall establish our own Labour Church.' [34] This duly happened, predominantly in areas where social friction had developed enough to harden attitudes towards Gladstonian Liberalism. The question remained, however, of what would happen to the moral effluence once the grit got properly into it.

The fate of the Labour Church movement gave a large part of the answer. Its founder and leader, the Socialist and Unitarian minister John Trevor, insisted in 1893 on the formation of the Labour Church Union that 'the Religion of the labour movement is not a class Religion, but unites members of all classes working for the abolition of commercial slavery'.[35] In practice, though, the majority of the movement's members, numbering about 2,000 by the mid-1890s, came from industrial Lancashire and the West Riding. According to the *Spectator*, describing a Labour Church congregation in April 1894, 'the bulk were men, decently dressed artisans and mechanics, some of the highest grade, all unless the look belied them, full of earnest expectancy'. The familiar Nonconformist strain was apparent: high-minded and improving working men, only rather more conscious of social issues than a generation earlier. But in the event, fully-fledged ethicalism proved incompatible with the new emphasis on more temporal matters. As early as October 1894, Trevor was complaining about the guest speakers at services who 'confine themselves to questions concerning the conditions of life, but never approach the problem of how to live'.[36] The times, however, were entirely with the peripatetic orators: often leading ILP figures like Hardie, Mann, Glasier and Snowden, they merely represented the most striking part of the ultimately secular, certainly non-theological, hymns, brass bands, social activities, and loose expression of ethical sentiments that comprised the weekly round of most Labour Churches. By the late 1890s, as Hardie opted for the 'labour alliance', it was clear that an essentially materialist nexus was dominant; and the Labour Churches, with Trevor a sick man, passed into fairly rapid decline. Even during the course of the 1890s, the blunting of the early idealism had been reflected by the political lecture topics discussed in the Churches, which changed in emphasis from the spread of Socialist ideas in the early 1890s to the less stirring subjects later in the decade of municipal growth and electioneering techniques. It may be that the Labour Churches had 'a distinct value, especially as tending to keep the movement from sinking into sordid materialism',[37] as Hardie put it, 'thoughtfully sucking his pipe', in an interview in 1897. Yet the ethical legacy it left was soggy – at best a cultural reference for a labour élite who were in many ways old-fashioned Radicals at heart – and one that was to be increasingly superseded by the more deadpan secularism of subsequent labour leaders.

In the eyes of the Christian Socialist Scott Holland, the apparent end of the Gladstonian hegemony was a stark fact of crucial importance. He wrote after the 1895 Election: 'Down goes the middle-class Radical-ism and the Nonconformist conscience. They lie smashed in ruins. . . . It will be an immense and most perilous shifting of centres.' [38] But Holland's fears were exaggerated. Booth instead uttered a central truth when he wrote fairly soon afterwards that 'among working men a kind of sublimated trade unionism is the most prevalent gospel; a vague bias towards that which is believed to be good for one's fellow men'. Various assorted phenomena help one to understand the nature of this sublimation. One was the increasing popularity from the 1860s of working-class spiritualism, especially prevalent in northern in-dustrial towns and offering (usually to ex-Methodists) cosy, immediate and non-judgemental family reunions. A similar diluting of older harshnesses was apparent in the tremendously popular, entirely non-theological revivalism of the American evangelicals Dwight L. Moody and Ira D. Sankey, who first toured Britain in 1873. Favourite tunes like 'Hold the Fort' and 'Safe in the Arms' relied entirely on their simplicity of melody, catchy repetitiveness, and banal sentimentalising. Hell seemed a spent force, Sankey's unwavering harmonium a more comforting alternative. The Welsh Revival of 1904 was more fervent, but similarly ethical rather than dogmatic, and likewise offering an engulfing spectacle. The journalist W. T. Stead described a typical meeting, lasting over two hours: 'Three-fourths of the meeting con-sists of singing. No one uses a hymn-book. No one gives out a hymn. . . . People pray and sing, give testimony; exhort as the Spirit moves them.' [39] Against such a background, the tendency during the late 1890s of Hardie's ILP towards woolly ethicalising becomes intelligible. Snowden, for example, wrote in the *Bradford Labour Echo* in January 1896: 'The desire for Socialism is a desire to loose the chains that have bound men's souls to the earth, and to set them free for higher things. Free from the struggle for existence, and freedom to develop the higher life. Socialists are to work until the day breaks and the shadows flee away.' The creation of this sort of aura, the dilution of Morris's authentic moral vision, took its toll. Even in 1929 only 8 out of 249 Labour MPs described themselves as either agnostics or atheists. Yet this creation of a blanket quasi-religious affirmation meant in the long run somewhat less than met the eye. A central figure at a more local indigenous level was Robert Blatchford, founder of the *Clarion* in 1891 and the frankly secular Clarion Cycling Clubs soon afterwards. He was an inspiring propagating Socialist who came by the beginning of this century to repudiate ethical as well as institutional Christianity as irrelevant to man's terrible condition. Len Youle, a veteran Sheffield labour leader born in 1890 into the family of a 'high-class' cutler who was also a Methodist lay preacher, described in 1970 the effect of reading Blatchford when young: 'I renounced the whole conception of religious teaching altogether. . . . For three weeks I hardly ever slept because I had omitted to get down on my knees and pray.' [40] The experience was formative. A deistic conceptual framework remained ('Whilst not going so far as being a positive atheist I was certainly an agnostic and would not accept the conformist idea of religion'), but on a conscious level these terms of reference became increasingly less relevant. In other words, the cultural by-passing of the morally improving ethic was what signified in everyday practice, not the absence of a new and positively non-deistic counter-culture in opposition to that ethic. The extent of this eminently empirical detachment was made clear in 1902 when organised labour stuck to its board schools and declined to support middle-class Nonconformity's campaign of resistance against Balfour's Education Act. And in the same year Scott Holland acknowledged this formal coming of the two cultures, a divide hastened by religion, even though *neither* culture now genuinely expressed religious concerns: 'War rages, great social changes are toward, disasters intervene, there are discussions on bread and education, but the adult male population of England and Scotland is watching its football matches.' [41]

Chapter 6

CULTURE

'I am asked to tell what the great mass of the workers in the North of England desire. It would be easier to say what they need. Many of them would ask for more wages, many for shorter hours of work, not a few for better racing "tips", or more beer.' [1]

So wrote Blatchford in 1894 about a recognisably modern outlook in an industrial society. The sense is of certain secular wants, and not just the basic 'Hard Times' needs, that now demand to be satisfied. Yet the evidence suggesting an ameliorated working class able by the end of the century to extend its material pleasures is by no means uniform. It is true that during the third quarter the 'killer' zymotic diseases like cholera and smallpox began to be successfully combated; while in Sheffield, for example, the death-rate fell (though the infant mortality rate did not) from 27·4 per 1,000 in the 1860s to 20·9 by the early 1890s. Nevertheless, the condition of working-class housing was still terrible and possibly even worsening; and behind it lay the continuing and still more severe phenomenon of poverty as such. Booth's findings in London were confirmed soon afterwards by Seebohm Rowntree in York, to the effect that 9·9 per cent of the people in that city were in 'primary' poverty, and 17·9 per cent in 'secondary' poverty. There was no falsifying sentimentality about these figures: Rowntree's estimate of a minimum subsistence diet was actually harsher than that provided at the York workhouse. And in 1907, Lady Bell calculated that a third of Middlesbrough's working-class families were either 'absolutely poor' or 'so near the poverty line' as to be 'constantly passing over it'. The background was the Great Depression of 1873–96, which caused heavy unemployment and little advance in real wages until the 1890s at the earliest, despite the falling price of certain imported foods. In accordance with the new militarism, the effects of this continuing pauperisation came increasingly to be seen in biological as much as old-fashioned moral terms, culminating at the beginning of the century with the Committee on Physical Deterioration. The shocking figures at the beginning of the Boer War are well known: in Salford alone, of the 12,000 who looked as if they might survive a medical test, 8,000 were absolutely rejected and only 1,200 fully accepted for military service, despite the dropping of pass standards to those of 1815. And in 1883, the working-class football team, Blackburn Olympic, had beaten the Old Etonians 2–1 in the FA Cup Final, despite giving their opponents an average of 28lb a man.

The question of food was obviously all-important. William Luby, who was born near Manchester in 1883 and worked as an assistant to a sweet-boiler in his early years, described on television in 1963 the daily scrounge. When asked: 'Were you eating at home at all?' Luby simply replied: 'When I could. When I could get it.' [2] Obviously it all came down to money: refrigeration and North American wheat undoubtedly did reduce the price of meat and bread in the last quarter of the century but this was at least partly counteracted by more expensive milk products and of course rents, the other great living expense, even leaving aside the question of job prospects and short-time. Rowntree more insistently than anyone else stressed family income as the great determinant. Thus at 15s a week: 'Breakfast and tea were identical; bread and margarine or dripping or treacle or jam, and tea. Dinner was rarely a two-course meal.' [3] Even in 'group C', 21s–30s a week, which Rowntree saw as the most representative, just out of the reach of 'secondary' poverty, bread and potatoes remained staple, the infant mortality rate high, and the daily intake of calories and protein nowhere near adequate. Milk was perhaps the single great arbiter. At over 30s a week, consumption averaged over two pints per head per week, but below that income reliance was placed heavily on tins of the condensed and sweetened variety, much cheaper but often leading to young children getting rickets. Similarly pernicious was the rising sale of margarine, which was new, cheap and utterly unvitamised. Nor was the problem of food adulteration seriously tackled until at least the 1880s. The general impression of grimness is well summed up by Stella Davies, writing about her Edwardian childhood in Rossendale, Lancashire, as part of an improving sort of family that in fact ate better than many: 'In my memory, we lived almost entirely on porridge, hot-pot, sheep's head broth, boiled cod, herrings, rice pudding and suet dumplings.' [4] Clearly the desire for something 'tasty', which Orwell emphasised at Wigan in the 1930s, had deep historical roots as the only way of offsetting such a stomach-turning diet.

We shall return to the question of choice, for food *was* beginning to become a matter of choice for some working-class families towards the end of the century. Nevertheless, the basic struggle for existence continued to remain for a long time the pervasive theme. Food was almost always bought in minute and therefore uneconomic quantities, with the many pawnbrokers and money-lenders (generally charging interest of 2d in the shilling) further exploiting the working-class lack of ready funds. Apart from suicide – which seems to have been fairly common –

the major alternative to this vicious circle was immortalised in the
song 'My Old Man said Follow the Van'. Or in Luby's words: 'Of
course, in those days one way of getting out of debt was to remove.
Naturally.' But this could at best be only a transient solution, a temporary stemming of often implacable circumstances. This sense of
living from a certain stage of life almost permanently on the edge,
heightened by the coming from the mid-1870s of mass cyclical unemployment, was brilliantly caught in Tressell's novel about building
workers in Hastings. Thus of Easton: 'As a single man he had never
troubled much if he happened to be out of work; he always had enough
to live on. . . . But now that he was married it was different; the fear of
being "out" haunted him all the time.' And Lady Bell in Middlesbrough
confirmed the 'spectre of illness and disability'. In this context, the
failure of the working class to reduce its birth-rate at anything like the
same pace as the rest of society from about 1877, the result of continuing hostility to contraception, was particularly significant. Breast-
feeding for up to two years in order to avert another pregnancy
remained common, but it was a miserable substitute. In an awful sense,
human life, a mouth to be fed, succumbed to the nineteenth-century
cash nexus. As Lady Bell wrote: 'to the weak and ailing mother the
child is looked upon often as more of a trouble than a joy, and if
insured its death is a positive benefit instead of a misfortune.' There
could be another side to the effects of this bruising existence: a sense
of animal vitality and devil-take-the-hindmost does sometimes come
through. But on the whole, at the everyday experiential level, one's
abiding impression is of weariness and pessimism, a profound fatalism
about the intractability of life's condition. One does not need to hear
the recording to sense the matter-of-factness in Luby's voice as he
related the scarred details of his life history.

Of course, the dehumanising involved in the industrial process, the
sharpening of the life/work dichotomy, and indeed the notion of alienation are all common enough concepts. One must still reiterate, however,
that precisely as the need to be in employment became more and more
imperative, and the rigour of the new factory discipline became increasingly formal, so the working class seemed to react by withdrawing
their primary, orientating energies from the function that gave them
their name. In an article whose tone was generally progressive, taking
pride in recent ameliorating reforms, W. A. Abram perhaps put the
matter a little strongly, but nevertheless indicatively, when he wrote in
1868 about the workmen of Lancashire: 'The omnipresent and probably
the strongest sentiment of this people is an inveterate repugnance to
factory-work, and a constant desire to get away from it.' [5] But 'repugnance' was in daily practice too strong a word, as Tressell, an
exasperated Socialist, caught exactly in his evocation of the working-

class attitude towards the irksome but eminently endurable phenomenon of work. One of his characters, Philpot, shouts 'Come on, Saturday!' just after 7 o'clock on Monday morning, yet is unable to perceive any remedy beyond the pin-pricks delusion of 'getting some of your own back'. This feeble recompense for ultimate acceptance of the existing system was expressed perfectly by Kipling in one of his *Barrack-Room Ballads*, called 'Cells':

> 'Yes, it's pack-drill for me and a fortnight's C.B.
> For "drunk and resisting the Guard!"
> Mad drunk and resisting the Guard –
> Strewth, but I socked it them hard!'

The negative response of wage-workers to the notion of paid holidays, slowly beginning to be given to salaried staff from the 1880s, was another example of this minimalist attitude towards work: no enthusiasm shown, therefore no favours asked. 'A man that wants paying without working is a drone to his fellow men' [6] was how a spokesman of the Sheffield Engine Drivers and Stokers Society put it in the early 1890s to the Royal Commission on Labour. This acceptance of the work ethic may have been a long way from the Smilesian inculcation of joy-through-labour, but, however unspontaneous, acceptance it was all the same.

Underlying this mediated form of deference – head down, do the work, try to forget about it – was the great psychological sense of social apartness. This took a specifically urban as well as class form. Alfred Williams, lamenting the general blinkered acceptance of the institution of overtime, chronicled [7] in some detail the materialist norms that prevailed in a Swindon railway factory early this century. Rural immigrants, seen as job-rivals, are bluntly told that 'all you blokes are fit for is cow-banging and cleaning out the muck-yard'. Moreover, although 'there is a great deal of talk, chiefly with a political bias, about the sheds, of getting back to the land', in practice very few opt for the low-paid life of the agricultural labourer. And: 'The beauties of wood and field, or hill and down, scarcely appeal to the average working man.' This suggestion of a thoroughly urbanised outlook fits in with the relative unpopularity of rambling as a form of working-class holiday; while at an even more ubiquitous level, Norman Douglas noted about girls' skipping chants in *London Street Games* (1916) that 'you'll not find much talk in these songs about sunshine and flowers and things like that'. Within the urban wen itself there existed, of course, the other main divide. Both classes – the one travelling above the inner-city viaducts, the other living below – clearly perceived the fact of the divide and increasingly gave up seeking a common bridging culture. Roberts has written of Salford at the turn of the century, though it could have been many other thoroughly industrial areas, that it was as parochial and inward-looking a community as any other in Europe at the time. Indeed, the industrial process established the formative pattern early. Thus at Preston in 1847, for all the social insecurity and recourse to removing, roughly 40 per cent of its working-class inhabitants were found to be living within 200 yards of where they had been ten years earlier. Half a century and much transport later, Booth reaffirmed the pattern as it existed in London: 'Migration rarely proceeds outside the little charmed circle of alleys where "old pals" reside: it is rather of the nature of a circular movement.'[8] One can attribute this confinement to several causes: to the propinquity to familiar faces; to the oppressive negative sense of feeling trapped, as in Morrison's Jago; and to a sturdier feeling, the working-class attitude that the world of villadom and the values it represented was not *their* world. Yet 'us' against 'them' can be a deceptive affirmation of independence if 'them' are tamely permitted to go on holding all the trick-taking cards. 'It can't never be altered. Human nature's human nature and you can't get away from it': the new and distinctive forms of working-class industrial culture that emerged in the second half of the century need attention, but one should also recall Philpot's view of 'the system' in order to put them into their correct, non-trick-taking perspective.

One manifestation of this essentially sullen resistance was continuing working-class antagonism during the century towards the police. This new form of social control was justifiably seen as representing an antipathetic middle-class cultural force. In the West Riding in 1857, the background [9] to Wakefield colliers meeting 'the blue locusts' in pitched battle at the Middlestown Feast in June was the context in which county police had been introduced there late the previous year. Early actions set the pattern: the police quickly clamped down on pubs and beerhouses operating in the hitherto immune out-townships of Leeds and Huddersfield during the hours of divine service; they also cleared the outlying roads of Wakefield, which, according to the *Leeds Times*, were regularly 'infested . . . with young men given to foot racing'; and in January 1857 they turned their attention to cock-fighting, another traditional aristocratic-cum-popular pastime. The showdown was inevitable – and eventually led to a not untypical barely tacit peace in which the police virtually abnegated responsibility for certain particularly rough areas. One of the skipping chants heard by Norman Douglas records nicely the popular view:

CULTURE 103

'I went down the lane to buy a penny whistle,
A copper comes by and pinch my penny whistle.
I ask him for it back, he said he hadn't got it –
Hi, Hi, Curlywig, you've got it in your pocket.'

Another 'snatcher' was the school attendance officer created by Forster's Act. He tended to be a former soldier or policeman, accustomed to carrying out orders, and was an enormously unpopular figure. Two main sources underlay this hostility. One was experienced by John Green, who was born in the 1830s into a Liverpool docking family and who, according to his great-grandson, 'stayed up late as a youth, studying by the glow of coals from the kitchen range', though 'at the risk of a belting from his father, who was illiterate'.[10] In a society, however, that was well on the way to being almost fully literate even before Forster, the other main source was less hostility to book-learning as such than a more specific economic consideration. The motivation was particularly strong with relation to the sweated industries not yet effectively protected by factory legislation. Lady Dilke reported in 1883 how she had overheard the informal confession of a female matchbox maker in Shoreditch: 'Of course, we cheat the School Board. It's hard on the little ones, but their fingers is so quick – they that has the most of 'em is the best off.'[11] Nevertheless, it is possible to make too much of the laments of an ostracised figure like John Reeves, whose *Recollections of a School Attendance Officer* described how in Bethnal Green in the 1870s 'the odium of the new system was largely thrown upon the visitors'. Quite a few working-class parents, especially in the north of England, saw the matter differently, recognised the importance of elementary education despite its current regimentation, and were from the 1880s enthusiastic participants as voters in School Board elections or even as candidates. From about the same time, moreover, at a more pervasive level, the early antagonism towards the attendance officers began to show signs of diminishing, as evidenced by the declining number of assaults on them. At both ends of the traditionally polarised working class the pressures were tightening: the would-be aspiring artisan was hardly going to find Forster's schools a potent springboard for the leap upwards; while even the unskilled labourer, let alone the new generation of semi-skilled, might find the three Rs a beneficial acquisition. In other words, the working-class attitude towards elementary education was moving towards fairly general acceptance and, among a minority, steady reform within its established framework. Certainly the gap between the educationally improving respectable and sunken non-respectable seemed by about the 1880s to be not nearly as operative or significant as before.

The late-century resolution of the drink question confirmed the decline of this major mid-Victorian divide: by the end of the century sentiments like 'the lips that touch liquor shall never touch mine' were rapidly losing their stigmatic power. Again, the contraction of attitudes was at both ends of the working-class axis. Per capita consumption of beer reached its highest figure of the century in 1876 at 34·4 gallons, from which point a fairly steady decline began. During the key years 1877–82 static or even falling real wages seem to have been combined with a widening of cheap consumer choices – especially refrigerated meat – in such a way that many housewives were able for once to put the squeeze on the proportion of domestic expenditure devoted by their husbands to alcohol. By the time the situation changed, and real wages again began to move upwards, precedents had been established, and for the rest of the century the proportion seems to have steadied itself at about 12 to 13 per cent, appreciably less than the estimates of even up to 25 per cent made a decade or so earlier. This decline of the Cruikshank caricature was matched by the eclipse of the dogmatically abstinent working man. Temperance reformers increased steadily in numbers during the last quarter, but, being predominantly middle-class in composition and headed by Liberal industrialists, their message assumed an increasingly sectarian aura. Apart from the obvious antagonism of the specifically drinking fraternity, working-class opposition comprised two main elements: one was a general distaste for authoritarian, legislative teetotalism – a major plank of the temperance campaign from the 1870s. The other was the usually Socialist-inspired rejection of the doctrine that drink was the prime cause of poverty and its traditional concomitant, slackness at work. The pub itself reflected this changing situation. Once posited as the extreme and sinful antitheses to the alternative chapel-centred culture, it now towards the end of the century became increasingly respectable, a place where the wife could be safely taken, and also began to rely on more than its drink and *bonhomie* alone with the appearance of rival attractions of secular entertainment. 'In order to succeed, each public-house now finds itself impelled to become more of a music-hall, more of a restaurant, or more of a club, or it must ally itself with thrift' was Booth's evidence. An irony indeed: frugality and Christmas savings schemes at the beer-house. Of course, for all this confusion of roles, the old temperance strain did continue to exercise a major pull, even if, as in the case of a Good Templar like Keir Hardie, the motive derived as much from a respectabilising background as sober-minded analysis. As a 6-year-old disarmingly told Booth: 'My father isn't class, he's always boozing.' Nevertheless, the usage *was* anachronistic: increasingly 'class' was a matter of the workplace and the home, leaving public cultural manifestations like the pub and chapel as fallible reflections of social status rather than certain determinants.

Even more unsuccessful than the temperance movement was the middle-class attempt, on a municipal basis, to transplant the culture of museums and art galleries into a working-class setting. Response was positive only when the new provisions chimed in with specific working-class needs. The free libraries, for example, were widely used, but almost solely for the purpose of taking out cheap fiction: while even a venture like Victoria Park, opened in 1862 and intended to beautify life in the East End, in practice had its lakes used as a huge bathhouse, with the police ineffectually resisting. Another middle-class improving campaign, equally futile, was the attempt to discourage betting on horse-races. By the end of the century all the commentators were agreed that the habit was increasing; and the warm accord given to victorious Derby owners like Lord Rosebery and King Edward indicated the sport's hazily populist connotations. Certain pre-'industrious' practices did, however, succumb. One was bare-knuckle fist-fighting, very much a pursuit for working youths and aristocrats; others, also perishing from about the third quarter, were the crueller forms of bloodsports. The main attack, however, was directed from the 1840s against the fairs and workers' holidays that symbolised an essentially casual, seasonal approach towards life. Many fell, perhaps most notably Bartholomew Fair and its attendant pleasures in 1855. Nevertheless, what is less often realised is the way in which an increasingly industrialised society created an array of what were virtually *new* fairs, largely patronised by the working class and looked upon with acute disfavour by the guardians of middle-class morality. Prime examples included Manchester's Knott Mill Fair at Easter, the Leeds Summer and Winter Fairs, and St Giles's Fair in Oxford, where, according to the *Oxford Magazine* in 1883, 'every class was fully represented except gentlefolks'.[12]

Chance, vitality and a sense of spectacle were the qualities that characterised these and many other forms of nineteenth-century working-class entertainment. Typical were the East End Penny Theatres (or 'Penny Gaffs') which from about 1830 until the commercial rise of the music hall in the 1870s offered intimate, gas-lit melodramas like *Othello* reduced to twenty minutes and new works like *The Blood-Stained Handkerchief or the Murder in the Cottage*. This affinity with the immediate and concrete was carefully noted by Booth, who observed of the open-air debates, often religious, at Mile End Waste on Saturday nights, Victoria Park on Sundays, that 'it is the fence, the cut and thrust, or skilful parry, that interests rather than the merits of the subject'. Elsewhere he wrote of a Saturday afternoon entertainment that took place while he was visiting 'poverty-stricken' Little Clarendon Street: 'A crowd had gathered at the further end of the street round two performers, each of whom in turn did feats of skill and strength while his companion turned the handle of the piano. . . . Upper windows were opened and heads craned out to see the show. Ha'pence were thrown into the performer's hat, and one lady giving a penny received back a halfpenny change.' But perhaps the best set-piece description of this life-renewing vitality comes in the 'Io Saturnalia!' chapter, describing a Bank Holiday outing to the Crystal Palace, in Gissing's *The Nether World* (1889). But, as Gissing himself stressed, there was a darker side to that day: not just the drunkenness and brawling, familiar enough themes, but also the ominous mindlessness, the stress on masculinity and imperialism, which was epitomised at the coco-nut shy where the 'object was a wooden model of the treacherous Afghan or the base African'. The working class had perhaps resisted one form of manipulation only to succumb to another. As a Baptist minister gravely informed Booth: 'Since the Jubilee there has been a tendency to spend more on luxuries.'

The image mattered: in 1878 the US Consul reported [13] that in Sheffield it was the 'ignorant poor' who were the most reluctant to eat foreign meats like corned beef despite their comparative cheapness. By the 1890s, however, with the spread of the slicing-out technique, corned beef was able to be sold in suitably small quantities and it began to enter the working-class diet despite its origins. But food not only had to be possible to purchase and convenient to eat, it also had to be, to return to Orwell's point, suitably 'tasty'. Jellied eels, tripe and black puddings were all favourites, but the great sign of the times was fish and chips, which got properly under way in the 1880s with John Rouse's original fish-and-chip frying range in the open-air market at Oldham. Institutes like the National Training College of Domestic Subjects attempted to wean working wives away from their addiction to things fried, but to little avail: partly because the board schools failed to teach domestic science, but more because of an innate hostility towards such extraneous foodstuffs as fruit and vegetables. There seemed to exist, as the 1904 Inter-Departmental Committee on Physical Deterioration sadly noted, a 'desire for some sort of sensation, comparable to the . . . dietary of pickles and vinegar'.[14] The natural auxiliary to wash this taste down was of course highly sugared tea. As late as the 1860s tea had been a drink from China and Japan for the few, but by the 1880s it was an altogether sturdier and more popular brew from India and Ceylon; while by the same decade only the United States came remotely within half of Britain's sugar consumption per head. 'A lifetime of unemployment mitigated by endless cups of tea' [15] began to beckon. The best-known of the entrepreneurs who brought cheap tea from sweated plantations was Lipton, who more than anyone personified the late-century 'retail revolution': brash, mass-producing, the tycoon with 'the common touch'. One of the most striking pictorial price cards [16] displayed outside his chain of grocery shops featured a hen on strike 'because of the low price of eggs'. Increasingly, this sort of populist approach became differentiated from the selling technique adopted towards the middle-class consumer, who by the end of the century was demanding at least the appearance of choice and individuality in the proffered goods. But for the working-class counterpart, the price of cheapness was uniformity: great mounds of readily divided food to be bought for cash, often late at night, at new multiple 'company' shops which spent money on publicity rather than on amenities; and increasingly standardised clothing and footwear also sold with the same overbearing emphasis on inexpense. 'Lewis's are the friends of the people, and Lewis's deserve the thanks of the people for providing these Splendid Suits of Clothes, which are suitable for Sunday wear or for business days, and the price is 30s always 30s' ran a typically deafening advertisement in 1883 'for Warehousemen, for Clerks, for Persons in all Stations of Life', with the final phrase – '30s always 30s' – repeated twenty-three times in two columns. There was no broaching that message, no room for bartering at the shop-counter: the time of the old 'moral economy', as it has been called,[17] was up.

It was still some while, of course, before the distinctively modern forms of a 'mass culture' had a thorough economic infrastructure built up around them. Working-men's football teams, for example, began in the 1860s as improving agencies, often under the auspices of local churches. Nevertheless, the signs were apparent – and perceived – that an industrialised society was making possible entirely new modes of recreation. Mass-circulation Sunday papers, 'penny dreadfuls', the first music halls – all these were early mid-Victorian signs of a low-standard 'mass culture' imposed from above for primarily commercial reasons. One might argue that the success of these ventures showed that the need was clearly there. Perhaps: but even if this was so, one must add that these were the new and arguably unnatural needs of a generation subjected in increasingly wide areas to concentrated industrialism. One of the most central experiences belonged to Thomas Wood,[18] an engineer brought up in Bingley, Yorkshire, who moved in the 1840s from a workshop to the enormous machine-making firm of the Platts Brothers in Oldham. There he earned 28s a week, but was aghast at working with men who 'turned out a large quantity of work with the requisite exactness without a little of the thought required of those who work in small shops'. Nor, as a Methodist, did he enjoy his new company: 'The men among whom I worked were wicked and reckless. Most of them gambled freely on horse- or dog-races.' And: 'There were very few who took care of their money; fewer still who went to a place of worship, or regarded the Sabbath in any other light than as a holiday. Their mode of living was different to the homely manner I had been accustomed to. Flesh meat, as they called it, must be on the table twice or thrice a day. A rough and rude plenty alone satisfied them.' These were the men to whom in quantitative terms the future belonged. One of the great working-class achievements has been to practise certain cultural modes with a skill and even subtlety that entirely belie the middle-class 'barbarian' taunt that, as it were, the 'flesh eating' habit suggests. But what could not be done was to create an urban culture effectively independent of either the newspaper proprietors, hack writers and music-hall managers or the disciplined industrial rhythm of the factory system. By about 1880 industrial workers were generally being granted the Saturday half-holiday as part of a wider process of intensified production; and the growth of professional football as a spectator sport in the North and Midlands mushroomed soon afterwards. One can hardly stress too much the sense of herding involved in this developing cultural pattern. A case in point was the friendly societies, whose numerical flourishing as insurance agencies after the Friendly Societies Act of 1875 concealed a deeper loss of intimate social activities and democratic lodge control. The crush of humanity in the 'gods' and on the terraces offered at best a reified substitute.

The coming of the annual holiday, Wakes Week, was an important regulative part of the industrial rhythm. In its own way, the background to the Blackpool era was a microcosm of nineteenth-century class relations. Back in the middle decades, the first excursion trains prompted thousands of Sunday day-trippers to visit new resorts like Margate and old ones like Brighton, where in 1862 an observer noted how the descending hordes 'bring their dinners with them in baskets, in sheets of old newspapers, and in pocket-handkerchiefs'.[19] The disapproving tone was significant, for during the 1860s the railway companies effectively sealed off the south coast from working-class trippers by raising fares and reducing the number of excursions. The mix had been found not to work. Then, in the 1870s, the Midland Company decided to reintroduce cheap holiday travel and thus virtually created Blackpool as *the* northern working-class resort. As Stella Davies recalled about the Wakes Weeks that were staggered through the summer: 'The overwhelming majority of people went to Blackpool, though some, eccentrically, went to Morecambe or even Rhyl. Blackpool, therefore, was full, at any one time, with neighbours from the same town and no one need feel isolated or lonely.' As one would expect, shibboleths were now strict: if Blackpool was working-class, then St Anne's nearby was most definitely not; while in the South, Margate was a resort for frankly secular pleasures, but Broadstairs one for Pooter's type. Moreover, as with other forms of working-class relaxation, the critics trained their guns. Baedeker in 1890 wrote scathingly of Douglas in the Isle of Man as 'practically one large playground for the operatives of Lancashire and Yorkshire' and added that 'their tastes have been so exclusively catered for, by the erection of dancing saloons and the like at every point of interest, so as to seriously interfere with the enjoyment of the scenery for its own sake'. At these resorts a tourist industry was quickly built up: Blackpool's population increased from 8,000 in 1871 to 47,000 by early this century; while skating rinks, big dippers and enormous dancing palaces all typified new technology catering for increasingly monolithic working-class tastes. But perhaps the most central symbol were the brass bands, the great musical attraction at these late-century resorts. They began as remarkable feats of improvisation by Lancashire and Yorkshire mill-hands in the 1840s and continued to expand in numbers for practically the rest of the century. By the 1880s, however, the competitive edge which had always been there had become sharpened into potentially cut-throat professionalism, culminating in 1888 at the Belle Vue Championship where, watched by a crowd of 8,000 who had been conveyed by fifty excursion trains, the judges were actually subjected to physical violence. In such an all-consuming atmosphere, older cultural conflicts – typified by the rivalry at the village of Wyke in Yorkshire between the pub-based Wyke Old Band and the ensuing Wyke Temperance Band – were again losing much of their relevance.

The development of working-class soccer revealed similar tendencies. Virtually defunct as a traditional sport after the incursions made by early industrialisation on open spaces, football was brought back to life in the 1860s by the middle-class products of the new type of public school, who saw the game as an admirable opportunity to instil manly character-building qualities into alien environments. It seems odd now to think that Nat Lofthouse's Bolton Wanderers were once a team called Christ Church FC run by well-meaning clergy. By the 1880s, however, working men themselves were taking the initiative and forming teams. A group of cutlers created Sheffield United, railway workers Manchester United, and Thames ironworkers West Ham, to name only a few. Along with the new teams came a new type of game, far more collective and now more concerned with passing than with the individualist approach favoured by the aristocrats like Lord Kinniard who continued to dominate the game until Blackburn Olympic vanquished the Old Etonians in 1883. On that famous occasion, the *Athletic News* reporter noted how the Olympic went in 'for wide crossing, whilst their opponents stuck to the close dribbling game'. Soon afterwards, the beginning of the Football League and legalisation of professionalism gave formal expression to the new mores: hard, competitive, encouraging fierce local rivalries, and on the field thoroughly team-based. The social consequences of this gritty professionalism seemed on the surface acute. Ernest Ensor expressed a typical 'educated' opinion when he wrote about 'The Football Madness' in the *Contemporary Review* for November 1898: 'The effect of League matches and cup ties is thoroughly evil. Men go in thousands, not to study and admire skill or endurance, but to see their team gain two points or pass into the next round. The end, not the means, is everything.' And he added: 'Gentleman can now only play Association football with each other, for they cannot risk plunging into the moral slough.' The apartheid was duly enacted: football-playing former public schoolboys began soon afterwards to compete for their own Arthur Dunn Cup; while for the majority who preferred to dirty their hands the other way, the growth of rugby union was already providing good amateur middle-class fun. Yet appearances were in an economic sense deceptive. The founder of the Football League was a shrewd Scots businessman called William McGregor; and Manchester United moved from the sidings to potential star status through the financial offices of J. H. Davies, a local entrepreneur. The working class may have provided the talent and paid at the gate, but, in an almost classical way, the profit-making shareholders of the limited-company football clubs were almost invariably top-hatted.

The almost simultaneous development of cricket represented in its professional state a more ostensible form of ethical as well as diversionary control. An anthology published in 1900 under the title of *Cricket* [20] was particularly full of inculcating material. O. R. Borradaile, Secretary of Essex CCC, took a military approach in his 'Hints to Young Cricketers': 'Do whatever the captain asks you to do, do it *immediately*, do not hesitate.' While Lord Harris, captain of Kent, after extolling cricket's selfless qualities and urging readers to 'play the game', went on: 'And there is one thing also most necessary, I think, and that is enthusiasm, having glory and pleasure in the success of your side; and that is an admirable quality, because it expands, it rises up by degrees to that very magnificent expression, "patriotism".' Harris was a persistent advocate: fifteen years earlier he had written in the *Contemporary Review* about how it was 'very much better that the teeming swarms of a city should be interested in something that will take them into the open air, than that they should spend their time in a stuffy taproom, talking maudlin politics over beer and pipes'. But it is doubtful whether this overt sort of propaganda was really effective. Unlike in soccer there was not even the illusion of popular participatory control over cricket. The Oval in London and Bramall Lane in Sheffield were the only test grounds sited in working-class areas; and Lord's, home of MCC, was aptly named. Nevertheless, in practice it was the working-class professionals who took the wickets and often had to make the runs. Suitably enough, within two years of Blackburn Olympic's footballing triumph, the Players regularly began to beat the Gentlemen at cricket. Moreover, as a spectator sport, large crowds were frequently attracted, especially at the Oval, where on August Bank Holiday 1892 a record 63,000 gate watched Surrey play Notts. The two aspects of this hierarchical populism showed themselves clearly in Yorkshire not long afterwards. In November 1896 the dashing amateur batsman F. S. Jackson stood as Conservative candidate at the Leeds municipal elections ('Vote for Stanley Jackson, the popular candidate'), only months before Lord Hawke, captain, summarily dismissed Bobby Peel for improperly watering the wicket. The new sort of 'pro' was instead the respectful and hard-working cricketer like Wilfred Rhodes, who in Smilesian fashion worked his way up from No. 11 to opener in England's batting order. Of course one can easily put the matter out of perspective: Attlee's obsession with how Haileybury were getting on was not an inevitable sign of deep-rooted political reformism. But too often 'the game is greater than the man' did mean precisely that.

The cheap mass press was of course the agency that disseminated information about football and cricket and kept up spectator interest. Its origins lay back in the 1840s when, after the decline of indigenous working-class papers like the *Poor Man's Guardian, Voice of the West Riding* and the *Political Penny Magazine*, a new and much less keenly radical cheap Sunday press was imposed from above. *Lloyd's Weekly* began in 1842, the *News of the World* in 1843, and *Reynolds' Weekly Newspaper* in 1850. By 1855, with the abolition of newspaper tax, their circulations were 96,000, 110,000 and 49,000 respectively. By 1863, after the abolition of paper duty, these figures were on their way to being trebled. Can one argue, though, that the end of the 'taxes on knowledge' was really that – that in these early years the widely read Sunday papers were more than the spiced-up pulp we have come to expect from their counterparts this century and tend to attribute to the 'Northcliffe Revolution' in the 1880s and 1890s? Possibly: a comparison of two randomly selected 'early' and 'late' issues of *Lloyd's Weekly Newspaper* – 24 January 1864 and 19 February 1893, circulation roughly 350,000 and 950,000 respectively – shows certain significant differences. Whereas a long editorial about the absence of political liberty in Louis Napoleon's France features prominently on page one of the earlier issue, the corresponding page of the 1893 paper is dominated by a report of Blackburn Rovers versus Sunderland. There were other contrasts inside. In 1864 news on page two of 'a dastardly outrage' near Leamington rubs shoulders with a sober item about the declining oyster fisheries of Ireland; page eight features an announcement of the forthcoming English version of Gounod's opera *Faust*, with the rider that 'there will be cheap prices, and the question of costume people may settle for themselves'; and page eleven has a very genteel gardening column and answers to self-improving correspondents. The 1893 copy has little of this, but instead has half a column of 'Jokes of the Day', a serial called *A True Story of a Snuff-Box*, and a consistent personalising of politics, in the same vein as Madame Tussaud's prominent announcement that she was now displaying 'Eminent People "At Home" '. Nevertheless, for all the differences, a basic and more important continuity remains. As Thomas Wright wrote in 1867 about 'the steady family man' settling down to his weekly read: 'He will go through the police intelligence with a patience and perseverance worthy of a better cause, then through the murders of the week',[21] before passing on to anything else. An advertisement in a north-eastern local paper of July 1868, proclaiming the choice articles in next Sunday's 'Lloyd's', confirms the primacy of this sensationalist appeal: 'The Emperor Napoleon on Assassination. Fearful stabbing case through jealousy. Terrible scenes at an execution. Cannibalism at Liverpool. A man roasted to death. A cruel husband and an adulterous wife.' [22] In this context the 'Northcliffe Revolution' – and the myth about his exploiting Forster's newly literate generation – seems unimportant. The appeal of the *Daily Mail* (1896) and its stable companions was anyway primarily to clerkdom, and its specific novelty lay at the outset essentially in its deployment of advertising. The harm, in other words, for such it surely was, had been done much earlier – before Forster, before Northcliffe – by newspaper owners feeding increasing quantities of rubbish to a readership whose critical faculties were by the end of the working week battered into submission. These owners took time to systematise their techniques, but even their early circulation successes were based on precisely the same appeal that prompted Orwell's family man of the 1930s to slump down after Sunday lunch to a good murder in the *News of the World*.

The commercial provision of trashy literature was similarly relentless. Between 1849 and 1856, Reynolds comfortably outsold Dickens with his *Mysteries of the Court of London*; while in 1887 the *Edinburgh Review* calculated that the weekly sale of serialised sensational novels, the penny dreadfuls, was somewhere over two million. These stories tended to be either vividly melodramatic or, as Lady Bell put it, romances in which 'the poor and virtuous young man turns out to be a long-lost son, and becomes rich and powerful'. Such escapist fictions were in no way authentic working-class products. Moreover, as Hoggart has stressed about their descendants, it is doubtful whether they even meant a great deal in the lives of the people who read them. Instead, they were simply a way of relaxing in a low-key way for an hour or two. The pity was, however, not only that this had to be so, but also that no authentic and relevant working-class literature developed at the same time as an alternative. Dialect literature, flourishing in the industrial north from about 1860 to 1885, was usually an inadequate substitute – though it *could* be powerful in a way reminiscent of the older oral tradition. Ben Preston's *I Niver Can Call Her My Wife* (1872),[23] the poem of a weaver on short-time, evoked with felt irony the sense of trying to be reconciled to a far from perfect situation after the promises of the Chartist had 'wattered my hoap':

> 'Yit a bird has its young uns to guard,
> A wild beast, a mate in his den,
> An' Aw cannot bud think at it's hard –
> May, deng it, A'm roarin' agen!'

Generally, however, dialect literature of this period preferred not to confront the economic question. Ben Brierley even went so far, in his *The Wayver of Wellbrook*, as to transmute the defiant weaver figure of the 1790s, the constantly recreated Jone o'Grinfilt, into a homely contented figure, happy just to have 'a quiet heawse nook, – a good wife an' a book'.[24] This acceptance of the urban condition, with all its material benefits, characterised Brierley's writings, as it did also the work of Edwin Waugh and John Hartley, the other best-known exponents of the genre. Waugh, from Lancashire, made his name in 1856 with the broadside *Come Whoam to thy Childer an' Me*, which immediately sold 20,000 copies; while Hartley, from Halifax, produced collections of dialect stories like *Yorkshire Puddin'* (1877), besides founding and editing the *Original Illustrated Clock Almanack*, which ran from 1865 to 1956, had a circulation of 80,000 by 1887, and was full of humorous sketches about contemporary events (usually local) and comforting or amusing mottoes. All three writers worked prodigiously hard and, seeing literature as a way of earning a living rather than as a calling, tended to try for a wide appeal by taking recourse in an essentially generalised view of social situations, that in practice seriously diluted the descriptive uniqueness of the working-class existence. Even the music hall, full of warm vitality, fell victim to the 'lowest common denominator' temptation and began to spread thinly and evenly.

In a sense, though, the commercial makings of this decline into vapidity were always there. When the middle-class actor Albert Chevalier practised for months before launching himself into the music hall in 1891 with a computerised rendering of 'Down at the Welsh 'Arp, Which is 'Endon Way', he was merely accepting the Fabian-type precept that an audience did in the end represent no more than a certain quantity of common 'potato love' dreams and aspirations. 'My Old Dutch' was everyone's life partner. Earlier, however, during the third quarter, the first music-hall songs had tended to be far more indigenous, rooted in local traditions and events, as in Ned Corvan's 'The Toon Improvement Bill, or Ne Pleyce noo te play' about the new railway station in Newcastle. This relatively unsentimental critique was replaced from about the 1880s by a new music-hall archetype, a sort of compound of Kipling's grumbling Tommy Atkins, the warm-hearted Cockney coster, and the experienced-yet-wholesome Marie Lloyd. At the archetype's best, sharpness of ironic detail was able to keep its head above the sentimentality, as in Gus Elen's best-known song:

> 'Oh! it really is a werry pretty garden,
> And Chingford to the eastward could be seen;
> Wiv a ladder and some glasses,
> You could see to 'Ackney marshes,
> If it wasn't for the 'ouses in between.' [25]

But even in this song, and much more in others of the same tradition, the pervasive sense of having to struggle on regardless comes through. Dan Leno, the great music-hall comedian, above all personified this weary fatalism and turned it into the anarchy of passivism. Thus he would consider 'The Egg' – 'a little round white thing' – and observe: 'You can't tell what it is thinking about. You dare not kick it or drop it. It has got no face. You can't get it to laugh. No, you simply look at it and say: "Egg".' [26] But Leno was already becoming outdated in his own life (1861–1904), at odds with the star system, the stratified seating system, and the insistence on broad-based variety entertainment (epitomised by Harry Lauder) that at least would please everyone a bit. The new music-hall comedian was Chaplin, who turned anarchism into whimsicality and duly went off to films, an even more remote form of shared mateyness; leaving Leno's mantle to be ultimately taken up by Samuel Beckett, hardly the people's expounder of the human condition.

All this, however, is not to suggest a whole class happily lapping up the new forms of urban culture as if they were some total panacea. As the values of the dialect poets suggest, one is struck in this last quarter of the century by the increasing home-centredness of everyday working-class life, the internal burrowing in the face of a harsh world. Even prostitution was affected by the ideal of cosy homeliness, as the for-midable mid-Victorian brothels began to yield to the more independent hostess, the woman 'sailing on her own bottom'. Morrison stressed the point in his first collection of stories, *Tales of Mean Streets* (1894). Only one of the stories, 'Lizerunt', was explicitly violent, while the twelve others deliberately evoked the 'deadly monotony and respect-ability of the mean streets' in the East End of London. Indeed, as Winnington-Ingram admitted later about coming to Oxford House in 1888: 'My first surprise about East London was its extreme respect-ability.' And almost all the evidence agrees that in the usual cheek-to-jowl working-class communities the very opposite of a libertine ethic tended to be the rule. Stella Davies has written about the stormy reaction of family and neighbours to a fiancée discovered kissing a cousin in about 1900: 'Poor Lilly! her partner in guilt did not marry her and, for no more than a snatched kiss, she became a marked woman. . . . She shortly left the district and it was not for many years that she married.' And within her family (as one of fifteen children), Davies recalls how once 'my mother told me that never in the twenty-six years of their life together had my father seen her naked'. These were not middle-class values: the far greater degree of working-class sexual satisfaction is proof of that. But equally they were respectable values, though very much of the self-respecting sort. Recent oral evidence [27] of this comes from the descriptions, by an elderly West Riding couple, of the late-Victorian one-up, one-down homes they grew up in in two large colliery villages near Barnsley. In the summarising words of the interviewer: the fireplace was the 'focal point of the house'; the table was usually a 'simple deal four-legged one', but 'if the family was "coming on in the world" the table might have turned mahogany-coloured legs, and these were then protected during the week by old woollen stockings with the feet cut off'; and 'on the mantelpiece might be a pair of Staffordshire pottery figures, cats or dogs and occasionally a mantel clock', though 'the poorer folk would go "next door" to tell the time'. The normative centrality of the family as an institution within this framework was clearly a *sine qua non*. The heightened significance of a kinsman's death said as much. Booth noted that 'even the poorest will pay £8 or £10 for a burial and then starve the week after', while Luby remembered funerals as 'the only times that we really did get good feeds'. This continuing centrality of the family had, however, as much of a calculative as an ethical basis. In life's many crises, there seemed no alternative to turn to: neither a welfare system nor a political agency. This lack of choice was particularly severe for a wife with children, as Lady Bell noted about the haggard mothers of Middlesbrough, expected to go on satisfying their husbands. Family life *might* bring happiness and pride, but at underlying, undermining root it was the only form of social security left in an industrial society, the one refuge from the fate Morrison described in 'A Street': 'Nobody laughs here – life is too serious a thing; nobody sings. There was once a woman who sang – a young wife from the country. But she bore children, and her voice cracked. Then her man died, and she sang no more.'

In such a milieu it was not surprising that there existed a continual undertow of violence *within* these mean and apparently monotonous streets. Near the end of his interview Luby was asked whether he ever now thought of 'the people who didn't survive the same kind of conditions'. He replied: 'Eh . . . not then. No, because it was the survival of the fittest – if I left a man behind, well, that's his fault. It wasn't mine.' And earlier he had confirmed the commonness of formal Sunday morning bare-fist fights to settle quarrels, adding that in each family 'one son was kept for that purpose, fighting'. Yet, as Roberts has shown,[28] these fights tended to derive less from explicitly Darwinian purposes as from the more short-term desire to satisfy certain norms of respectability. He cites as a typical immediate cause of a street punch-up: 'One wife waved, for instance, a "clean" rent book (that great status symbol of the times) in the air, knowing the indicted had fallen in arrears.' This housewife may of course simply have wanted to be involved in a fight for a fight's sake, but the point was that she chose such upright ground from which to initiate proceedings. And elsewhere Roberts writes of how the proletarian caste system in Salford at the turn of the century was determined not only by job skills and resultant wages, but also by more moral considerations, with 'bookies' runners, idlers, part-time beggars and petty thieves, together with all those known to have been in prison whatever might be their ostensible economic or social standing', forming, apart from the professionally immoral and the poor-house occupants, 'the base of the social pyramid'. But with job status and mores in practice inextricably linked, the potential for internal working-class cultural stratification was of course infinite. The fifty-nine skilled prizewinners (in contrast to the eight semi- and unskilled) at the 'Working Men's Flower Show' held in Edinburgh in 1870 seemed to live in a different world to, say, the estimated 44,000 illiterate adult bargees of the same decade. Nevertheless, although one cannot gainsay such a contrast, it is possible to exaggerate its significance. Gissing said much when he wrote in *The Nether World* about the animal-spirited Clem (the most convincing character in the novel) and what she wanted out of life: 'Her ambitions were essentially gross. In the way of social advancement she appreciated nothing but an increased power of spending money, and consequently of asserting herself over others. She had no desire whatever to enter a higher class than that in which she was born; to be of importance in her familiar circle was the most she aimed at.' Aspirations within a class were not, in other words, at all incompatible with consciousness of belonging to that class or even positive repudiation of the values of another class.

Thomas Wright, an essentially improving writer, perceived as much when he wrote in 1868 that 'it is better to be "had" sometimes than from over-suspicion to refuse such help as it is in your power to give to a case that may be one of real distress'.[29] Moreover, as the century went on, an element of reinsurance perhaps began to enter into charitable help for the temporarily less fortunate. We have seen how occupational changes were beginning to reduce the gap between the skilled and the unskilled; and the survey on unemployment in London conducted by William Ogle in 1887 showed how the phenomenon by no means exclusively affected the low-paid and must therefore have been a considerable source of worry to those who considered themselves part of the labour élite. Recent oral hearings,[30] conducted by the Social Science Research Council about working-class life at the turn of the century, have added a measure of confirmation about this solidifying tendency: 'The occupational mobility revealed is surprising . . . it has proved very difficult to discover the families of "labour aristocrats".' As has been suggested, a new and broader-based more-or-less skilled 'aristocracy' was perhaps emerging – but the point remains significant. Ultimately, however, working-class modes were less a question of straight economics than much deeper-rooted values. The man who worked with his hands *always* felt himself quite different from the white-collar wearer. Even in the 1860s, Oppenheimer anticipated Booth's conclusions by noting how both the 'rough' and the 'solid' elements of the working class lived in the same streets in St Giles. And the many ground-level observers round the turn of the century agreed about the quality of rugged generosity that kept even the most deprived communities going in the absence of state or philanthropic services. As a nurse told Booth: 'How the poor live when they are helpless remains a mystery, save for their great kindness to each other, even to those who are strangers. This is the great explanation. It is nearly always the neighbours.' Arguments and fights, yes, but there was another side to all-in proximity, even while bitterness in the form of rivalry continued to gnaw away at the heart. Moreover, linked to this underlying solidarity was a distinct sense of social apartness and consequently keen nose for 'betrayal'. When in *The Nether World* Jack Bartley is cornered by the police and starts blabbing about his fellow-accomplice, 'several voices from the crowd shouted abusively at the poltroon whose first instinct was to betray his associate'. Gus Elen put it another way in ' 'E Dunno where 'E Are': [31]

> 'Jack Jones is well known to ev'rybody
> Round about the market, don't yer see,
> I've no fault to find wiv Jack at all
> When 'e's as 'e used ter be.
> But some 'ow since 'e's 'ad the bullion left
> 'E's altered for the wust,
> When I sees the way 'e treats old pals
> I am filled wiv nuffing but disgust.
> 'E says as 'ow we isn't class enuf,
> Sez we ain't upon a par
> Wiv 'im just because 'e's better off –
> Won't smoke a pipe, must take on a cigar . . .'

In the context of these sort of sentiments, summed up by the Jago's motto 'thou shalt not nark', one can understand how the great working-class achievements since the Industrial Revolution have been of an essentially (though still incomplete) collective and horizontal nature. Orwell made this point in the 1930s: 'The English working class do not show much capacity for leadership, but they have a wonderful talent for organisation. The whole trade union movement testifies to this; so do the excellent working-men's clubs – really a sort of glorified co-operative pub, and splendidly organised – which are so common in Yorkshire.' [32] And, indeed, it was the late-nineteenth-century development of the working-men's clubs, a cultural transplant of the hearth-side ethic for manual workers, that showed precisely why the working class has taken so long to get beyond the stage of non-trick-taking organisation.

The independence and vigour of the working-men's clubs was never in doubt after the firm rejection of middle-class patronage in 1884. Booth noted how 'in many cases the members do all the repairs and alterations of the club after their own day's labour is done'. Moreover, for a few years after 1884 a spirit of determined if eclectic radicalism seemed to prevail in the clubs. Well-attended though often very melodramatic club drama productions flourished; and also popular were mock trials, the 'Judge and Jury Class', similarly participatory and therefore emancipating. But even in the late 1880s the signs were that the clubs were beginning to turn into almost solely social institutions. Penny readings of writers like Shelley, Leno, Dickens and Kingsley did continue, but were rapidly giving way in popularity to Club Concerts and the 'Free and Easy'. Brass or string bands, Glee Clubs and Minstrel Troupes all became increasingly common forms of club activity. By the 1890s there could be no doubt about the trend. In June 1891 the *Club and Institute Journal* lamented [33] the fact that 'as is well known, lecturers have a poor chance of getting an audience, no matter how clever or gifted they may be, while the comic singer and the sketch artiste, however lacking in real ability, can always draw a hall full'. And inevitably, as this entertainment became more professional, including an increasing hire of music-hall performers, so, as Booth put it, 'the social side tends to become more important than the political'. This is not to put forward a simplistic theory of degrading 'bread and circuses': the high moral order of working-class mutualism in everyday life has already been suggested. Yet in a cultural extra-parochial sense there does seem to have taken place towards the end of the century a certain loss of high seriousness, an inability to develop more abstract qualities of analysis. Thomas Hancock, the most socially committed of the late-century Christian Socialists, subsequently looked back from

a disenchanted perspective on the early 1880s: 'In that hopeful generation, when the Devil had scarcely begun to infect the poor in our dear
fatherland with his anti-Christian plague of Imperialism, there were
wage-workers serious enough to be Secularists, too serious to be
gamblers and jingoes, and with sufficient love for their neighbours and
their nation to look for some great Revolution like that promised by
the Blessed Virgin to the poor, the humble, and the hungry. . . .' [34]
One does not have to accept all the details or indeed the tone to perceive
its potency: the working class, dug deep into an independent defensive
position, failed in a cultural and ideological as much as a political sense
to move on to the offensive. Hancock underestimated the problems
involved, of leadership as well as of environment, but the substance of
his charge remains.

Chapter 7

SOCIALISM

1880 — 1895

' *"Do you smoke, Leno?" were his first words, after the usual greeting.
I replied "No; but I snuff". "Then have a pinch with me", was the
rejoinder.*' [1]

Such were J. B. Leno's impressions of his first encounter with the
fellow-poet William Morris. The stamp was unmistakable. On another
occasion Morris declared: 'If I were to work ten hours a day at work
I despised and hated, I should spend my leisure, I hope in political
agitation, but I fear in drinking.' [2] Unfortunately, few of the English
middle-class Socialists of the 1880s possessed either the open-handed
manliness or the deeply-felt awareness of the working-man's down-
trodden condition that Morris did; and none, including Morris, had
the strategical acumen to inspire in late-Victorian Britain an authentic
form of practical class-conscious Socialism. Perhaps one should not
be unduly critical. For all the socially unsettled atmosphere of the
1880s, especially in 'Outcast London', the persistent quietism of the
organised working class seemed for most of the decade to continue
steadfast. Three working-class Lib.-Lab. MPs were returned in 1880 –
Burt, MacDonald and Broadhurst – of whom Broadhurst, also Secretary of the National Liberal League, the new and quite ineffective
LRL's successor, especially distinguished himself by procuring an
invitation in 1884 to visit the Prince of Wales at Sandringham. 'Wielded
by the middle-class politicians for party purposes' [3] was how Morris in
1883 described with some justice the trade union leadership. Quite
different were the aspirations of his generation of Socialists. A fairly
typical example was William Clarke: son of a small Norwich businessman, educated at Cambridge, an under-employed journalist in London,
an advanced Liberal in the 1870s, and an ethical propagandist against
industrialism in the early 1880s, he turned in about 1885 to Fabian
Socialism and more specifically social questions with the heady aim [4]
of forging a 'union of culture with labour'. At its most extreme, this
tendency produced not so much 'false' consciousness as non-conscious-
ness. The young Ramsay MacDonald (only a marriage away from
middle-class intellectualism) envisaged Socialism in 1887 as 'a stage in

the process of intellectual development';[5] and in 1892 Engels (never
a respecter of English Socialism) described as either ignorant 'neo-
phytes' or 'wolves in sheep's clothing' the 'people who, from the
"impartiality" of their superior standpoint, preach to the workers a
Socialism soaring high above their class interests and class struggles',
attempting 'to reconcile in a higher humanity the interests of both the
contending classes'.[6] It was a fair criticism. Significantly, this dis-
interested loftiness often derived from the failure of earlier attempts to
recast society by exploiting almost mechanically mass grievances.
'Socialism had only to be put clearly before the working classes to
concentrate the power of their immense numbers in one irresistible
organisation'[7] was how Shaw towards the end of the 1880s looked
back ironically on the mood of a few years earlier. When this tactic
failed, as in a Shavian sense it palpably had by the time of his observation, then the middle-class Socialists of the mid-1880s drifted with
few exceptions into either obscurantism or progressivism. As a result,
when a new quasi-Socialist phoenix did arise in the 1890s, far more
indigenous and working-class, it turned into a movement quite bereft
of theoretical rigour.

The Englishman whose interpretation of Marxism exercised (in a
negative sense at least) the widest influence was H. M. Hyndman. Out
of London's Radical and Republican clubs of the 1870s, his Democratic Federation coalesced in 1881 with initial intentions comprising
a mixture of standard electoral proposals and George-inspired talk
about the nationalisation of land. The alliance was short-lived: all but
one of the Radical working men's clubs soon left the Federation in
protest against its relentless attacks upon Gladstone's Irish policy;
while Hyndman himself, true to the totality of his Tory background
and as early as 1880 inspired by reading *Das Kapital* in French while
stopping over in Salt Lake City, pushed on towards what he regarded as
thorough-going Socialism. In November 1883 he established himself
as the theoretician of the movement by bringing out *The Historical
Basis of Socialism in England*; in January 1884 the first issue of *Justice*
appeared; in April he debated in public with Bradlaugh; and between
August and October the Federation became the Social Democratic
Federation and adopted a recognisably Socialist programme. Under
this name it lasted well into this century – persistent, hectoring, never
more than sporadically popular-based in patches of London and
Lancashire, both traditional if changing resistants of Liberal influence.
Explanations of this ultimately undistinguished record have justifiably
emphasised the Federation's sectarianism and its mechanical theory of
revolution. Unaware of Marx's *Critique of the Gotha Programme*,
Hyndman and the other SDF theorists believed firmly in the rule of

the 'iron law of wages' and consequently dismissed as irrelevant the attempts by evidently reactionary trade unionists to improve their standard of living. 'The most stodgy-brained, dull-witted, and slow-going time-servers in the country'[8] was Hyndman's view in about 1886 of these men. Nor was he in much better harmony with the mood of the new unionism: Mann, Champion and Burns all had to leave the Federation in order to activate with freedom. Instead, Hyndman in the most challenging years of his career, 1886–7, put his trust almost boyishly in conspiratorially-led mass insurrection. A journalist recorded the leader's mood on 'Black Monday', the West End window-smashing 8 February 1886: ' "No one knows what we shall do", said Mr Hyndman impressively; "not even ourselves. Probably we shall disappear for six months altogether. . . . One thing is certain . . . we dare not go back even if we would" '.[9] It was a futile tack: the residuum who sang 'Rule, Britannia!' on their way back to the East End needed more than an adventure-loving cadre to be shaped into effective revolutionary action; while the entirely secular basis of the Federation meant that in terms of active membership it was perforce over-dependent on London's declining politically-conscious artisan tradition. In more solid, factory-based areas, an altogether different ethic operated, focused (even in revolt) on a vaguely ethical and thus still essentially Liberal axis. 'Hyndman Hall, home of the SDF, remained for us mysteriously aloof and through the years had, in fact, about as much political impact on the neighbourhood as the nearby gasworks': in this respect at least, Roberts's classic slum was undoubtedly typical.

The Toryism of England's best-known Marxist *qua* Marxist was crucial. Even when Hyndman accepted the need to reconcile his cataclysmic urge to a more mundane platform – in particular the reforming proposals connected with matters like housing, education and hours that he called in 1883 'stepping-stones to a happier period'[10] – he never attempted to erase his extraordinary social mark. He stressed his army and county cricketing past, always wore a silk top hat at meetings, and unashamedly played the market in order to subsidise his Socialism. As early as 1881 Engels was referring to Mrs Hyndman's 'self-satisfied garrulous husband';[11] and Tom Mann later wrote in his *Memoirs*: 'At almost every meeting he addressed, Hyndman would cynically thank the audience for so "generously supporting my class". Indeed, he brought in my class to an objectionable degree.' Nevertheless, in a movement virtually without a concrete past, the well-spoken gentleman had his appeal. For as Mann went on: 'It was no small matter to know that in our advocacy of the principles we had learned to love, which on so many occasions brought forth stinging criticisms from the Press, Hyndman's ability to state the case comprehensively, logically, and argumentatively was at our disposal always.' Yet the case itself was faulty: for besides his economic and strategic misreading of Marx, Hyndman also believed in, if not imperialism for imperialism's sake, then certainly a strong and influential armed presence abroad. This did not mean that Hyndman perniciously steered the working-class membership of the SDF into these treacherous waters with him, for in practice most of the rank-and-file kept their own minds in this respect. But what it did mean was that when the organised working class attained something like political independence within a context as traditionally self-determining as the Boer War, then the role of Hyndman's SDF (still the most Marxist English body) was negligible in both a short- and a long-term sense. The pity was that the furtherance of Marxism in this country was so dependent upon a man of Hyndman's qualities at the very time that classical *laissez-faire* competition was rapidly being superseded by imperialism and monopoly capitalism. The shame was doubly acute in the context of the political existence of William Morris, who not only had a far more generous vision of Socialism, but also came much closer to understanding the changing motive forces of late-century capitalism. As early as December 1884, after barely a year as a member, Morris left the SDF to form his own Socialist League. Dislike of Hyndman's flag-waving nationalism, over-bearing personality, and brandishing of the 'turnip bogie' of instant revolution were all present in Morris's decision. But the split itself was messy and seemed to outsiders too much a question of high-level bickering. The bulk of the SDF's membership (encouraged by Morris's impulsive decision to form a new organisation rather than take over the existing one) stayed with Hyndman, despite the majority of the executive backing Morris. Yet at least the split came sooner rather than later. Morris himself wrote to his wife shortly before the formal divide: 'All this is foul work: yet it is a pleasure to be able to say what one thinks at last.' This was indeed true – even though in his own lifetime what Morris said was hardly heard enough.

'Apart from the desire to produce beautiful things, the leading passion of my life has been and is hatred of modern civilisation,' wrote Morris in his 1894 'How I Became a Socialist' article. The influence of Ruskin was manifest. In a lecture given in 1880 – one of several about the social nature of art – Morris looked to the time when 'the "residuum" of modern civilisation . . . will become the great mass of orderly thinking people, sweet and fair in its manners, and noble in its aspirations' as 'the sole hope of worthy, living, enduring art'. But Ruskin's noble-minded paternalism was only a stage. The symbol of Morris's further development was the relative recession in his own mind of his firm, with which sort of exclusive activity he had been feeling increasingly disenchanted, at one point turning angrily upon a client, the ironmaster Sir Lowthian Bell, and declaring that 'I spend my life in ministering to the swinish luxury of the rich'; and by the end of 1883 England's most famous living craftsman was a committed Socialist. The personal price was a heavy one, with most of his friends abandoning him. A letter written by Morris in October 1885 to 'Georgie' Burne-Jones reflected the mood of these difficult early years: 'You see, my dear, I can't help it. The ideas which have taken hold of me will not let me rest: nor can I see anything else worth thinking of. . . . One must turn to hope, and only in one direction do I see it – on the road to Revolution: everything else is gone now. And now at last when the corruption of society seems complete, there is arising a definite conception of a new order . . .' [12]

There is little doubt now that what Morris meant by this was Marxism: as early as 1884 his French copy of *Das Kapital* needed rebinding because of wear and tear on it; his reiteration during the 1880s of Marx's distinction (not made public until 1891) between Socialism and Communism indicated a period of close contact with Engels; and in 1885 he categorically asserted as pivotal his conviction that 'the creation of surplus value being the one aim of the employers of labour, they cannot for a moment trouble themselves as to whether the work which creates that surplus value is pleasurable to the worker or not'. The realisation of this inexorable characteristic of capitalist society became an increasingly dark consideration in Morris's thought, even jaundicing his response to the Arts and Crafts movement which he above all had inspired. 'Any one who professes to think that the question of art and cultivation must go before that of the knife and fork does not understand what art means, or how that its roots must have a soil of a thriving and unanxious life,' Morris wrote in his 1894 retrospect. Economics-as-morality: this was the core of Morris's teaching – a doctrine going far beyond a materialist grab for the unchanging means of production – as he gave the best years of his life to trying to imbue organic values into an intolerable society. His Communism was utopian, his faith in the emancipatory potential of egalitarian relations limitless. To his liberal acquaintances who complained that the individual would suffer in the initial post-revolutionary period of centralised Socialism that would precede Communism, his answer was simple: 'We are prepared to face whatever drawbacks may accompany this new development with equanimity, being convinced that it will at any rate be a great gain to have got rid of a system which has at last become nearly all drawbacks.' [13]

Yet in 1934 it fell to Baldwin to deliver the address on the occasion of Morris's centenary and describe him as a 'great, glorious, jolly human being'. Not that he was not: but the tone and the orator remain as a measure of Morris's immediate failure as the practical Socialist who aimed higher than any of his contemporaries. This was certainly not because of any poetic haziness. The tone of his despatches to younger Socialist League activators was invariably clear-sighted: 'I now see the absolute necessity of discipline in a fighting body, which of course in no sense resembles the Societys of the future',[14] to J. L. Mahon in 1886; and 'I am glad to hear that you are getting *solid* up there. . . . Staying power is what we want, the job before us being so egregiously long', to Bruce Glasier in Glasgow the following year. This sense of settling down to a lengthy uphill haul comes through all too clearly in the 'Socialist Diary' which Morris kept in the early months of 1887. Time and again he records his dismay at being unable to get through to even Radical working audiences, once bluntly writing *à propos* of a lecture at Hammersmith Radical Club that 'the frightful ignorance and want of impressibility of the average English workman floors me at times'. Yet in a sense Morris was unrealistically disappointed. At the heart of the Socialist League's lack of broad-based appeal was his insistence that any engagement in parliamentary activities would be 'deadly to that feeling of exulted hope and brotherhood that alone can hold a revolutionary party together'. But if such an approach precluded mass participation in the League, more modern examples than Broadhurst alone surely confirm the justness of Morris's analysis. As Lansbury recorded in his autobiography in 1928: 'From the sheltered libraries, reading and dining rooms of the House of Commons it is a little difficult to realise the class war and all these two words mean in moral, mental and material degradation to those who remain in the mental and material abyss.' A similar purity underlay Morris's studied detachment from sectional trade unionism: 'Our business, I repeat, is the making of Socialists. . . . When we have enough people of that way of thinking, *they* will find out what action is necessary for putting their principles in practice.' Morris clearly meant this deeply, for he was writing in 1890 in the very process not only of being by-passed by the working-class new unionism and growing desire for independent representation, but also of resigning from the Socialist League after his defeat of the pro-parliament section in 1887 had pushed it ever more into the hands of a group of East End anarchists quite alien to his way of thinking. After this blow (the germ of the gloomy opening passage in *News from Nowhere*) Morris accepted the need for a certain degree of tactical *rapprochement* with the times: machines were permissible if used appropriately to cut down on unavoidable drudge; and even the election of Socialist MPs might be useful as a means of maintaining local political consciousness. Above all, Morris insisted, Hyndmanesque fractionalism must be avoided if a broad front was to be created against the common enemy. The fundamental purity remained unadulterated. In March 1895, the year before he died, he reiterated his most central theme: 'I have thought the matter up and down and in and out, and I cannot for the life of me see how the great change which we long for can come otherwise than by disturbance and suffering of some kind.' There were never any easy ways out for Morris. Therein lay his greatness, but also at the same time the difficulty which the small but significant body of working-class adherents experienced when they attempted to fulfil his precepts.

Whether under the auspices of the SDF or the SL, what Socialism provided for mentally aspiring engineers like Tom Mann and John Burns, and tough unskilled labourers like Harry Quelch, was not just a discipline and mode of thought but a positive and revolutionary alternative social system. The high moral tone of the mid-1880s, not yet gone soggy, was the response of men to whom the acceptance of Socialism as the method of regeneration was as a religious revelation. 'Something more than good machinery is necessary if really good results are to be obtained' [15] affirmed Mann about this time. And: 'The baser sides of our nature must be beaten down that the higher and nobler side may develop'. Henry Snell, a follower of Morris, caught the atmosphere of these few years in his description of Socialist activities in Nottingham, where working-class members of the two bodies combined harmoniously: 'Our practice was to ride out on a penny farthing from the saddle of which, the machine being kept in the perpendicular by comrades standing either side, I and others preached the new gospel.' [16] By about 1887, however, the moral fervour of the small groups of working-class Socialists was giving way to more gritty considerations increasingly divorced from the movement's stubbornly theoretical middle-class leadership. In London certain branches of the SDF started to concentrate on specific reform issues, the controversial 'palliatives', thus foreshadowing Lansbury's 'Poplarism' of the next decade. While in the North the young J. L. Mahon of the SL was in 1887 successively stirred by the potential Socialism of striking miners in Northumberland, defeated by Morris over the question of parliamentary candidates, and swept into dreams of independent glory by the initial success of his North of England Socialist Federation. But the tightrope was narrow, the overbalancing perhaps inherent. Mahon wrote in *Commonweal* in October 1887, two months before he formally left the SL: 'The method of Socialist propaganda must not be merely, or mainly, preaching rigidly pure principles which the masses of the people *cannot* grasp, but taking hold of the working-class movement as it exists at present, and gently and gradually moulding it into a Socialist shape.' So Mahon went his logical way in 1888 – acting with Champion behind Keir Hardie at Mid-Lanark, taking a leading part through the Scottish Land and Labour League in the formation of the Scottish Labour Party, and beginning *The Labour Elector* with Burns and Mann. The middle-class Glasier expressed a justified worry when he wrote in *Commonweal* about Mid-Lanark: 'I trust this attempt to force Socialism into the strife of "practical politics" and the rut of party contest will not prejudice the miners of Lanarkshire against listening to and accepting our teaching upon its own merits in future.' But of course (being seemingly impossible to have it both ways) it did. Tom Maguire – another of the working-class 'parliamentary' Socialists forced to wean himself away from the SL – experienced similar pressures. In 1890, anticipating the paring-down trend of the decade, he was only able to retain the support of the Leeds new unionists by pushing hard and almost exclusively for labour representation as an end in itself. For all the quasi-Socialist aura of the subsequent ILP, Maguire saw well what was happening. 'People call themselves Socialists, but what they really are is just ordinary men with Socialist opinions hung round, they haven't got it inside of them' he remarked with much sadness shortly before his death in 1895. The contempt expressed by the middle-class Socialists of the 1880s for time-serving had perhaps only encouraged a new and subtler form of the vice to develop very soon afterwards.

Fabian Socialism too had in 1887 its own 'grit-split' of significant consequences. The crystallising event was 'Bloody Sunday', the Trafalgar Square demonstration of 13 November ostensibly over Ireland, in practice over free speech, that was broken up by mounted police with a brutal ease which finally convinced the middle-class Fabians of the impossibility of trusting to an insurrectionary working class. Ever since its foundations in 1884 as part of the general blast against *laissez-faire* assumptions, from Whistler upwards in terms of Socialist commitment, the composition of the Fabian Society had always suggested a small group of high-powered propagandists likely to disengage themselves from the sterner realities of class conflict. Sidney Webb in particular, brought in from the Colonial Office and increasingly influential in breaking off Fabian relations with the SDF, never felt the least inclination to become a street-fighting man. Even Hubert Bland, one of the instinctively more extreme Fabians, flatly wrote in 1886 after 'Black Monday' that 'the revolt of the empty stomach ends at the baker's shop'.[17] George Bernard Shaw, for all his inextinguishably rebellious nature, likewise felt disbelief about the actual revolutionary potential of the working class. Trafalgar Square, which he found a petrifying experience, offered vivid confirmation. As he wrote to Morris: 'I object to a defiant policy altogether at present. If we persist in it, we shall be eaten bit by bit like an artichoke.' And another embryonic middle-class revolutionary, E. Rhys, wrote the day after Trafalgar Square: 'I am done with the Socialist League. The

Fabians are the men for my money.' [18] The route towards 'permeation', the peaceful infiltration of Fabian ideas into the minds of men of reason, clearly beckoned. Shaw declared in 1892 in one of the Society's characteristic retrospective trumpet-blasts: 'In the middle of the revengeful growling over the defeat at the Square, trade revived; the unemployed were absorbed; the *Star* newspaper appeared to let in light and let off steam: in short, the way at last was clear for Fabianism.' [19] Yet for Shaw himself, this apparent smoothing of the path was not a recipe for deceit. Certainly he had lost faith in the revolutionary working class, but equally he knew full well that persuasion alone would never be sufficient to wrest the concessions from the established order necessary to create an authentic Socialist society. 'A good man fallen among Fabians', Lenin once justly called him. Shaw's sympathies were entirely with Ruskinite regeneration, but his pessimism could not allow him to subscribe to that creed in practice. 'An army of light is no more to be gathered from the human product of nineteenth-century civilisation than grapes are to be gathered from thistles' he wrote in 1889 in *Fabian Essays in Socialism*. This wistful desire for something more total than the strategy of 'permeate and trim and compromise' remained constant and comes out at odd moments in tracts and plays written during the 1890s. 'Give us hundreds of thousands, as you can if you try hard enough, and we will ride the whirlwind and direct the storm' he ended the 1892 survey with a resonant appeal for popular support. But this was not forthcoming, not only because it was not there, and Shaw had to wait until the 1930s and Soviet Russia for a society of suitably magisterial quality.

The appeal that Stalin's Russia was also to make to the Webbs was apparent in Sidney's affirmation as early as 1889 that 'the essential contribution of the century to sociology has been the supersession of the Individual by the Community. . . . Socialism is the product of this development.' [20] This was obviously not a moderate, liberal vision of society's future. But it did have the gradualist advantage of seeking to be implemented through an agency, the State, already in operational action. Even Clarke, though far more ethically motivated than Webb, likewise stressed in his contribution to the 1889 *Fabian Essays* bureaucrats rather than capitalists, municipalisation rather than working-class muscle-power. Underlying this emphasis was a basic Fabian revision of Marxist economic theory. The key notion of surplus value was discarded in about 1887, to be replaced by a theory of rent on the one hand, very much in the Mill 'unearned increment' tradition, and marginal utility on the other, which maintained in a counter-Ruskinite way that in the utilised market everyone got what their productive contribution entitled them to. It was an uninspiring body of thought: provided that certain excesses were abolished, and certain minima standards of hours, sanitation and educational training were established, then within a controlled labour market there would be all possible encouragement for efficiency and technological progress, none at all for slackness and casual waste. Within this framework, trade unions were encouraged to build up a clear-cut collective bargaining mechanism, since in Fabian neo-classical economic terms there existed a built-in safeguard against unions attempting to extract greater rewards than their output warranted. As the Webbs put it in *Industrial Democracy*: 'Even the most aggressive members of a Trade Union discover, in an increase of the percentage of unemployed colleagues whom they have to maintain, an unmistakable and imperative check upon any repetition of an excessive claim.' There was nothing apocalyptic, no call to arms, about that type of logic. And a year earlier the Society's Policy Report announced simply enough to the Congress of the Second International meeting in London in 1896: 'The Fabian Society begs those Socialists who are looking forward to a sensational historical crisis, to join some other Society.' Socialism for the Fabians had become a medicine, its doses to be measured out only by qualified doctors.

It certainly seemed so to Morris, who continued indomitably to insist on moral attainment and class conflict. While the Fabians were tempering the political struggle, Morris, in one of his last articles, dismissed as 'a futile hope indeed' the notion that with the advance of 'civilisation' and ease of production so 'the possessing classes will be able to spare more and more from the great heap of wealth to the producing classes'. Instead, 'nothing better will happen than more waste'.[21] So Morris died denying the possibility of peaceful Socialist change with the same vigour which he had shown from soon after the Trafalgar Square episode. This contrast with the vaunted Fabian moderation had been deliberate, heightened by the publication first of Edward Bellamy's utopian vision of syndicated happiness in *Looking Backward* (from the year 2000) and then of *Fabian Essays in Socialism*, which soon sold 25,000 copies. He countered the first by presenting an alternative utopia in *News from Nowhere*, the second in his review of the *Essays* in the pages of *Commonweal*. There he criticised the Fabians for setting aside 'the clear exposition of the first principles of Socialism . . . for the sake of pushing a theory of tactics, which could not be carried out in practice; and which, if it could be, would still leave us in a position from which we should have to begin our attack on capitalism all over again'. And of Webb in particular: 'He seems to enjoy all the humiliations of opportunism, to revel in it.' This is not to suggest that Morris was opposed in a dogmatic way to all that Fabianism was trying to achieve. In his *Communism* lecture of 1893, perhaps the richest expression of his political thought, he accepted the good work that the London County Council (established in 1889 and at the outset a Fabian stronghold) was doing in respect of free libraries, public parks, and other like forms of municipal improvement. But then in a haunting passage he went on to wonder whether 'the tremendous organisation of civilised commercial society is not playing the cat and mouse game with us socialists' and if 'the Society of Inequality might not accept the quasi-socialist machinery above mentioned, and work it for the purpose of upholding that society in a somewhat shorn condition, maybe, but a safe one'. Socialism of the heart was what mattered, not the conversion of voters and politicians to the authorising and implementation of State-Socialist measures. The difference was absolute and gave an historic quality to the words Morris exchanged with Webb after the latter had lectured at the Hammersmith Socialist Society in October 1895: 'The world is going your way at present, Webb, but it is not the right way in the end',[22] Webb revealed years later when asked what Morris had said. And by 1931 Shaw at least was publicly admitting that the false turn had after all been taken by the Fabians. He wrote in the Preface to that year's edition of the Essays: 'When the greatest Socialist of that day, the poet and craftsman William Morris, told the workers that there was no hope for them save in revolution, we said that if that were true there was no hope at all for them, and urged them to save themselves through Parliament, the municipalities, and the franchise. . . . It is not so certain today as it seemed in the eighties that Morris was not right.'

Indeed, in a specific working-class sense it is doubtful whether even in the 1890s things were really going Webb's way. Based in London, where the Metropolitan Radical Federation was increasingly becoming a cog in the Liberal Party electoral machine, neither the Fabians nor the SDF managed to take advantage of the desire for a new independent political force related to new unionism and working-class representation. The SDF failure was especially palpable. Mann, Burns and Thorne were all Socialists prominently associated with the new unionism; in October 1891 five out of the seven new members of the LTC executive were also SDF members; and in 1891–2 local election results showed how well an SDF candidate could fare in London if he was also a trade unionist. But Hyndman remained resolutely apart from labour matters, thereby consigning the SDF to be a significant force only at a localised rank-and-file level. This sense of a non-Liberal political vacuum waiting to be filled was also behind the temporary, even more circumstantial surge of Fabian popularity in the early 1890s. It was hardly courted by the London executive. When asked in January 1891 about the desirability of forming a new working-class party, Sidney Webb wrote in his most dampening way to The Workman's Times that 'the nature of an Englishman seems to be suited only to a political fight between the two parties – the party of order and the party of progress'. And a year later Shaw informed the same paper that the idea of an independent Labour Party 'turns out to be nothing but an attempt to begin the SDF all over again' because it likewise 'wants to make the pies first and find the plums afterwards'. It was very much in the context of this attitude that the great majority of the new provincial Fabian societies (up from twelve in 1890 to seventy-two by January 1893) passed into the ILP camp once the new organisation was under way. As W. H. Utley, a Fabian lecturer visiting the North, had sadly noted, his audiences 'seemed to be more interested in immediate political problems' than 'improving their minds by listening to lectures'.[23] So the London Fabians shrugged off with few qualms the political infant in the provinces and settled down to the struggle for the intellectual control of progressivism. Only once did they seriously seek to determine the course of independent working-class politics – with their January 1894 'Plan of Campaign' seeking to persuade the TUC to back fifty non-Liberal candidates – but it was an unconvincing gambit decisively repudiated. The new initiative clearly lay elsewhere. Morris in April 1887 had addressed a mass rally of Northumberland miners and had found it 'very inspiriting to speak to such a big crowd of eager & serious persons'.[24] Returning to London the next day the cocknified contrast had seemed unbearable. It was a paradigmatic experience: the immediate future of Socialism lay in the industrial north and, for all the sectional and ethical pitfalls, the 'Mahon path', despite the subsequent vagaries of Mahon himself, was in an Hegelian sense at least the necessary one.

The key figure in this coming of working-class representation was Keir Hardie. As late as 1886, in his role as leader of the Ayrshire miners, he still favoured a moderate industrial policy along the lines established by Alexander MacDonald and also (as an active Good Templar) continued to stand for essentially self-help, temperance values. Two developments then caused him to change direction and to choose the more horizontal course of working-class solidarity. One was the general spread of Socialist propaganda in industrial West Scotland under the auspices of Mahon's Scottish Land and Labour League. This threatened to undermine the old-style leadership by its forceful demands for eight hours and independent representation. The other was the absence of Liberal protest when hussars suppressed with considerable violence striking Lanarkshire miners at Blantyre in February 1887. The effect of this on Hardie was profound. Not only did he turn on [25] trade union leaders like Burt and Broadhurst as 'dumb dogs who will not bark', but he also committed himself to the cause of working-class candidates. He stood at Mid-Lanark in 1888 against a Liberal barrister candidate as well as a Conservative, and in 1892 successfully at West Ham South against a Conservative only. He thereupon made his famous trumpet-accompanied entry into Parliament and, as 'member for the unemployed', laid the foundations of the image he was never to lose as the sturdy cloth-capped labour pioneer. Yet the break with his Radical past was by no means total. At Mid-Lanark he affirmed his basic Liberal allegiance in matters of policy, and eschewed (as also at West Ham) any specifically Socialist tenets. This continuing orientation was at the root of Hardie's increasing disassociation between 1888 and 1893 from H. H. Champion, who organised the Mid-Lanark campaign but was linked with secular middle-class London Socialism and also more specifically with using Tory money to finance the *Labour Elector*. The paper collapsed in 1890 and Champion never recovered his former weight in the movement for independent representation. The ILP disavowed him in 1893 and soon afterwards he went into permanent exile in Australia, leaving behind as his parting shot the warning to the fledgling working-class political movement that 'the Liberal Party has a strong stomach and will swallow anything'.[26] It was a fair enough caution. As Hardie wrote to Burns in May 1891 about the Liberals: 'Like yourself, I believe we have more hope from that party than from the other.' He went on: 'But this applies to the rank & file only & not to all the leaders, & to prevent possible misunderstanding, the less said about this "hope" the better.' [27] The note of guilt was indicative: Hardie knew that independent representation was the card to play whatever the ideological situation. Moreover, he felt no inclination at this stage to compromise his political position (that of a Radical disenchanted by Liberal middle-classness) to the stringently economic demands of organised labour. 'The Labour Party will be a distinct organisation from the Trade Unions'[28] he had declared in 1887; and in 1891 he resigned as Secretary of the Ayrshire Miners. A specific labour alliance seemed in Hardie's eyes at least as yet superfluous.

The immediate 'independence' roots of the extraordinarily eclectic ILP were scattered far more widely than Yorkshire alone. In Newcastle three labour candidates had been elected to the school board as early as 1888; in Leicester the local Trades Council had representatives on both the School Board and the Town Council by 1891; while in Cumberland the local branch of the Labour Electoral Association (the generally dormant organisation initiated by the TUC in 1886) issued in January 1892 a Radical but strongly independent manifesto. But the heart of the ILP, both numerically and spiritually, was in the industrial West Riding, where between 1889 and 1892 new and predominantly Socialist trades councils were formed in Halifax, Huddersfield, Keighley, Spen Valley, Dewsbury and Batley, and Brighouse. During 1892 all the various types of labour organisations were pulled together through the agency of Joseph Burgess's *The Workman's Times*, finally assembling at Bradford in January 1893 to form the Independent Labour Party. The choice of site was entirely suitable. A bitterly fought, unsuccessful six-months' strike of the wool-workers at the large Manningham Mills was the immediate background to first Ben Tillett of the Dockers' Union splitting Illingworth's vote at West Bradford in 1892 and then Fred Jowett (a former member of the SL) being elected to the town council later in the year. Jowett's subsequent campaigning during the 1890s over issues like housing and school meals became typical of the way in which at a specific everyday level – through mediums like town councils, school boards and trade councils – concrete distinctions were maintained between the political working class and the still predominantly individualist Liberal middle class. This sense of a gritty and indigenous fighting body undoubtedly played a major part in the growth of the ILP. Frank Jackson recalled by contrast what he had to struggle against when he joined the Coventry branch of the SDF in 1902: 'The big propaganda against us was that we were a branch of the German Socialists. The greatest part of the efforts of the comrades were spent on this. It was in some respects, in my view, due to this that the ILP was formed.'[29] Inevitably, though, this often led to an insular disregard for 'continental' theory. Even in January 1893 Tillett successfully opposed the proposal to call the new party the 'Socialist Labour Party' on the grounds [30] that he wished 'to capture the trade unionists of this country, a body of men well organised, who paid their money, and were Socialists at their work every day and not merely on the platform, who did not shout for blood-red revolution, and when it came to revolution, sneaked under the nearest bed'. Nevertheless, the ILP was at the outset ignored by stolid trade unionists (and indeed by the SDF leadership, equally stolid in its own way), and was instead dominated by young and earnest Socialists from trades councils who ensured the defeat by ninety-one votes to sixteen of an amending motion by Mahon against the object of the party being 'to secure the collective ownership of the means of production, distribution and exchange'. Moreover, the underlying spirit in these early years – one of a basic ethical revolt against individualist hypocrisy – was quite different from that of any of the movement's working-class predecessors. One of the party's Yorkshire pioneers, Margaret McMillan, wrote in her autobiography: 'It was called the Independent Labour Party. In reality it was a new religion – a heresy.' The choice of spiritual but unabstracted metaphor was illuminating, the position of the Congregationalist rebel Keir Hardie as leader appropriate.

Significantly different in tone was the 'Clarion' strain within the ILP. The mood of Blatchford's Manchester-based movement was essentially that of good cheer and fellowship, inspiring an ethical approach to life that was generous rather than pious. It was also specifically Socialist. In May 1892 Blatchford not only took a full part in the formation of the Manchester and Salford ILP, but he also willingly accepted the SDF-inspired 'Fourth Clause' that forbade members from voting for any other party. Blatchford was no lover of the sectarian Social Democrats, but in a manifestly inegalitarian society he believed strongly in Morris's aphorism that 'no man is good enough to be another man's master'. Indeed, the influence of Morris and a generally Ruskinite analysis was extremely strong on Blatchford. Even in 1890 he had written in his widely read column in the *Sunday Chronicle*: 'Believe me, my lads, it is necessary not only to improve your conditions but to improve yourselves. Moreover, you must *begin* with yourselves.' Two years after the founding of *The Clarion*, and the rise of its circulation to about 90,000, this emphasis culminated with the publication in 1893 of *Merrie England*, which within a year came out in penny form and sold a million. The irony of the title showed Blatchford's concern about the continuing of dreadful social conditions; and much of the book consisted of, as it were, super-charged 'Facts for Socialists'. The central stress, however, was on how a surfeited civilisation needed to be replaced by older and less industrial self-sufficient productive forms. In the light of this belief Blatchford felt little enthusiasm for sectional trade union matters; while towards the increasingly systematic electioneering methods of the ILP he felt positive antipathy, especially in the context of the rejection of the 'Fourth Clause' at Bradford in January 1893. In particular he believed [31] Hardie – whose *Labour Leader* became nationally based from 1894, destroying *The Workman's Times* and in the end severely mutilating *The Clarion* – to be 'vain, greedy, crooked and bumptious' as well as a prig. And in the same letter, written to Glasier in 1900, he looked back on the mid-1890s: 'Hardie must be a journalist, and a "leader", and John Burns must be a statesman. God's love. So I hung the sword up in the lumber-room and took to planting cabbages.'

The caustic 'leader' reference was inspired by Hardie assuming the position of President of the ILP between 1894 and 1896 before the alternative role of 'Chairman' was created. In these years Hardie shaped the party firmly in his own determinedly independent image. On the one hand the London Progressivism of Burns was allowed to pass into the Liberal camp; while on the other the SDF connotations of Mann were discreetly played down by the provincially-based executive even after he became national Secretary in February 1894. Behind Hardie's dominance lay the general feeling that he more than anyone had discovered how to carry independent working-class Socialism to the mass of the population. In 1894 the number of ILP branches reached 400 and encouraging by-elections were fought. Moreover, while ILP candidates stressed concrete issues like eight hours and freedom of trade union action, and local branches were particularly vigorous in the fields of housing and education, Hardie in Parliament was making his name on the unemployment question and flatly referring to the 'flabby imbecility known as Liberal-Labourism'.[32] Everything built up to a peak in 1895: the annual conference flamboyantly proposed pensions for everyone at the age of 50; and the newly centralised party organisation seemed clearly geared to produce results. In the event, the 1895 Election proved even more catastrophic for the ILP than for the Liberals. All twenty-seven candidates were defeated (including Hardie at West Ham) and neither the SDF nor the trade union strongholds indicated any substantial measure of support. The proletarian leader had gone too far too fast in his bid to win over the entire working-class world to the politics of independence. The Webbs in particular relished Hardie's plight. After contentedly referring to the demise of Gladstonian Liberalism, Beatrice went on in her private assessment soon after the Election: 'The ILP has completed its suicide. Its policy of abstention and deliberate wrecking is proving to be futile and absurd.'[33] It was a suggestive analysis: the Liberals would have to become 'New', while the ILP for its part would have to moderate its Socialism and look rather more patiently to prosaic labour. The way was clearly open for a specific, socially-concerned Progressivism, though somewhat more ethical than the Webbite variety. To understand this retreat of the next few years, and to explain why the TUC plumped for pure sectionalism in 1895 (excluding even trades councils' representatives as well as non-unionist politicians like Hardie himself), it is clearly necessary to consider in more detail the recent past of organised labour. But if that now seems to us an indisputable historical perspective – in the sense that the ILP chose to live by working-class votes and therefore had to adjust to working-class voting habits – one should at least realise that a choice was involved. As Blatchford, classless son of a travelling theatrical family and the most popular journalist of the decade, vainly implored in 1894 with a voice whose inspiration it is not difficult to guess: 'Let us make Socialists first, and organise them next . . . .'[34]

The growing centrality of this relationship between Socialism and trade unionism perhaps justifies a brief coda on the question of work itself. Morris in particular insisted (in contrast to Carlyle) that work was something that should not be done for the need or glory of it but instead for the joy. He realised how impossible this was in late-Victorian capitalist society and, in most vital respects, anticipated Marx's doctrine of alienation that has been revealed this century. Morris perceived only too clearly how critical the question of work satisfaction was in the attainment of what Gramsci was to call *senso commune*,[35] that is an authentically integrated common culture. Yet when Blatchford under Morris's inspiration pursued much the same theme, he was treated in 1909 to a condescending 'Progressive' sneer [36] by Ramsay MacDonald to the effect that '*Merrie England* is like a man fully explaining a motor-car by describing a wheelbarrow'. Shaw, however, included the theme in his 1931 retraction. Instead of following Morris's insistence on shorter hours and more leisure for *everybody*, twentieth-century capitalism had, Shaw argued, permitted heavy unemployment in order 'to keep the workers working as long as before, or longer, and to increase the number or the luxury, or both, of the leisured rich'. Unemployment, as Shaw realised, divided the working class not only in an obvious occupational sense, but also in terms of alienation at the workplace itself. Even leaving aside the question of alienated labour in the sub-divided factory system, the sheer economic necessity of having to work inexorably long hours in order to stay employed inevitably made for *general* disenchantment (or at the least disengagement) from the work function itself. But as Foster [37] has shown in connection with Oldham, it was the *few* who did find satisfaction at the workplace who had the energy and commitment during the third quarter of the century to put the political brake on the working-class discontent of the Chartist period. Similarly, it was a minority of the working class – not necessarily satisfied with the work function but at least responding positively towards it – who subsequently lay behind the fairly rapid growth of efficiently organised, fully industrial trade unionism; and provided that these representatives have gone on making satisfactory bargains with the employing class, the rank-and-file has tended this century to remain relatively passive, desiring only like Philpot to get through to the end of the week and pay-day. Lockwood has written of 'privatisation',[38] Hyman of 'an alienated, "instrumental" orientation to work and the union'.[39] Yet for all this there remains an underlying solidaristic aspect, which one must include in a perspective on the labour-centred politics of the 1890s. Goldthorpe and Lockwood quote the American sociologists Kornhauser, Sheppard and Mayer: 'Our study of auto workers contributes rather striking evidence that it is possible for wage-earners to experience vast social and economic gains and yet remain steadfastly union orientated in their political views.' [40] The point is surely applicable also to twentieth-century 'Fabian' Britain. And although Morris would have preferred no auto workers, and Dagenham materialist aspirations are not his, at least working-class communitarian values remain recognisably similar to the ones he admired during his visit to Northumberland in 1887 and which subsequently came to dominate the formative labour alliance thirteen years later.

Chapter 8

LABOUR

1885 — 1900

'Everyone is on strike; so, landlords, do not be offended.
The rent that's due we'll pay you when the strike is ended.' [1]

So sang striking London dockers in August 1889. Such was their *élan*
that it did indeed seem for some time afterwards that with the exception of the blackguard of the piece – C. M. Norwood, Chairman of
the Joint Dock Committee – everyone would find satisfaction in the
vindication of the dockers' claims. To veteran labour leaders it was as
if the working class was waking up from a prolonged slumber. 'Not
since the high and palmy days of Chartism have I witnessed any
movement corresponding in importance and interest' [2] wrote G. J.
Harney at the end of September. The dock strike was not the first
manifestation of the upsurge of hitherto spasmodically organised and
seemingly unskilled labour, but it was undoubtedly the most famous
and influential. For a few months afterwards, during the winter of
1889–90, an astonishing proliferation of new unionism took place. In
South Wales alone, confectioners and tramway workers as well as
dockers and railway workers began for practically the first time to
take collective militant action. For all his well-tried scepticism, Engels
found the phenomenon rich in promise: 'These new trade unions of
unskilled men are totally different from the old organisations of the
working-class aristocracy and cannot fall into the same conservative
ways.' [3] Tom Mann, active Socialist and inspiring organiser of the
London dockers, keenly held to the same hope. Writing with Tillett
in 1890 in reply to a recent reaffirmation of 'New Model' principles by
George Shipton, Mann delivered a fundamental pledge of intent about
the new unionism: 'Poverty, in our opinion, can be abolished, and we
consider it the work of the trade unionist to do this. We want to see the
necessary economic knowledge imparted in our labour organisations,
so that labour in the future shall not be made the shuttlecock of
political parties. Our trade unions shall be the centres of enlightenment,
and not merely the meeting-place for paying contributions and receiving
donations.' [4] It was a poignant hope: the Dock, Wharf, Riverside and
General Labourers' Union, of which he was President and Tillett

Secretary, ultimately became the Transport and General Workers' Union; and Will Thorne's Gasworkers and General Labourers' Union – the other great Socialist-inspired creation of 1889 – was to turn into the National Union of General and Municipal Workers. Moreover, the seeds of the transmutation into monolithic, unbending organisations, quite as sectional in their own way as their Junta-ridden predecessors, were apparent at the very outset of the new unions' existence.

The specific economic context of the new unionism was the upturn in trade which gave wage labourers a chance to make up for the highly-publicised hard times of the mid-1880s. But if this was a well-known cyclical phenomenon, the opportunity to press employers was especially welcome as a means of alleviating the intensification of labour as well as direct wage-cutting which had accompanied the ending in the 1870s of Britain's industrial monopoly. The systematic employment of virtually unorganisable women (as in the West Riding woollen textile industry in the 1880s) was a clear indication of these pressures at work; while the formation of the National Labour Federation in 1886 and Tyneside and National Labour Union in February 1889 for the North-Eastern semi-skilled, and the National Amalgamated Labour Union in 1888 for Swansea dockers, were all indications – even before Thorne's gasworkers, Maguire's Leeds builders, and Mann's dockers – of counter-measures. The impulse to associate was, however, more than merely an expression of the desire to reap hard while the economic going was good. It was also the hopeful affirmation of a certain job status, the sense of having acquired a certain limited semi-skill, whether real or conventional and often machine-operating, that demanded various quasi-craft privileges of its own. Inevitably, this only affected in a significant way specific occupational groups in specific geo-economic circumstances. In Hobsbawm's words, the North-East and NAUL was built on 'ships and engineering, Barnsley and Nottingham on iron, steel and pit-top men, Hull on docks and shipyards'. [5] More than anything, this essentially parochial dynamic, seeking to create a succession of unrelated 'closed shops', lay behind the extremely patchy early development of the theoretically 'general' new unionism. Suitably, when the Tyneside and National Labour Union became the National Amalgamated Union of Labour in 1893 (but deceptively national, simply deriving its strength from Sheffield rather than Newcastle), it was able to look back with a sense of debt to its firmly down-to-earth Burt-encouraged Lib.-Lab. origins. Moreover, as Champion noted in 1890, the Socialists who were so prominent in the previous year's dock strike had been welcomed by the rank-and-file far less for their doctrines than for their organisational ability in a particular situation of stress.

Indeed, the need for an initially high degree of centralised organisation was probably inherent if these unions of less than highly skilled (even if somewhat skilled) workers were to be effective. As T. R. Threlfall, the old-timer Secretary of the Labour Electoral Association, wrote somewhat maliciously in *The Nineteenth Century* in October 1892 about the 'flatness' of the new unions at the recent TUC in Glasgow: 'Their leaders are paying the penalty of responsibility and office. . . . Experience is after all proving that a substantial balance at the banker's, although devoid of poetry, has many consolations for the members of a union.' But this was only a partial perspective: the new unionist dawn of 1889–90 was false, as much because of the employers' counter-offensive which immediately followed it as on account of its somewhat limited nature at inception.

The fortunes of the gasworkers were in some ways symbolic of those of new unionism in general. Thorne, who was brought up as a general labourer and joined the SDF in 1884, insisted at the outset that contributions should be kept down to 2d a week instead of the usual 1s, that the tag 'General Labourers' be added to the union's name in order to catch the casual yard-labourers who were otherwise easily trained to become blackleg stokers, and that benefits be confined to strike pay only. Such a broad-based plan was undermined early on: the various district branches demanded sickness and funeral benefits and Thorne reluctantly gave way. Moreover, early industrial successes proved transient. The Gas, Light and Coke Company agreed to eight-hour shifts in August 1889, but the South Metropolitan Company resisted and, through the use of police-protected blacklegs, managed to combat the strike action of December 1889 to February 1890 at a cost to Thorne's union of £10,000. But elsewhere, the much more explicitly Lib.-Lab. Birmingham Amalgamated Society of Gasworkers, Bricklayers and General Labourers had managed in November 1889 to wrest a 48-hour week out of the Birmingham Corporation. The toast at the celebration breakfast held by the union at the Town Hall was instructive:

> 'Here's to the men who are willing to work,
> The employer that's willing to pay,
> And here's to the men who have striven to get
> The gasmen their eight-hour day.' [6]

This tone of social concord had its effect, especially when trade began to decline again about 1891. Though emphasising the strategy to be only a temporary expediency, Thorne stated bluntly in his annual report for 1892 that 'strikes, through whatever cause, should be avoided wherever possible'.[7] Moreover, while in principle holding to the boundlessly horizontal slogan of 'one man, one ticket, and every man with a ticket', Thorne in practice followed the Birmingham example and increasingly concentrated during the second half of the decade on solid provincial recruitment of labourers employed by municipal authorities. This made recognition very much easier, the great test of a normalised give-and-take relationship that private employers with access to a labour surplus were still reluctant to concede to only semi-skilled unions. This is not to posit a major diluting of belief on Thorne's part: he had little practical alternative, and in the event did well to recover membership figures to almost 48,000 in 1900 after a decline in the early and middle years of the decade. Moreover, he and his labour group managed in 1898 to gain control of West Ham Town Council, from which base he pushed vigorously for the fulfilment of specific demands like the compulsory eight-hour day, improved housing, and the taking of tramways into public ownership. And soon afterwards, one of the motifs of 1889, the following of a different path to Hyndman and Morris, achieved fruition in a certain sense at least when Thorne was responsible more than any other Socialist for persuading other trade unionists to accept the ILP's offer of alliance in the cause of independent parliamentary representation.

The muted splendour of Thorne's achievement stood out in contrast to the tribulations suffered during the 1890s by the waterfront workers, the other great rebels of 1889. At the outset in August the 'aristocratic' stevedores had only agreed to make common cause with the London dockers because of contiguity of livelihoods, the lightermen because they had their own grievances to redress. 'He had always refused to speak under the red flag' revealed *Reynolds' Newspaper* about the lightermen's leader, Wigginton, a Radical concerned to refute employers' charges that the strikers were Socialist. He need not have worried: Hyndman protested, but Burns declined to raise the red flag during the well-disciplined processions through the City. In this atmosphere Cardinal Manning flourished. He wrote of the strike leaders that they were 'very reasonable' and had 'broken with the Socialist Theories, and are simply industrial and economic'; [8] and after winning the dockers their tanner, he even found himself the next year portrayed on banners alongside ones of Marx at London's first great May Day demonstration. In practice, though, it was a quickly devalued sixpence: mealtime deductions virtually wiped out the improved rate of pay; while in organisational terms, not only did the stevedores and various watermen stick closely to their own unions after the strike, but also the foremen and permanent labourers decided against joining the Dockers' Union. In this situation, against the odds, the leaders sought to create union homogeneity and labour discipline by putting a 'ring fence' round the docks. In stern words Mann informed a mass meeting in November 1889 that his union was 'determined to eliminate the riff-raff: the wretched wastrels that have disgraced the Docks', and that 'the end of this week we close our books'.[9] The policy failed: no docker was going to support decasualisation if it meant putting him or his mates out of a possible job. Instead, after a year of 'ca'canny', which Mann tried unsuccessfully to speed up, being well aware that the employers would only grant recognition in certain economic circumstances to more purposeful work forces, the tide turned inexorably against the union. In the declining trade of the winter of 1890-1 the Joint Dock Committee took the opportunity to decasualise on their own terms. A system of classes was introduced, partly determined by medical tests, giving the companies exclusive job control and pushing the residuum (class 'C') of roughly 5 or 6 per cent into an acceptably detached minority position from the rest of the dock labourers. As Llewellyn-Smith, a contemporary historian of the strike, had hopefully anticipated, 'the self-respecting labourer will no longer be demoralised and manufactured into the loafer'.[10] The Dockers' Union itself could only accept the trend: contributions were raised from 2d a week to 4d in 1890 and the next year it introduced the usual gamut of sickness and funeral benefits. But there was no irresistible glide towards solid and secure expansion, for its industrial power had already been effectively broken. Tillett's union steadily declined in numbers over the decade; and the Shipping Federation (formed in September 1890) was able with ease to bring in blacklegs to defeat strike action. Jobs meant everything – and market forces dictated market responses on both sides.

A similarly uncompromising dialectic was enacted in provincial ports, most significantly in Liverpool and Hull. J. Havelock Wilson's National Amalgamated Union of Sailors and Firemen (active since 1887) struck twice in Liverpool during the first half of 1889, but failed to win the issue of job control. Wilson thereupon saw the need to consolidate and without delay told a mass meeting at Liverpool in July that 'neither the men nor the officials of the union have any intention of permitting another strike to take place if it can possibly be staved off by arbitration or otherwise'.[11] And, true to his sectionalist Lib.-Lab. persuasions, Wilson had positively allowed his seamen to enter into alliance with the employers against striking Liverpool dockers in March 1890. Here, likewise, the question of job control was central: the National Union of Dock Labourers, recently founded in Glasgow, had only been able to set up its Liverpool branch on the premise that it was to be concerned not with benefits but with being able to enforce effective non-blacklegged strike action; while for its part, the Employers' Labour Association, formed in February 1890, was well aware that in a long-term period of falling profits for the shipping companies it was vital to be able to keep labour costs down by employing non-union men wherever possible. Once again the employers had their work made easy for them. The benefits-orientated carters and flatmen never joined in, while after a few weeks the foremen in particular began to drift back towards employment on any terms. Thus the companies kept control of the hiring of casual labour; and waterfront unionism in Liverpool was only saved by the common-sensical abilities of James Sexton, who became General Secretary of the National Union of Dock Labourers in 1893 and managed to make some organisational sense out of what was virtually a caste system. In Hull, in the same year that Sexton took over in Liverpool, defeat was complete. The apparently strong branch of the Dockers' Union there struck over the question of the Shipping Federation's establishment of a Free Labour Exchange and were roundly defeated in seven weeks. Solidity was strong during the actual struggle, but dissipated practically overnight once the union had lost control over the dispensing of jobs. Such was the scale of the defeat that for the rest of the century Tillett's Dockers' Union actually had fewer members in Hull than the National Free Labour Association. 'It behoves the toilers first to organise and then to sympathetically set about the task of reform',[12] observed Tillett with the circumspection born of vanquished hopes in his annual report later that year.

An indication of new unionism's difficulties during the 1890s was Tom Mann's essentially gadfly role. Originally an engineer like Burns, he followed a very different course from his colleague of 1889, who was elected MP for Battersea in 1892 and soon moved over to the progressive Liberals, finishing up in 1914 as President of the Board of Trade. Mann by contrast remained as President of Tillett's union and forcibly insisted in his 1890 pamphlet that 'the key-note is to ORGANISE first, and take action, in the most effective way, so soon as organisation warrants action, instead of specially looking to Government'. Then in the mid-1890s Mann accepted political responsibilities with the ILP until disenchantment with this followed also in about 1897. Finally, in 1898, dismayed by the internal divisiveness revealed by the engineering lock-out, he founded the Workers' Union in what he regarded as a decisive attempt to fulfil his precept of 1890 that 'clannishness in trade matters must be superseded by a cosmopolitan spirit'. The union's generic title was a token of Mann's wide-ranging aims. Accordingly he held out against the provision of de-militating benefits, tried to ignore the dampening remarks of first Dipper of NAUL and then Thorne, and insisted that 'we do not propose to refuse to enrol those who present themselves simply because another Union exists willing to enrol them, as in some instances existing Unions have not organised more than 5 per cent of those in the trade'.[13] It was a fair point, but the omens were not good. As early as 1892 those in explicitly general

unions only comprised some 13 per cent of total trade union membership; and Dipper's NAUL had only flourished relatively because – unlike
the much more ambitious National Labour Federation which it
virtually took over in the early 1890s – it confined itself in practice to
certain occupational groups (like the surface workers in collieries
around Sheffield) and provided funeral and accident benefits rather
than strike pay alone. Under these auspices 'general' unionism proved
in the 1890s a misnomer, failing especially to organise the great mass
of low-wage women workers. And Mann's Workers' Union was in the
event similarly unsuccessful in terms of fulfilling classic 'general'
principles. Though it made certain ground during the favourable
economic conditions of 1898 to 1900, it succumbed soon after its
formation to the benefits snare and as a result appealed not to the key
unorganised drifting element, potential anarchists, blacklegs, or 'angels
in marble' all of them, but instead only to not entirely unskilled
labourers already in regular employment. Thorne's prognostications
were thus confirmed: Mann emigrated not long afterwards to Australia
and Thorne's own focus switched to the political attitudes of the older
unions which, for all the impetus given to their activites by the new
union 'explosion', were rooted in a working tradition established long
before the transpontine dramas of 1889 played out before packed houses.

Mann had voiced a growing opinion by declaring in 1886: 'The average
Unionist of today is a man with a fossilised intellect, either hopelessly
apathetic, or supporting a policy that plays directly into the hands of
the capitalist exploiter.'[14] Certainly Broadhurst, Secretary of the
TUC's Parliamentary Committee, justified Mann's sense of outrage.
'No great national labour contest has occurred to strain the resources of
our unions or to disturb the relations between capital and labour',[15] he
noted with satisfaction in his report for 1888. Yet it is doubtful whether
Broadhurst in the few years before his tacitly enforced retirement in
1890 was still really typical of the mood of even the 'old' unions. In
the mid-1880s especially one senses widespread resentment against the
tendency of employers to stretch to their utmost carefully built-up
mid-Victorian trade regulations. In July 1884, for example, a masons'
representative called Annand complained[16] to the Aberdeen Trades
Council about the relentless overtime in the stone-cutting trade,
especially in 'the many small yards which had sprung up of late years,
and where those employed were chiefly young lads or apprentices'. In
Hull the next year the Liberal shipowner Norwood, already a marked
man for his opposition to Plimsoll, was opposed by the distinctly non-
Socialist local labour group even though this had the effect of letting
the Tory in. And between 1885 and 1887 three successive presidential
addresses at the TUC (one of them delivered by Threlfall) revealed an

awareness of 'the system' and stressed their particular concern about unemployment and undue labour intensification by employers. In this context the demand for the eight-hour day increasingly became the single dominant question: in 1887 the ASCJ accepted it; in 1889, among others, even Broadhurst's Operative Stonemasons rebelliously did likewise; and finally, at Liverpool in 1890, the TUC as a whole voted in favour of the principle. Against this background, and also the sub-sequent history of the new unionism, one should not make too much of the contrast which Burns noted [17] at the 1890 Congress between 'workmen' like himself and the 'aldermanic' representatives of the older unions, with their 'very good coats, large watch-chains and high hats'. The second item alone Thorne had been presented with after securing eight-hour shifts at the Beckton gasworks the previous year. Moreover, Burns was mistaken both quantitatively and qualitatively when he regarded the acceptance of eight hours in 1890 as a portent of authentic victory for new unionism and even Socialism. Between 1892 and 1894 the average new unionist strength was 107,000 out of a total TUC membership of 1,555,000; and to most trade unionists the accept-ance of eight hours meant not so much Socialism as a necessary ex-tension of protective trade regulations. For all the rhetoric, of Mann, of Hardie, of the young ILP, the eight-hours movement remained of relatively low political import – certainly until 1897, when Congress at last made up its mind to press for legislative rather than local industrial implementation of the principle. Typical of the *extent* to which Glad-stonian Liberalism was able to ride out the policy-making pressures of this economic factor was the episode which took place at Sheffield in 1894. There the local crafts-dominated trades council supported the Liberal rather than the ILP candidate at the Attercliffe by-election even though one of their own men, Charles Hobson, had been displaced as Liberal candidate after pressure from party headquarters in London. This low-profile pursuit of limited objectives, quite unacceptable to the young MacDonald, was confirmed by the excluding constitutional changes enacted at Cardiff in 1895. In more ways than one, the older delegates knew their place.

Mann's bold assertion of 1890 that 'no longer can the skilled assume with a sort of superior air that they are the salt of the earth' proved basically unfounded at the workplace as well as within institutional trade unionism. Despite all the pressure from intensifying employers and semi-skilled machine operators, differentials seem to have been resolutely maintained right up to 1914. This was partly done by getting in quickly on new machines and adjusting their use to standard entry-controlled practices (as in the case of printers), but more often by simply playing up the traditional skilled/unskilled shibboleth as much as possible. Robert Knight's Boilermakers were a classic example in this respect.

After a long struggle during the 1880s between skilled sub-contracting platers on the Wear and their helpers, the Society unashamedly acted in liaison with the local employers to bring in 700 blacklegs to oust the unrepentant helpers. There were many other instances during this period of a similarly inflexible sectionalism. Yorkshire spinners, for example, gave little encouragement during the 1890s to the development of the powerloom weavers' unionism in the West Riding which after several checks culminated in the Textile Workers' Federation of 1900. One of the weavers' leaders, Ben Turner, later recalled: 'The weaver was looked down upon by the overlookers, and . . . a woollen spinner and a woolsorter despised the company of men in ordinary grades of labour.' [18] Above all, it was the trade societies within the building industry which remained most faithful to the premises of their mid-Victorian growth. The General Secretary of the ASCJ said it all in an address of October 1889: 'The great strike of dock labourers which, during the past month, absorbed almost the whole attention of the public, caused us serious anxiety, fearing it should interfere with the progress of work in which our members are engaged.' [19] And soon afterwards Coulson of the Bricklayers' replied when he was asked to help the new United Builders' Labourers' Union: 'You cannot do it. I myself tried to help Kenney. It is impossible to organise labourers.' [20] Yet the irony was that in actual occupational practice this sort of lofty distinction was becoming an increasingly artificial one. It seems unlikely that the spinners kept their distance from the weavers purely for the reason that their skill was of a different order; and in Aberdeen the secretary of the local branch of the Ironmoulders' Union, writing in 1898 to ironworkers' labourers who were complaining of being blacklegged by ironmoulders during strike action, unwittingly admitted that 'in a moulding shop it was a difficult matter to define what was really moulding work and what was labourers''.[21] Before long, however, the fineness of the point would be rumbled and everyone would have to bow in more or less the same direction to the mechanised god. Instead, the relatively short-term future at least of organised labour lay less with Applegarth's successors than with the more recognisably modern heavyweights – and in particular the miners, whose face-working 'aristocrats' were far too populous (representing about half the work force) for them ever to attain an authentically vertical state of mind.

Yet it was the powerful voting force of coal which, together with cotton, determined the TUC's constitutional decisions of 1895. This retrenchment was not so much an indication of hostility to the notion of independent representation as such as a flat expression of unwillingness to help others on the part of miners and spinners who often lived in occupationally solid enough areas to be able to elect and subsidise their own MPs. James Mawdsley, Lancashire-based leader of the sub-contracting cotton spinners, was to express this mood well when in 1900 he condemned the LRC as 'an attempt to saddle another organisation on the shoulders of that patient carrier of burthens – the British workman'.[22] A year earlier, as befitted the architect of the 1893 Brooklands Agreement that had established peace in the cotton industry for almost two decades, he had run with the young Churchill at Oldham. There he stated his political philosophy: 'I am not going to starve myself, or to ask workpeople to starve themselves, for the idea that their grandchildren might be well off. I want a little of that well-off business myself, and if I cannot get it by any other system I am going to make the best of the system we have.'[23]

One counterpart to this patchwork rise in the standard of living was the popularity in the industrial North of comfortable dialect literature; another was the quickening growth of the Co-operative movement, and in particular the consumer-controlled Co-operative Wholesale Society, which in 1886 decisively rejected the 'bounty to labour', but whose goods increased in value from less than £150,000 in 1882 to over £2,500,000 a year by 1900. Producers' co-operation grew by contrast far more slowly, tending to centre on technologically threatened groups like boot-and-shoe makers in the East Midlands. Among consuming co-operators, miners were especially prominent. An observer in Derbyshire, writing in 1893, described a community sturdily carving out a niche for itself: 'At Hucknall Torkard, where there are three large collieries, the men are great co-operators, holding all the shares themselves, and providing themselves with the best of everything at the lowest price. They have also put in force the Allotments Act . . . and nearly every man has his bit of highly cultivated ground.'[24] This was very much the background for the politically conservative phenomenon of Lib.-Labbism. Eleven such members were elected in 1886, six of them miners: Burt, Crawford, Charles Fenwick and John Wilson in the North-East, Benjamin Pickard in Yorkshire, and William Abraham ('Mabon') for the Rhondda in South Wales. All were Nonconformist, all with the exception of Crawford (who had died) were still there in 1900. Within the context of this broader tradition, the fact that the 'aristocrats' of Northumberland and Durham, together with Abraham's South Wales miners, declined in 1888 to join the pro-eight hours and anti-sliding-scale Miners' Federation of Great Britain was not in the long term of critical importance. Pete Curran of the ILP found this out when he stood in 1897 at a by-election in Barnsley (the headquarters of the MFGB) against the Liberal pro-eight hours mine-owning candidate. Pickard gave the Liberal his support and Curran was stoned by miners in Wombwell. It was a consistent enough action: eight hours bank to bank was what they wanted, not control of the means of production, distribution and exchange.

Yet eleven years later the miners committed themselves to support of the Labour Party, and the success of Keir Hardie's labour alliance strategy – the abandoning of high-sounding Marxian revolutionary slogans – was confirmed. One should not be surprised: the industrial tenacity of late nineteenth-century Lib.-Labbism, especially after the harrowing lessons of the 1870s, has been too often underemphasised; likewise the fact that the real turn-about was made by Hardie in the late 1890s, not the miners a decade later. The activities of the rank-and-file in proudly exporting Durham provide plenty of evidence [25] of local workplace resistance to employers' wishes. 'Cavilling' in particular – choosing who-works-where by lot rather than by colliery management – provided a primitive but perennially effective form of job control. And in 1892, after the leadership had accepted the owners' claim for a 10 per cent reduction in wages according to sliding-scale principles, the Durham miners themselves voted against this by over three to one. Elsewhere, in MFGB territory, the Derbyshire miners' leader James Haslam noted somewhat guiltily after the 1893 lock-out had ended in a settlement mediated by Rosebery: 'We are not surprised at the uneasiness manifested among our Members. . . . No one likes reducton in wages.' [26] Yet as continuing rank-and-file allegiance indicated, Lib.-Lab. mining leadership had much to commend it in specifically trade unionist terms. Reliable, long-lived, sensible of being able to be treated as equals at the negotiating table, and concerned with such concrete matters as rescue work and additional payment for miners who had to use safety lamps, men like Wilson and Pickard cannot be glibly dismissed. With these qualities there went also a redoubtable sense of independence. 'Men living surrounded by all the luxuriousness which wealth can command . . . cannot possibly form a correct view as to the life's wants of working men',[27] declared a circular as early as 1884 after discussion at that year's Conference of the Miners' National Union about middle-class MPs. Burt's fellow-members were one expression soon afterwards of this independent mood, but more common was the increasingly frequent election of miners' leaders to local councils, school boards, and boards of guardians. It remained an unambitious form of working-class politics, but it was undoubtedly an emerging one. Yet it was not in vain that Gladstone had spoken of 'masses not classes'; and 'Lib.' continued as important as 'Lab.'. In an understanding of how (and at what price) Hardie managed to make what was to be the linking bridge, the Yorkshire mining leader Ned Cowey, the miners' representative from 1893 on the TUC parliamentary committee, is a central symbolic as well as substantive figure. Frederick Rogers, first Chairman of the LRC, described Cowey in his autobiography and in so doing seemed to evoke exactly the evolving, somewhat paradoxical nature of late nineteenth-century Lib.-Labbism: 'A giant in stature, with a leonine head and face, energy and passion were his chief characteristics. . . . He had been brought up in one of the religious sects, and the poetry of the Old Testament was in his blood. His interests were few . . . but one subject always stirred him to poetry and passion, and this was the need for workmen in Parliament.'

Booth's phrase about trade unionism transcended by a certain ethicalism is clearly pertinent. In 1881 Burt, 'The Pitman gan te Parlemint', had criticised [28] the Irish anti-coercionists who were asking the trade unions 'to support the Irish tenant-farmers who were fighting a great battle on behalf of the cause of labour'. Instead, Burt argued that an appeal based on 'some great chivalrous idea' like 'the legislative independence of Ireland' would be far more suitable; and in Gladstonian phrase he insisted that 'class feelings, class distinctions, and class prejudices are fast dying out, and the sooner they are altogether obliterated the better'. But when class did come visibly to matter again, the Bulgarian idea declined for its part to die out and instead remained to crucial effect. The classic instance of this emerging turn-of-the-century configuration was in highly industrial Nonconformist South Wales. The effect of the Local Government Act of 1888 was particularly important there, not only in standard Nonconformist fashion driving out the landed aristocrats, but also within Nonconformity itself giving the working-class mining leaders the chance to fill a political niche as recompense for the way in which lower middle-class colliery officials were increasingly monopolising the lay offices within the actual chapels. Mabon as a trade union leader managed to a considerable extent to fill the ethical vacuum left by this growing working-class alienation from institutional Nonconformity, but he himself kept up his connection as a lay preacher with the Nazareth Calvinistic Methodist Chapel in Pentre and only with the utmost reluctance abandoned the social concord of sliding-scale settlements. This belated but decisive turning-point came in 1898, when against Mabon's advice the South Wales miners struck after the owners had formally refused to accept the principle of the minimum wage. Great suffering resulted and 'Mabon's Day' (the once-a-month holiday) was lost, but the employers eventually accepted the principle in theory and in October the explicitly anti-sliding-scale South Wales Miners' Federation was formed, affiliating to the MFGB the following year. The new Federation remained resolutely Lib.-Lab. in its politics and showed little warmth towards the ILP, which it regarded as over-ambitious and even (in comparison with Mabon) ungodly. Yet in 1900 Keir Hardie secured election at Merthyr against both his expectations and opposition to his candidature on the part of the Federation's leaders. An extract from one of his speeches conveys the tone of his campaign:

'My programme is the programme of Labour. My cause is Labour's cause – the cause of Humanity – the cause of God. . . . I first learnt my Socialism in the New Testament where I still find my chief inspiration.' [29] So the rank-and-file miners voted for this working man of the right sort; and the influence on Hardie of 'Coom-to-Jesus Philip' (or Snowden as he was known outside Yorkshire) thus scored its first electoral success.

For some time after the defeats of 1895 the ILP had been in a state of indecision. Membership fell from 35,000 to 20,000 in about a year, but pleasure over 'the Sedan of the "Great Liberal Party" ' forestalled an immediate re-evaluation of strategy. However, in a later issue of the same paper which used that over-certain phrase, the *Liverpool Labour Chronicle*, Burgess in April 1897 argued that 'our attitude towards Liberal/Labour men is precisely the attitude of which we complain when Social-Democrats accuse us of compromise' and looked instead to a common working purpose to 'weld the forces of labour into one harmonious whole'. Hardie half took the point: he accepted the need for a broader-based non-sectarian appeal, the seeds of the labour alliance, but was not prepared to accept the relative Socialist rigour involved in formal unity with the SDF. This reservation was reinforced by internal ILP developments later in the year. Mann resigned his Secretaryship, the influence of working men like Curran and Burgess waned, and the rise to executive prominence of the far more middle-class trio of Glasier, Snowden and MacDonald foreshadowed the coming of an eclectic non-Marxist ethical progressivism. Glasier it was who at the Annual Conference in 1898 jettisoned the plan for unity already voted for by members of both the ILP and the SDF. 'Is it not, think you, better for a land that there may be one straight, flat, unfertilising central canal?' [30] went his winsome appeal. It was a decisive moment: the rejection of Marxism in favour of progressivism gave the ILP not only contemporary intellectual respectability, but also a fundamentally Liberal-centred outlook, capable of attracting even guarded trade unionists in certain industrial circumstances. Glasier himself did not relish the mundane realities of the labour alliance – 'this tendency to constantly refer to sexual matters by Scotchmen when provoked is a very ugly fact' [31] he once noted after being interrupted by drunks at a meeting in Ayrshire – but he was prepared to accept it as a numerical and financial necessity. But the key figure was MacDonald, who made much of his lowly origins but partook socially and intellectually of a diluted form of wistful middle-class Socialism. As Bland once exclaimed of it: 'It seems that we are to work for socialism, fight for socialism, even die for it, but not, for God's sake, to define it.' [32] There was much to the charge, as was shown by the 'ILP Programme' that MacDonald drafted together with Hardie for publication in *The Nineteenth Century* in January 1899. The article described the ILP as being 'in the true line of the progressive apostolic succession' and added about the British Socialism which it claimed to represent: 'It trusts to no sudden changes, it needs no beginnings afresh, it works under the conditions it has found, its constructive methods are chiefly adaptation and rearrangement, its ideals are the growths of the past, its work is to proportion and complete the present.' And inevitably, with the usual progressive view of collectivism-as-Socialism in contrast to selfish nineteenth-century individualism: 'If Marx's position in economics became untenable tomorrow, the case for Socialism as an improved system of production and distribution would not be touched.' Of surplus value not a word, of electoral alliances over 'questions of immediate reform' a lot: fame had become the spur.

In this situation the Fabians ought to have flourished. Socialism was not 'a panacea for the ills of human society, but only for those produced by defective organisation of industry and by a radically bad distribution of wealth' had been one of their central tenets of 1896. But Fabian progressivism was ultimately total in spirit, not piecemeal. This led them in immediate political terms towards some sort of tacit alliance with the apparently bolder, socially reforming wing of the Liberal Party under Rosebery and Haldane; and, in the event, towards support with this wing for the Boer War. In a striking passage in *Fabianism and the Empire* (1900), Shaw attacked the other Liberal wing, Gladstonian in outlook, which 'still clings to the fixed-frontier ideals of individualist republicanism, non-interference and nationalism [i.e. self-determining nationalities], long since demonstrated both by experience and theory to be inapplicable to the present situation'. Suitably, it was over support of the war that MacDonald resigned his Fabian membership. And indeed, the future of progressivism lay in many ways with the spirit of more ethical institutions like the Rainbow Circle and William Clarke's *Progressive Review* in which MacDonald had begun to participate from the mid-1890s. It is true that the apparent mark of Fabian gradualism remained: 'The state is not the instrument of a class but an organ of society' [33] MacDonald was to declare in 1909; while back in 1893 Hobhouse, in *The Labour Movement*, insisted that 'no sweeping interference with private property is either possible or desirable', instead putting his trust in 'gradual steps' and affirming that 'the progress of public enterprise admits of indefinite extension, and at each step some fragment of Land or Capital passes to the community'. But for all the collective orthodoxy of this progressivism, the Gladstonian spirit was nevertheless clearly recognisable. Hobhouse affirmed the need for a change-of-heart as well as ownership, while MacDonald was to state his belief in an even vaguer ethical objective: 'The man through whom

Socialism is to come is not . . . the man toiling with the muck', but rather 'the man of ideals . . . the man in whose intelligence religion and sense of what is of good report will have a dominating influence'.[34] The Boer War was crucial in the consummation of this nebulous strain. From one side, the ILP passed an anti-conscription resolution as early as its fateful 1898 Annual Conference; and from the other, the Liberal journal, *The Speaker*, showed which way the wind was blowing (and which ultimately Campbell-Bannerman caught) by changing its editorship in 1899 from one that supported Rosebery to that of the progressive Radical J. L. Hammond, who believed in the historical centrality of Gladstone and the Irish nation, stood firm against Chamberlain at the Colonial Office and the Boer War, and was to praise the LRC in 1900 for its similar moral fortitude. In this way the origins of the Edwardian popular-based 'New Liberalism' were apparent in the very making of the Labour Party.

The Boer War itself was by no means the occasion for displays of mass jingoism as is often thought. The dockers at the Victoria and Albert Docks who demanded that all ships be garlanded in celebration of the relief of Mafeking were a famous but untypical example. Not even the propagandist use of the brass band movement – in particular the 'Absent-minded Beggar' concert of January 1900 at the Albert Hall that was sponsored by the *Daily Mail* and performed by eleven brass bands – was in practice enough to get the masses chanting. Recent research [35] on the contrary indicates a basic working-class indifference to the war. Very few working-men's clubs even discussed the matter; and those that did tended to express opposition. Nor, once the war had started, was working-class volunteering either very striking in its numbers (especially when the drum was sounded after 'Black Week' in December 1899) or even particularly patriotic in its motivations. One perennial motivation was unemployment. Another was described by a warehouseman volunteer in *Club Life* in May 1901: 'It was to escape for a time the monotony of existence, and if other volunteers were only to speak the truth they would tell you the same thing.' The other two great patriotic phenomena of the war were also less than they seemed: Mafeking hysteria was the response to a human rather than an imperial drama; and working-class voting in the 'Khaki Election' of 1900 seems to have closely followed not the flag but the candidates who offered tangible measures of social reform. As for the breaking-up of anti-war meetings, once again it seems to have been the medical students who were primarily responsible. Yet if there was no imperialist fervour, equally lacking was any Bulgarian agitation. Above all there was the absence of a great unifying figure like Gladstone to fire the forces of old-fashioned Radicalism that still remained powerful in the more traditional, solidaristic occupational areas like the mining communities. Blatchford in particular was more and more out on a limb. He objected to the labour alliance, writing of 'the average trade unionist' that 'he is narrow, and shallow, and selfish, and he objects very strongly to the trouble of thinking, and to the efforts of understanding'; [36] while as for the war, he saw it as wicked and perceived the capitalist market forces at work, but was aware also of the attitude of the Boers towards the coloured natives and in the end gave his support to the British soldiers in the field, the only people with whom he could identify. Hardie's position intellectually was comparable to that of the pro-North campaigners in the early 1860s: full of moral passion, but an essentially cardboard understanding of the issues. This worked in Merthyr, but was on the whole ignored by a working class which either left the war alone or opposed it as a check on the advancement of more concrete social questions. Nevertheless, the ethical stance did help to create a certain basis for unity during 1899 and 1900 between Hardie and the old-fashioned Gladstonian trade unionists who formed the majority of the 'labour' part of the alliance leading up to the LRC. It also put Hardie in line with the shift in Liberal progressive thinking. And once the LRC grew slowly but inexorably into a progressively influenced Labour Party, then it could start to try and fulfil not only the specific material wants expressed by the 1900 electorate, but also the flabby ethical aspirations cherished by the ineffectual opponents of Chamberlain's war.

A German coal miner, Ernst Dückershoff, wrote in *How the English Workman Lives* (1899) on the basis of a stay in Newcastle: 'Trades Unionism and politics are kept distinct in this country. It would be to the disadvantage of the working classes themselves to sever themselves in the matter of politics from the middle classes, since the attitude of the latter towards the workman has been friendly.' But Dückershoff's rose-tinted spectacles betrayed him: the attitude of the middle class towards organised labour had been far from friendly during the 1890s and by the time he wrote the above trade unionism was at last moving towards a coherent and apparently independent political position. First Lord Wemyss's National Free Labour Association of 1893, then the Employers' Parliamentary Council established in 1898, had spearheaded a counter-attack against the trade union rights of industrial action seemingly established in the 1870s. Significantly, these explicitly aggressive employers tended to be strongly Conservative, which in intellectual terms permitted the progressive 'New Liberalism' to fill the anti-*laissez-faire* gap now vacated by the old paternalist Oastler-and-Sadler Tory tradition. The attack derived partly from a repressive response to the new unionism and partly from a general tightening of economic conditions and profit margins. In working action it took two

forms: one was the systematic importation of blackleg labour; the
other the legal barrage against 'intimidating' picketing, which at first
affected only certain unions but soon after the formation of the LRC
was then broadened through the Taff Vale ruling into a more general
attack on actual trade union funds. Both elements – free labour and the
undermining of industrial action – were involved in the relentlessly
executed lock-out of the ASE between July 1897 and January 1898. The
success of the attack was central not just because the ASE was (in the
words of the *Birmingham Trades Journal* in July 1897) 'the boast and
pride of trade unionism in this country'. It was also crucial because of
the nature of the ASE, a union caught between two worlds. Its work was
thoroughly modern and was to become of key importance this century;
and in 1896 it elected a declared new unionist, George Barnes, as its
General Secretary as the prelude to taking in some 20,000 semi-skilled
planers, borers and so on as members over the next five years. Yet these
were in a sense enforced concessions: the society's basis had always been
craft skill, it tried its hardest to take over the new machines, it militated
in 1897 against the attempt by employers to reduce differentials, and
the resultant lock-out showed the glaring tension between the skilled
and their labourers. This underlying conservatism was reflected in
Barrow, where in July 1897 the ASE district committee rejected the
national council's offer of Mann as a rallying speaker and instead preferred [37] Burns, who 'would have more weight with the general public
and also would be more acceptable to our members'. The shock was
all the greater then when such a socially respectable union was so
roundly defeated. Again the apposite comment came from Birmingham,
where David Jones of the Patternmakers, and also Treasurer of the
local trades' council, voiced in January 1898 the thoughts of many
skilled unionists: 'The one great truth which the recent dispute has
demonstrated is that in the future, political action is the workers' only
hope.' [38]
     For Hardie at least it was a propitious sentiment. In his editorial in
The Labour Leader for 14 January 1899 he asked rhetorically about the
non-participation at recent by-elections: 'What excuse can we of the
ILP give for not fighting?' And he answered: 'There is one reason, and
one alone, why this is . . . the case – lack of funds.' It was true enough.
The Leicester ILP was typical when it complained in its annual report
that year that its income of roughly £200 p.a. 'barely suffices to cover
the necessary expenses of organisation, leaving all election expenses to
be raised by special collections'; [39] and if an ILP candidate did get to
Parliament, then it cost another £400 p.a. to keep him. But as Hardie
went on in his editorial: 'Arrangements are in progress for bringing
the trade union, co-operative and land movements into closer fellowship with the ILP. Work of this kind cannot be rushed . . .' In the

event, in trade union terms anyway, formative arrangements were reached far quicker than Hardie could have expected. The union which proved Hardie's benefactor was the ASRS, which possessed its own collective traditions, however suppressed by the companies, and declined to recruit from the labourers working in the railway workshops. There was little encouragement therefore for the General Railway Workers' Union, which was formed in 1889 under Champion's auspices after the ASRS had declined to drop its subscription from 5d a week. Accordingly the GRWU went the way of most new unions, its numbers declining from 14,000 in 1889 to 4,000 by 1895. But for the ASRS itself these were by no means entirely static years. Even before the formation of the GRWU it had accepted the principle of the minimum wage; and in 1890 it prosecuted hard-fought but largely unsuccessful strike action in several areas. A certain moderation followed: friendly benefits were kept going despite a drop in the subscription to 3d a week, and in 1893 the Hull dockers were only cautiously supported. But in an industrial context of barely remitted working conditions, a fundamental bitterness remained against the companies for refusing to grant recognition to the union. This took several forms: first the influx of ILP men to a position of parity on the ASRS executive by about 1897; then the all-grades campaign of the same year attempting to wrest recognition from the employers; and finally, after that failure, the acceptance in 1898 by the new General Secretary, Richard Bell, a non-ILP man, that over large as well as specific issues independent representation in Parliament had become indispensable. His union therefore tabled a motion accordingly, which at the TUC at Plymouth in September 1899 was accepted by 546,000 votes to 434,000, against the opposition of coal and cotton, but with the support of most of the new unions, above all the gasworkers, and the occupationally undermined engineers, boot-and-shoe operatives, and various long-established craft societies. It was a holy enough alliance, but hardly cataclysmic: its criteria were far too pragmatic for that.

On 27 February 1900, when the Labour Representation Committee took shape on a day of 'dreary, dripping rain' [40] at the Memorial Hall in Farringdon Street, there was likewise no great meeting of minds. The trade union delegates, representing somewhat less than half of all the members of the TUC, remained for the most part almost as distrustful as before of the political careerism of the ILP in general and over-stated ethicalism of Hardie in particular. They were also aware that they were being used financially and must have sensed the puzzled contempt which someone like Snowden felt towards them. 'A very commonsense lot, probably quite competent at their own job, but hardly the kind of men you would expect to find at the barricades when the Social Revolution came' [41] was his characteristically cool subsequent assessment. The actual proceedings were controlled by Hardie with the dabbest of hands. First he won the trade unionists over to his side by leading the opposition to an SDF resolution demanding 'a distinct party, with a party organisation separate from the capitalist parties based upon a recognition of the class war'.[42] Then he won their support for the conference's key amendment, which left out as much as it put in and demanded the establishment of 'a distinct Labour group in Parliament, who shall have their own whips, and agree upon their policy, which must embrace a readiness to co-operate with any party which for the time being may be engaged in promoting legislation in the direct interests of labour'.[43] And finally he managed to secure for the representatives of the nominally Socialist parties five places on the LRC's committee of twelve, despite the fact that they represented only 23,000 members, the trade union delegates over half-a-million. Of these five committee members, two were to come from the ILP, who also provided MacDonald for the central position of Secretary, he being the only delegate who could afford to take up the job unpaid. At first this all seemed of only theoretical interest. The Lib.-Labbers held their seats in the October election; and of the ILP candidates only Hardie was returned. Nevertheless, the average vote was almost twice that of 1895; and the momentous Taff Vale ruling was on its way. Soon, with the help of a secret pact with Herbert Gladstone, the Labour electoral bandwagon would begin to roll.

Yet one should not be bemused by the progressive umbrella: it remained a contingent protection. Better housing, municipal amenities, decasualisation, proper regulation of hours and labour, freedom to bargain – these were all things which most trade unionists wanted and the 'New Liberalism' was prepared to embrace, but there is little evidence that their electoral provision critically cut across the working-class voter's sense of class identity. Indeed, the secret of Keir Hardie's leadership was his ability not only to stay within these orthodox intellectual lines (Socialism/New Liberalism-as-collective-action), but also to emphasise in blunt, sectional, cloth-capped fashion, as he did in 1907, that 'to dogmatise about the form which the Socialist State shall take, is to play the fool'.[44] As he himself privately observed very shortly after the meeting at the Memorial Hall: 'One thing struck me very forcibly – the determination of nine-tenths of the Trade Unionists present to have a strictly independent party.'[45] One of these men was Frederick Rogers, an obscure but curiously relevant figure. A trade unionist known only in bookbinding circles, he seems to have become the LRC's first chairman precisely because of his acceptably bipartisan lack of renown. He believed strongly in his class and resented the ILP trend towards middle-class leadership. But at the same time Rogers was a craftsman fighting against the advance of the machine, a Radical workman in full possession of the self-determining ethical strain, who interpreted Socialism as State construction and accordingly criticised it on the grounds that 'it ignores utterly the human side of things, and emphasises only the economic, and therefore it is rejected as an interpretation of life by the thoughtful poor'.[46] The very phrase 'the labour movement' combines perfectly this duality – the material slog transcended by a notion of the spiritual – and retains extraordinarily powerful connotations. Yet in the end misleading. Hardie believed that he was creating a broad-based party by entering into the labour alliance, but in actual fact organised labour at the turn of the century constituted only about one in five of the country's adult male labourers. Behind Farringdon Street lay a nether world which one can only hope to approach in cultural rather than in institutional terms. There the word 'movement' meant little, the notions of progress even less. Life instead was a question of grinning, sometimes, and bearing it, always. The performer was Albert Chevalier; and the locale became in due course a lowly stop on the Monopoly board. But through all the distancing the spirit remains of the music-hall song about the husband being mocked after his wife receives an unexpected legacy:

> ' "Wot cher!" all the neighbours cried,
> "Who're yer goin' to meet, Bill?
> Have yer bought the street, Bill?"
> Laugh! I thought I should 'ave died,
> Knock'd 'em in the Old Kent Road!' [47]

POSTSCRIPT

1900 — 1914

'If I had the power and the authority, I have no doubt that I could come to terms with the leaders of the Labour Party in the course of half a morning.' [1]

This affirmation in October 1901 by Herbert Gladstone clearly presaged the secret electoral pact that, as Liberal Chief Whip, he was to conclude two years later with MacDonald of the LRC. Indeed, there seems from a certain perspective something almost definitive about Gladstone's sanguinity. One thinks of the infant Labour Party, too timid even to call itself by that name until after the 1906 Election, tagging along deferentially under the wings of the Liberals up to 1914, and yet within ten years and far before its due time shot to power by the profoundly accidental consequences of the Great War – it is a well-known thesis that rightly sees 1900 as a deceptively round-numbered turning-point. Nevertheless, it ignores much: the steady provincial growth of local Labour Parties a long way from the world of Westminster politicking; the specific and unprecedented heightening of industrial tension between 1911 and 1914; and above all, the long-term social and economic solidifying factors that, far more than the universal male suffrage at last granted in the 1918 Representation of the People Act, gave an illusory quality to the Liberal hope of permanently consensual politics. The Secretary of the Liberal Progressive Council in Battersea, stronghold of the Burnsian middle way, tacitly admitted as much when in June 1909 he addressed a warning to the Battersea Labour Party that 'if they wish to be identified with the Battersea progressivism of the future they must make up their minds to accept a programme which will not affright persons who pay rates'.[2] The class lesson that Chamberlain had learnt in the 1880s remained even more central a quarter of a century later. Typically, it was the unremitting individualism of the owners, rather than any apocalyptic conversion to Socialism, that underlay the miners' decision in 1908 to affiliate to the Labour Party. This MacDonald realised, for he remained steadfast to the original premises of the labour alliance, even if the restless Hardie, whose best days were now passing, sometimes did not;

and MacDonald went on playing the class-conscious but non-doctrinal 'independence' card for all it was worth, even while trying to persuade the ILP diehards to his left that the nascent Liberal-promulgated Welfare State was the real Socialist molloy. The triad is a familiar one: the small Socialist intelligentsia, the trimming Labour politicians, and the large and resolute but also sectionalist trade unions. From about 1910, however, a new and potent element was added, that of militant albeit distinctly minority rank-and-file working-class Socialism, providing not only a strident voice increasingly destined to be heard regardless of Sarajevo, but also the imponderable historical joker to set against any slide-rule analysis about the inevitability or otherwise of the Liberal Party's post-war electoral decline.

The determining event in labour history at the turn of the century was the famous Taff Vale case. The narrative is briefly told: following the victimisation of a signalman on the Taff Vale railway, the ASRS was chivvied in 1900 into a supporting strike by James Holmes, the local union organiser and an active Socialist; the railway company reacted quickly by drafting in Collison's Free Labour Association; and, a year after the conflict which ensued, the House of Lords ruled that the union was legally responsible for the damages incurred by its members in a strike situation. Bell himself of the ASRS was not displeased: 'a useful influence in solidifying the forces of trade unionism and in subjecting them to wholesome discipline' [3] was his view of the ruling. But this response changed when in January 1903 the actual Taff Vale damages were announced, amounting in all to a bill of £42,000 for the ASRS; and politically this ominous precedent, apparently turning the clock back over thirty years, quickened the general process which the earlier ruling had already set in motion. Trade union membership of the LRC by the end of 1903 was up to 956,000 and, as Beatrice Webb had observed during the 1902 TUC, the 'dominant note of the Congress is a determination to run Labour candidates on a large scale, and faith in the efficacy of this device for gaining all they require'. [4] Yet for all the earnests of intent, especially from 1903 the Parliamentary Fund of a penny per annum from each affiliated union member, the LRC in practice only operated, and then not always effectually, as a hard-fought compact between different interest groups. A confidential circular to ILP branches issued [5] by Hardie in May 1905 was in this respect instructive. After noting the decision to request the LRC to organise a mass meeting in London of the provincial unemployed, he went on: 'By this means, we hope to make the gathering a huge success, whilst we get the credit.' But in fact 'labour' by no means accepted that the million should merely provide the petrol while the 20,000 or so members of the Socialist parties simply sat behind the wheel and steered. As Tillett put it forcefully at the 1907 Labour Party Conference, 'the Trade Union official who did something towards adding a shilling to the wage and to put more food upon the table of the worker was doing a greater work than sentimental men talking about theories'.[6] In the event Tillett's motion to exclude the Socialists failed, but far more narrowly than the counter-motion to exclude all non-Socialists. 'Independence' continued as the agreed motif of compromise. Nevertheless, 'independence does not mean isolation',[7] as David Shackleton, Secretary of the Cotton Weavers, had reiterated in his presidential address to the LRC in 1905. And indeed, unbeknown to most, MacDonald of the ILP politicians had already taken the point and acted on it.

The central push behind MacDonald's pact with Gladstone in 1903 was as much financial as purely electoral. As early as during the 1900 Election Cadbury, the manufacturing Quaker, had given the LRC a £500 hand-out on the understanding that it was not to be used with an anti-Liberal purpose; while by definition the purse-strings held by the affiliated unions demanded deference to their innate political caution. As it happened, the pact, which eventually gave Labour a free run in about thirty seats generally confined to areas where Liberalism was weak and trade unionism strong, caught the prevailing political wind nicely. The dominant issue up to and including the 1906 Election was Chamberlain's tariff campaign, which in reaction brought together Liberals and organised labour in seemingly timeless Cobdenite harmony. The outcome was a free-trading landslide, with the Liberals coming conclusively to overall power, confident also of the support of not only the thirteen Lib.-Lab. mining MPs, but also the thirty members under the Labour whip, only seven of whom were ILP men rather than trade unionists. Not surprisingly, the Parliamentary Labour Party, in accordance with the LRC's carefully non-Socialist election manifesto and encouraged early on by the Trades Disputes Act of 1906 redressing the Taff Vale ruling, wavered only rarely from strictly union matters in its initiation of legislation. Even such a standard Socialist demand as the nationalisation of the mines and railways was in practice upheld less as a fundamental principle than as a specific way of improving working conditions in the particular industries. J. R. Clynes of the Gasworkers recalled in his *Memoirs* how in these early days after the 1906 Election he and his fellow Labour MPs were 'burning with impatience to set the world to rights', but soon sobered up for a lifetime at Westminster as they came to appreciate that 'behind the cumbrous formalities of Parliament lies the wisdom of long experience'. For Hardie, veteran MP and by temperament explorer rather than settler, the sensation of being surrounded by the laggard representatives of his own creation was peculiarly galling. After a weary reference to the tyranny already exercised by Cotton and soon to be shared by Coal, he went on in a letter to Glasier in December 1908: 'There are times when I confess to feeling sore at seeing the fruits of our years of toil being garnered by men who were never of us, and who even now would trick us out.' [8] Significantly, at this very time there was blowing up, in the context of recession and high unemployment, a groundswell of rank-and-file ILP opposition to the inertness of the Labour Party's leadership. Yet within months its sorry extinction only demonstrated the implacable parliamentary logic and ideological confines of Hardie's own labour alliance.

Behind this bout of internal conflict lay also the recent Socialist revival. The number of ILP branches went up from 292 in 1905 to 426 only a year later; while the *Labour Leader*, from 1903 the official ILP organ rather than Hardie's personal property, by 1906 had a weekly circulation of some 24,000 copies. Increasingly, dissatisfaction with the parliamentary leadership, and MacDonald's ultra-evolutionary form of Socialism, began to express itself. This dissent was formalised in 1907 with the successful candidature, unauthorised by the Labour Party, of the young firebrand Socialist Victor Grayson at the Colne Valley by-election. And before long Grayson was launching a series of bruisingly emotive attacks on the party's lack of resolve in getting through a Right to Work Bill. For a time, during the autumn of 1908, it seemed that Hardie, Curran and even Snowden (at odds with MacDonald's increasingly overt habits of accommodation) would spearhead an ILP drive to infuse a measure of broader social concern into the Labour Party. But once again, exactly as in the late 1890s, it was the existence of Hyndman's unacceptably sectarian organisation, now called the Social Democratic Party, which knocked the Socialist stuffing out of the ILP. The retraction came in February 1909, when the newly formed Joint London Right to Work Committee, on which the SDP was represented and which was already disavowed by the older, trade-union dominated National Right to Work Council, unsuccessfully petitioned the Labour MPs to back an unemployment demonstration timed to take place on the same day as the opening of Parliament. The ILP Easter conference a few weeks later offered appropriate confirmation: Hardie, Glasier, Snowden and MacDonald joined together by resigning from the executive as a gesture of apartness from Grayson *et al.*; for in MacDonald's words, unconsciously recalling the assumptions of the 1890s, 'the opposition between parliamentary procedure and the question of how to deal with the unemployed is purely a fictitious one'.[9] For Grayson in particular, the effects of this show of solidarity at the top were conclusive. In January 1910 he lost Colne Valley, in December he polled only 408 votes as a Socialist at Kennington, and in 1911 he joined with the SDP, the *Clarion* group, and some disenchanted

ILP branches to form the electorally insignificant British Socialist Party. Despite its personal interest the Grayson episode had perhaps added up to rather less than met the eye, for in parliamentary terms at least, inevitably the dominant concern of the Labour Party leadership, the central problem still remained – that of absorbing Liberalminded trade unionists while yet attaining a distinct identity apart from the actual Liberal Party. Ten years on from the formation of the LRC, predominantly the same minds were continuing to wrestle with this same, inherently emaciating dilemma.

The decision in 1908 by the MFGB (including by this stage both Northumberland and Durham) to affiliate to the Labour Party threw the issue into a particularly sharp focus. 'What then becomes of Socialism?' [10] was the characteristic question asked by Shaw, who realised that, for all the assiduous work done by ILP propagandists in the coalfields, the decision was essentially a sectionalist one based on specific industrial criteria, exemplified by the worsening problem of how to keep up already vulnerable wage rates in a period of geologically determined falling productivity, together with the traditional political grievance, aggravated during the 1900s, of not being able to persuade local Liberal caucuses to accept even perfectly harmless mining candidates. These complaints were particularly significant in the South Wales coalfield, where Lib.-Labbism, still somewhat shaky after 1898, suffered the additional blow of a decision by the Lords soon after Taff Vale to award damages to the Glamorgan Coal Company of £57,562 against the South Wales Miners' Federation. Yet exactly as Shaw had suspected, political caution and traditional voting habits did not suddenly cease to be the norm after 1908, whatever the heightening of the social and industrial stakes or the passing of popular Nonconformity. Thus the sixteen Federation MPs (excluding the unrepentant Burt, Wilson and Fenwick) who were elected in January 1910, although theoretically committed to an independent Labour Party, in practice held fast to their local Liberal ties and almost to a man declined to start up any rival Labour bodies. MacDonald, as Chairman of the Parliamentary Labour Party from 1911, accordingly found himself in a difficult situation. He certainly could not afford to lose a catch as large as almost three-quarters of a million miners. Nor in fact did the absence of three-cornered electoral fights particularly worry him: 'independence does not mean isolation' continued to make good evolutionary sense. But equally, MacDonald knew how imperative it was that the Labour Party as a whole did not alienate the ILP organisational work-horses in the constituencies. A typical grumble came from J. Thornhill, an active ILP propagandist in Derbyshire, who wrote to MacDonald in January 1911 about the local Federation MP: 'Talk about being loyal to the Labour Party, why, Harvey does just what he likes. Why not

let him go to the Liberal Party, and finish deceiving innocent miners ?' [11]
MacDonald played the situation skilfully, demanding from the local
Miners' Associations specifically Labour candidates, backed by an
independent organisation, to replace the older generation that was at
last (including Harvey himself early in 1914) beginning to die off.
This compromise, based as ever on the distinct but limited concept of
'independence' and evolved in the context of the number of Federation
MPs declining amidst disputes and electoral defeats to ten by 1914,
seemed by the outbreak of the war to have begun to check the slide.
Some twenty-seven MFGB candidates would have stood at the 1915
Election and many of these would probably have been engaging, even
against MacDonald's will, in three-cornered contests. The golden age
of Lib.-Labbism was over; and with the gradual disappearance of
that stubborn but ultimately manageable phenomenon (thanks as much
as anything to the local intractability of Old Liberalism), it was increasingly apparent that the Parliamentary Labour Party would also
have to be looking to its left, if perhaps not to its extreme left, in order
to keep the rough-hewn part of the labour alliance intact.

There were few signs that MacDonald, by now deeply committed
to the role of the responsible parliamentarian, was capable of fulfilling
this new task. The inadequacy was not altogether intrinsic: Mac-
Donald's approach to the political growth of the Labour Party had
come to seem, if not an unimpeachable orthodoxy on account of its
ideological indistinctness, certainly extremely difficult to replace, the
more so as prevailing political circumstances seemed to serve only to
validate the evolution of such a modest and respectabilising strategy.
First the Osborne Judgement of 1909, when the Lords effectively
banned the payment of political contributions by trade unions, and
then the constitutional crisis, an issue apparently comparable to free
trade in its broad-based democratic connotations, helped at constituency
level to hold together the working alliance in many areas between
Liberals and Labour. In the event, though, the Labour Party fared
indifferently in the 1910 Elections, securing no more than forty-two
seats, including the successful MFGB candidates, and making little
impact in the few three-cornered contests. The Liberals, relatively
speaking, did not do much better, though remaining in office; and it
was clear that the assertion of propertied middle-class consciousness
against Lloyd George's Budget meant the effective end of the Progressive alliance, triumphant in 1906 but ultimately always a forlorn
attempt to transcend the profound class implications of the 1886 divide.
Moreover, at the other end of the alliance, even though MacDonald
was able to persuade the Labour Party of the need not to rock the boat
until at least Osborne was reversed (which it was in 1913), not even
he could secure authentic acceptance of Lloyd George's 1911 National

Insurance Act, the consummation of the New Liberalism. Snowden boldly condemned the contributory character of the scheme as 'unadulterated, sixty year old, individualism' [12] and was joined in this criticism by Hardie, Jowett, Thorne and Lansbury. It is true that MacDonald won the day, taking along with him most of the trade-union MPs and the cautious party secretary, Arthur Henderson, but it was a hollow victory, attained only by persuading the Liberal government to offer the payment of MPs as bait. Beatrice Webb described the prevailing mood when she wrote in her diary in October 1912: 'The Labour MPs seem to me to be drifting into futility . . . J. R. MacDonald has ceased to be a Socialist, the Trade Union MPs never were Socialists, Snowden is embittered and Lansbury is wild.' [13] Moreover, there was a real sense in which this very *type* of activity, the workings of a small parliamentary pressure group, seemed in danger of losing its unquestioned primacy. MacDonald's response to Syndicalism was typical and entirely unsatisfactory: 'the impatient, frenzied, thoughtless child of poverty, disappointment, irresponsibility' [14] he called it in 1912. Significantly, Snowden shared to a perhaps even greater degree this distaste for extra-parliamentary industrial action. Between them the old ILP men were in peril of being outflanked.

Sidney Buxton, President of the Board of Trade, said as much when he told the Cabinet shortly after the 1912 national miners' strike of 'the almost complete collapse of the Labour Party in the House as an effective influence in labour disputes'.[15] And indeed, 1911–14 were years of high employment and massive industrial unrest, during which trade-union membership increased from 2,565,000 in 1910 to 4,145,000 by 1914 and the Parliamentary Labour Party could only watch impotently as the use of blacklegs several times led to bitter clashes between troops and strikers. Yet much about the pattern of events, the ultimate disappointing of hopes, was singularly reminiscent of 1889–90. The astonishing growth of the Workers' Union, from 4,500 members in 1910 to 143,000 by the war, was especially deceptive. The principal source of recruitment was those semi-skilled engineers who, in the scornful words of an ASE Report for June 1913, deign to 'consider themselves trade unionists as soon as they can get a button in their coats'.[16] The tone is a familiar one, but in practice these semi-skilled men, for all their involvement in the Black Country Strike of 1913, were attracted primarily to the Workers' Union by the benefits offered and certainly thought of themselves as as different from the general labourer as they were from the craftsman. A similar sectionalism applied also to the three central 'heavy' occupational groups. The recently created National Transport Workers' Federation struck successfully in 1911, but when the London waterfront workers tried again in 1912, following renewed threats of pressure from the Port of

London Authority over the question of job control, they received minimal support outside London and the strike was crushed with blacklegged ease. The Liverpool dockers in particular had gained all they required during 1911, hammering out a hiring compromise with the owners, and saw no point in jettisoning that. The railwaymen likewise retreated with the odds in their favour. There was a national strike in August 1911, instigated by rank-and-file disaffection with the processes of reconciliation, but it only lasted a few days, was bought off by Lloyd George waving the patriotic flag, and failed to secure union recognition. The miners too, striking nationally for a minimum wage, were after only a few weeks bullied by the MFGB executive in April 1912 into accepting the government's extremely fudgy Minimum Wage Act. In this context, it is probable that the vaunted 'Triple Alliance' developed during 1914 between the transport workers, the railwaymen and the miners was less a declaration of industrial war than a cost-reducing device to prevent the financial losses incurred by the loss of work consequent upon another union's isolated strike. The alliance also represented a closing of the ranks in order to bring recalcitrant elements outside the particular unions more into line. Yet potentially there was far more to it than that essentially defensive orientation. Thorne, addressing the NTWF Conference in June 1914, observed that if the railwaymen 'agreed upon a national strike it would mean that the whole of the transport workers and the miners would become involved' and that 'if that were so, then there would be no need for a railway strike'.[17] Such an ambivalent statement suggests most pregnantly how in an entirely uninstitutional sense the areas of industrial debate were perceptibly widening in these years immediately before the war. For all its elusiveness the question of Syndicalist influence remains central.

The formal influence exercised by the doctrine – demanding direct industrial action in order to abolish the profit motive and ultimately private industrial ownership – was of course limited. Herbert Booth of the Nottinghamshire coalfield subsequently described what happened when a group of young Syndicalist miners from South Wales, all heavily under the influence of the returned Tom Mann, arrived to spread the word: 'They were in the County about a week, then, nothing more was heard of them. As for the pamphlet *The Miners' Next Step*, nobody wanted it.' [18] Mann himself, though the key inspiring figure in the 1911 Merseyside transport strike, soon found himself forced to concentrate during it on the issues of wages and labour solidarity rather than any more novel industrial objectives. While in South Wales, the first wave of young Syndicalists, fresh from Ruskin College, Oxford, in 1909 and by 1911 well represented on the SWMF executive, inevitably divided before long into those who merely toned up the

Mabon tradition, with its politically reformist premises, and those who held on to something more revolutionary. The two factions, represented by George Barker and Noah Ablett respectively, met at Trealow in November 1912 to debate [19] the question of nationalising the mines, which in effect meant a debate about Progressivism's cherished theory of the neutral state. Barker stressed the practicality of the nationalisation proposals, especially in terms of safety and productivity, and added that 'you can enjoy them now and not have to wait for some subsequent generation'. Ablett countered by mocking Barker's vision of 'a happy little family' of citizens comprising ex-owners and ex-serfs alike and went on: 'The future does not lie in the direction of bureaucracy. . . . It lies in the democratic organisation and eventual control of the industries by the workers themselves.' Of course the formal political future *did* lie with Barker and bureaucracy, but even so, quite apart from the continuing entirely non-ideological root working-class social and cultural resistance to the de-classifying assumptions of Progressivism, the prevailing intellectual atmosphere was far more challenging than Barker's complacent Howell-like jibe – 'it is no good bringing German theories from books here' – might suggest. The keen struggle between the two new Labour daily newspapers revealed as much. The *Daily Herald* (April 1912) was informal, eclectic, sympathetic to Syndicalism and the suffragettes, hostile to the 'cat and mouse' qualities of the New Liberalism, and had a circulation of around 100,000. The *Daily Citizen* (October 1912) was official, toed the MacDonald line, was run by circulation-minded professional journalists recruited from the Northcliffe stable, was supported financially by the major trade unions, and sold around 165,000. The *Citizen* died with the coming of war, while the *Herald* went on as a lively oppositional voice. But the sword proved mightier than the pen, for the very elements who had sustained the *Citizen* were precisely the men who ensured that in August 1914 the Labour Party lent its support to the transcending cause of a national war.

Few can have expected otherwise. When Hardie at the 1911 Labour Party Conference proposed strike action in the event of war, he was successfully resisted on behalf of the labour alliance by Henderson, who argued that 'such a policy would divert attention from that part of their present work that they had recently taken up, namely, parliamentary action, and upon which they had had so much to say during recent years as being the instrument of the social and economic salvation of the workers of this country'.[20] Equally significantly and more realistically, he added that 'they were not sufficiently well informed as to give a lead to the workers in favour of a general strike'. In fact, as James Larkin found out when he made his bid for all-out support during the 1913 Dublin transport strike, the prospect of any sort of general strike was anathema to the firmly entrenched leaders of organised labour in England. So also in August 1914, when, as the ILP was declaring that 'across the roar of the guns, we send sympathy and greetings to the German Socialists',[21] and even MacDonald was opposing the war and thus renewing his Socialist standing, remarking privately that 'in three months there will be bread riots, and we shall come in',[22] the Labour Party as a whole, dominated by solid trade unionists and shrewdly guided by Henderson, eschewed rhetoric and permitted its members to vote with their restless feet in response to Kitchener. And in a way suitably enough: action had always spoken louder than words in the world of labour and would indeed continue to do so as the cruel follies of war soon began to leave their imprint on the working-class consciousness. For though the war may have broken Keir Hardie's heart, he more than anyone should have known that when the red-hot flame of Socialism is cooled in order that the ungloved may approach, then unromantic experience alone will be the determinant of political action.

Select Bibliography

BOOKS

R. D. Altick, *The English Common Reader* (1957).
R. Page Arnot, *William Morris* (1964).
Michael Barker, *Gladstone and Radicalism* (1975).
Zygmunt Bauman, *Between Class and Elite* (1972).
Frank Bealey and Henry Pelling, *Labour and Politics, 1900–1906* (1958).
Asa Briggs and John Saville (eds), *Essays in Labour History* (1960).
Asa Briggs and John Saville (eds), *Essays in Labour History, 1886–1923* (1971).
Kenneth D. Buckley, *Trade Unionism in Aberdeen, 1878–1900* (1955).
V. E. Chancellor (ed.), *Master and Artisan in Victorian England* (1969).
S. D. Chapman (ed.), *History of Working-Class Housing* (1972).
P. F. Clarke, *Lancashire and the New Liberalism* (1971).
H. A. Clegg, Alan Fox and A. F. Thompson, *A History of British Trade Unions Since 1889*, Vol. 1 (1964).
G. D. H. Cole, *A Century of Co-operation* (1947).
Margaret Dalziel, *Popular Fiction 100 Years Ago* (1957).
E. T. Davies, *Religion in the Industrial Revolution in South Wales* (1965).
H. V. Emy, *Liberals, Radicals and Social Politics, 1892–1914* (1973).
John Foster, *Class Struggle and the Industrial Revolution* (1974).
W. Hamish Fraser, *Trade Unions and Society: The Struggle for Acceptance, 1850–1880* (1974).
Alfred Fried and Richard M. Elman (eds), *Charles Booth's London* (1969).
Roy Gregory, *The Miners and British Politics, 1906–1914* (1968).
D. A. Hamer, *Liberal Politics in the Age of Gladstone and Rosebery* (1972).
Brian Harrison, *Drink and the Victorians* (1971).
J. F. C. Harrison, *Learning and Living, 1790–1960* (1961).
Royden Harrison, *Before the Socialists* (1965).
Harold R. Hikins, *Building the Union* (1973).
E. J. Hobsbawm, *Labour's Turning Point* (1948).
E. J. Hobsbawm, *Primitive Rebels* (1959).
E. J. Hobsbawm, *Labouring Men* (1964).
J. A. Hobson, *John Ruskin, Social Reformer* (1898).
Richard Hyman, *The Workers' Union* (1971).
K. S. Inglis, *Churches and the Working Classes in Victorian England* (1963).
Louis James, *Fiction for the Working Man, 1830–1850* (1963).
James B. Jefferys, *Labour's Formative Years* (1948).
Gareth Stedman Jones, *Outcast London* (1971).
P. J. Keating, *The Working Classes in Victorian Fiction* (1971).
Thomas Kelly, *A History of Adult Education in Great Britain* (1962).

F. M. Leventhal, *Respectable Radical: George Howell and Victorian Working-Class Politics* (1971).
J. C. Lovell, *Stevedores and Dockers* (1969).
Alasdair MacIntyre, *Secularisation and Moral Change* (1967).
A. Allan Maclaren, *Religion and Social Class* (1974).
A. M. McBriar, *Fabian Socialism and English Politics, 1884–1918* (1962).
Ross McKibbin, *The Evolution of the Labour Party, 1910–1924* (1974).
Hugh McLeod, *Class and Religion in the Late Victorian City* (1974).
Robert Moore, *Pit-Men, Preachers and Politics* (1974).
Kenneth O. Morgan, *Keir Hardie* (1975).
A. E. Musson, *British Trade Unions, 1800–1875* (1972).
George Orwell, *The Road to Wigan Pier* (1937).
Henry Pelling, *The Origins of the Labour Party, 1880–1900* (Second edition, 1965).
Henry Pelling, *Social Geography of British Elections, 1885–1910* (1967).
Henry Pelling, *Popular Politics and Society in Late Victorian Britain* (1968).
Henry Pelling, *A History of British Trade Unionism* (Second edition, 1972).
Stanley Pierson, *Marxism and the Origins of British Socialism* (1973).
J. A. R. Pimlott, *The Englishman's Holiday* (1947).
Sidney Pollard, *A History of Labour in Sheffield* (1959).
Richard Price, *An Imperial War and the British Working Class* (1972).
Frederick Rogers, *Labour, Life and Literature* (1973 reprint).
J. D. Rosenberg, *The Darkening Glass: A Portrait of Ruskin's Genius* (1961).
Edward Royle, *Radical Politics, 1790–1900: Religion and Unbelief* (1971).
John F. Russell and J. H. Elliott, *The Brass Band Movement* (1936).
John Saville, *Ernest Jones: Chartist* (1952).
Brian Simon, *Education and the Labour Movement, 1870–1920* (1965).
E. P. Thompson, *William Morris: Romantic to Revolutionary* (1955).
E. P. Thompson, *The Making of the English Working Class* (1964).
Laurence Thompson, *Robert Blatchford* (1951).
Paul Thompson, *Socialists, Liberals and Labour* (1967).
Dona Torr, *Tom Mann and His Times* (1956).
Chushichi Tsuzuki, *H. M. Hyndman and British Socialism* (1961).
H. A. Turner, *Trade Union Growth, Structure and Policy* (1962).
Martha Vicinus, *The Industrial Muse* (1974).
John Vincent, *The Formation of the Liberal Party, 1857–1868* (1966).
James Walvin, *The People's Game* (1975).
E. R. Wickham, *Church and People in an Industrial City* (1957).

Note: titles of more detailed individual trade union histories may be found in Clegg, Fox and Thompson, in W. Hamish Fraser, and in issues of the *Bulletin of the Society for the Study of Labour History.*

ARTICLES (excluding those cited in the notes)

V. L. Allen, 'The Origins of Industrial Conciliation and Arbitration', in *International Review of Social History* (1964).

R. Bean, 'The Liverpool Dock Strike of 1890', in *International Review of Social History* (1973).

Patrick Brantlinger, 'The Case against Trade Unions in Early Victorian Fiction', in *Victorian Studies* (1969–70).

J. B. Brown, 'The Pig or the Stye: Drink and Poverty in Late Victorian England', in *International Review of Social History* (1973).

G. D. H. Cole, 'Some Notes on British Trade Unionism in the Third Quarter of the Nineteenth Century', in *International Review of Social History* (1937).

Stephen Coltham, 'George Potter, the Junta, and the *Bee-Hive*', in *International Review of Social History* (1964, 1965).

A. E. P. Duffy, 'New Unionism in Britain, 1889–1890', in *Economic History Review* (1961–2).

W. Hamish Fraser, 'Trade Unions, Reform and the Election of 1868 in Scotland', in *Scottish Historical Review* (1971).

Christopher Green, 'Birmingham's Politics, 1873–1891', in *Midland History* (1973).

P. S. Gupta, 'Railway Trade Unionism in Britain, c. 1880–1900', in *Economic History Review* (1966).

Brian Harrison, 'Religion and Recreation in Nineteenth-Century England', in *Past and Present* (1967).

R. J. Holton, '*Daily Herald* v. *Daily Citizen*, 1912–1915', in *International Review of Social History* (1974).

Janet Howarth, 'The Liberal Revival in Northamptonshire, 1880–1895', in *Historical Journal* (1969).

Robert Kelley, 'Midlothian', in *Victorian Studies* (1960–1).

C. B. Macpherson, 'Politics: Post-Liberal-Democracy?', in Robin Blackburn (ed.), *Ideology in Social Science* (1972).

R. I. McKibbin, 'James Ramsay MacDonald and the Problem of the Independence of the Labour Party, 1910–1914', in *Journal of Modern History* (1970).

W. F. Mandle, 'Games People Played: Cricket and Football in England and Victoria in the Late Nineteenth Century', in *Historical Studies* (1973).

Paul Meier, 'An Unpublished Lecture of William Morris', in *International Review of Social History* (1971).

Kenneth O. Morgan, 'The New Liberalism and the Challenge of Labour', in *Welsh Historical Review* (1973).

Tom Nairn, 'The English Working Class', in Robin Blackburn (ed.), *Ideology in Social Science* (1972).

Richard N. Price, 'The Working Men's Club Movement and Victorian Social Reform Ideology', in *Victorian Studies* (1971–2).

John Saville, 'The Ideology of Labourism', in Robert Benewick *et al.* (eds), *Knowledge and Belief in Politics: The Problems of Ideology* (1973).

Lilian Lewis Shiman, 'The Band of Hope Movement', in *Victorian Studies* (1973–4).

Peter Stead, 'Working-Class Leadership in South Wales, 1900–1920', in *Welsh Historical Review* (1973).

Trygve R. Tholfsen, 'The Intellectual Origins of Mid-Victorian Stability', in *Political Science Quarterly* (1971).

E. P. Thompson, 'The Peculiarities of the English', in *Socialist Register* (1965).

Anthony S. Wohl, 'The Bitter Cry of Outcast London', in *International Review of Social History* (1968).

Note: the *Bulletin of the Society for the Study of Labour History* provides a store of articles, abstracts and reviews germane to the period, too numerous to be listed here.

Notes

NOTES TO CHAPTER 1

1 John Saville, *Ernest Jones: Chartist* (1952), p. 106.
2 Ben Brierley, *Home Memories and Recollections of a Life* (1886), pp. 36, 89.
3 J. B. Leno, *The Aftermath* (1892), pp. 22, 69.
4 Howell Collection, Bishopsgate Institute, London. This is the ultimate source of all the material here relating to Howell.
5 Asa Briggs, *Victorian People* (1965 Pelican edition), pp. 179, 181.
6 Simon Nowell-Smith, *The House of Cassell* (1958), p. 42.
7 James Hole, *Light, More Light !* (1860), pp. 56-7.
8 J. F. C. Harrison, *A History of the Working Men's College* (1954), p. xvii.
9 Hole, op. cit., p. 116.
10 Sidney and Beatrice Webb, *The History of Trade Unionism* (1894).
11 R. W. Postgate, *The Builder's History* (1923), p. 188.
12 J. E. Mortimer, *History of the Boilermakers' Society*, Vol. 1 (1973), p. 201.
13 E. P. Thompson, *The Making of the English Working Class* (1968 Pelican edition), p. 309.
14 Mortimer, op. cit., p. 65.
15 S. Higgenbottam, *Our Society's History* (1939), p. 33.
16 R. V. Clements, 'British Trade Unions and Popular Political Economy, 1850–1875', in *Economic History Review* (1961), p. 87.
17 Henry Collins and Chimen Abramsky, *Karl Marx and the British Labour Movement* (1965), p. 87.
18 Saville, op. cit., p. 194.
19 Asa Briggs (ed.), *Chartist Studies* (1959), p. 371.
20 Torben Christensen, *The Origin and History of Christian Socialism* (1962), p. 234.
21 *Transactions of the Historic Society of Lancashire and Cheshire*, Vol. 105 (1954), pp. 137–85.
22 Philip Magnus, *Gladstone* (1954), p. 160.
23 John Vincent, *The Formation of the Liberal Party* (1966), p. 233.
24 Royden Harrison, *Before the Socialists* (1965).
25 F. M. Leventhal, *Respectable Radical* (1971), p. 43.
26 Harrison, op. cit., p. 166.
27 Ibid., p. 123.

NOTES TO CHAPTER 2

1 Quintin Hoare and Geoffrey Nowell Smith (eds), *Selections from the Prison Notebooks of Antonio Gramsci* (1971), p. 12.
2 V. W. Bladen, 'The Centenary of Marx and Mill', in *Journal of Economic History*, Supplement (1948), p. 33.
3 Humphrey House, *The Dickens World* (1940), p. 203.

4 E. P. Thompson, *The Making of the English Working Class*, p. 193.
5 Dover Beach.
6 Edward Alexander, *Matthew Arnold and John Stuart Mill* (1965), p. 17.
7 A. B. Hopkins, *Elizabeth Gaskell* (1952), p. 81.
8 Edgar Johnson (ed.), *Letters from Charles Dickens to Angela Burdett-Coutts* (1953), p. 298.
9 Thomas Carlyle, *Chartism* (1840), p. 17.
10 E. T. Cook and Alexander Wedderburn (eds), *The Works of John Ruskin*, Vol. 37 (1909), p. 7.
11 Charles Kingsley, *Alton Locke* (1877 edition), p. xlv.
12 J. B. Leno, *The Aftermath* (1892), p. 49.
13 Torben Christensen, *The Origin and History of Christian Socialism* (1962), p. 29.
14 G. D. H. Cole, *A Century of Co-operation* (1944), p. 98.
15 Peter R. Allen, 'F. D. Maurice and J. M. Ludlow', in *Victorian Studies* (1967–8), p. 473.
16 Frederic Harrison, *Autobiographic Memoirs*, Vol. 1 (1911), p. 159.
17 J. B. Jefferys, *Labour's Formative Years* (1948), p. 59.
18 Philip N. Backstrom, Jr, 'The Practical Side of Christian Socialism in Victorian England', in *Victorian Studies* (1962–3), p. 323.
19 Kingsley, op. cit., p. lvi.
20 Royden Harrison, *Before the Socialists* (1965), p. 77.
21 Frederic Harrison, op. cit., Vol. 1, p. 258.
22 Peter Coveney (ed.), *Felix Holt, The Radical* (1972 Penguin edition), Appendix A.
23 Ibid., p. 607.
24 *Fortnightly Review* (1879), p. 382.
25 John D. Rosenberg, *The Darkening Glass* (1961), p. 140.
26 *The Works of John Ruskin*, Vol. 17, p. lxxxix.
27 Ibid., Vol. 18, p. 264.
28 B. Patch, *Thirty Years with G.B.S.* (1951), p. 239.

NOTES TO CHAPTER 3

1 H. J. Dyos and M. Wolff (eds), *The Victorian City*, Vol. 1 (1973), p. 198.
2 Royden Harrison, *Before the Socialists* (1965), p. 183.
3 H. J. Hanham, *Elections and Party Management* (1959), p. 303.
4 D. R. Moberg, *George Odger and the English Working Class Movement, 1860–1877* (1954 London Ph.D. thesis), p. 269.
5 Harrison, op. cit., p. 287.
6 Ibid., p. 229.
7 *Nineteenth Century* (1878), p. 35.
8 *The Eastern Post* (30 June 1872).
9 J. B. Jefferys, *Labour's Formative Years* (1948), pp. 191–2.
10 N. P. Howard, 'The Strikes and Lockouts in the Iron Industry and the Formation of the Ironworkers' Union, 1862–1869', in *International Review of Social History* (1973), p. 427.
11 *The Darlington and Stockton Telegraph* (13 March 1869).
12 W. H. G. Armytage, *A. J. Mundella* (1951), p. 102.
13 Ibid., p. 102.
14 Ibid., p. 127.

15 J. E. Williams, *The Derbyshire Miners* (1962), p. 140.
16 E. Welbourne, *The Miners' Unions of Northumberland and Durham* (1923), p. 146.
17 Williams, op. cit., p. 142.
18 A. J. Youngson Brown, 'Trade Union Policy in the Scots Coalfields, 1855–1885', in *Economic History Review* (1953–4), p. 36.
19 Welbourne, op. cit., pp. 160, 175.
20 Youngson Brown, op. cit., p. 36.
21 Harrison, op. cit., p. 300.
22 K. A. Mackenzie, *Edith Simcox and George Eliot* (1961), p. 39.
23 W. J. Davis, *The British Trade Union Congress*, Vol. 1 (1910), p. 67.
24 *The Eastern Post* (25 August 1872).
25 This despite the pioneering work of Stan Shipley, *Club Life and Socialism in Mid-Victorian London* (1971).
26 Philip Magnus, *Gladstone* (1954), p. 262.
27 R. T. Shannon, *Gladstone and the Bulgarian Agitation, 1876* (1963), p. 115.

NOTES TO CHAPTER 4

1 Philip Henderson (ed.), *The Letters of William Morris* (1950), p. 190.
2 Margaret B. Simey, *Charitable Effort in Liverpool in the Nineteenth Century* (1951), pp. 101–2.
3 Thomas Wright, *Our New Masters* (1873), p. 5.
4 Gareth Stedman Jones, *Outcast London* (1971), p. 326.
5 E. P. Thompson, *William Morris: Romantic to Revolutionary* (1955), p. 164.
6 *The Bradford Observer* (10 February 1888).
7 Harold Pollins, 'Transport Lines and Social Divisions', in Ruth Glass (ed.), *London: Aspects of Change* (1964), p. 43.
8 John R. Kellett, *The Impact of Railways on Victorian Cities* (1969), pp. 387, 406.
9 Stedman Jones, op. cit., p. 154.
10 H. J. Dyos, 'Railways and Housing in Victorian London', in *Journal of Transport History* (1955), p. 15.
11 Thompson, op. cit., p. 16.
12 Stedman Jones, op. cit., pp. 207–8.
13 Sidney Pollard, *A History of Labour in Sheffield* (1959), p. 90.
14 J. A. R. Mariott, *Modern England, 1885–1932* (1934), p. 164.
15 Harold Perkin, *The Origins of Modern English Society, 1780–1880* (1969).
16 H. V. Emy, *Liberals, Radicals and Social Politics* (1973), pp. 12–18.
17 D. A. Hamer, *Liberal Politics in the Age of Gladstone and Rosebery* (1972), p. 80.
18 Michael Barker, *The Formation of Liberal Party Policy, 1885–1892* (1972 University of Wales Ph.D. thesis), p. 18.
19 Peter Fraser, *Joseph Chamberlain* (1966), p. 44.
20 Henry Pelling, *Popular Politics and Society in Late Victorian Britain* (1968), p. 3.
21 Fraser, op. cit., p. 51.
22 C. H. D. Howard, 'Joseph Chamberlain and the "Unauthorised Programme" ', in *English Historical Review* (1950), p. 486.
23 Ibid., p. 487.
24 Michael Barker, *Gladstone and Radicalism* (1975), p. 25

25 John Vincent and A. B. Cooke, *The Governing Passion* (1974), p. 13.
26 Hamer, op. cit., p. 218.
27 Ibid., p. 228.
28 Michael Barker, *Gladstone and Radicalism*, p. 196.
29 Hamer, op. cit., p. 227.
30 Barker, op. cit., p. 134.
31 M. Ostrogorski, *Democracy and the Organisation of Political Parties*, Vol. 1 (1902).
32 Barry McGill, 'Francis Schnadhorst and Liberal Party Organisation', in *Journal of Modern History* (1962), p. 37.
33 William Stewart, *J. Keir Hardie* (1921), p. 92.
34 J. R. Vincent, *Pollbooks* (1967), p. 50.
35 P. F. Clarke, 'The Progressive Movement in England', in *Transactions of the Royal Historical Society* (1974), p. 167.
36 Roy Jenkins, *Asquith* (1964), p. 97.
37 E. P. Thompson, *The Making of the English Working Class*, p. 11.
38 J. F. C. Harrison, *Learning and Living* (1961), p. 239.

NOTES TO CHAPTER 5

1 *Karl Marx and Friedrich Engels On Britain* (1954), p. 159.
2 K. S. Inglis, *Churches and the Working Classes in Victorian England* (1963), p. 9.
3 David Martin and Michael Hill (eds), *A Sociological Yearbook of Religion in England*, Vol. 3 (1970), pp. 101–2.
4 David M. Thompson (ed.), *Nonconformity in the Nineteenth Century* (1972), pp. 141–2.
5 Evelyn Waugh, *A Little Learning* (1964), p. 109.
6 Inglis, op. cit., p. 60.
7 W. S. F. Pickering, *The Place of Religion in the Social Structure of Two English Industrial Towns* (1958 London Ph.D. thesis).
8 Hugh McLeod, *Class and Religion in the Late Victorian City* (1974), p. 86.
9 A. F. Winnington-Ingram, *Fifty Years' Work in London* (1940), p. 10.
10 McLeod, op. cit., p. 86.
11 W. Morris, 'An Old Potter', (ed.), *When I Was A Child* (1903), p. 235.
12 John Burnett (ed.), *Useful Toil* (1974), p. 291.
13 McLeod, op. cit., p. 50.
14 J. H. Y. Briggs, 'Image and Appearance', in *The Baptist Quarterly* (1969), p. 27.
15 Inglis, op. cit., p. 335.
16 McLeod, op. cit., p. 124.
17 F. Boulard, *An Introduction to Religious Sociology* (1960), p. 37.
18 Edward Royle, *Radical Politics, 1790–1900* (1971), p. 11.
19 Inglis, op. cit., p. 42.
20 Brian Simon, *Education and the Labour Movement, 1870–1920* (1965), p. 82.
21 Inglis, op. cit., p. 173.
22 Ibid., p. 84.
23 Richard Mudie-Smith (ed.), *The Religious Life of London* (1904), p. 202.
24 G. Kitson Clark, *Churchmen and the Condition of England, 1832–1885* (1973).
25 Harold Begbie, *Life of William Booth*, Vol. 11 (1920), p. 165.

26 Susan Budd, 'The Loss of Faith', in *Past and Present* (1967).
27 Robert Robson (ed.), *Ideas and Institutions of Victorian Britain* (1967), pp. 227–8.
28 J. C. C. Probert, *Primitive Methodism in Cornwall* (1966).
29 Robert Moore, *Pit-Men, Preachers and Politics* (1974), where the whole problematic is examined.
30 J. E. Williams, *The Derbyshire Miners* (1962), p. 234.
31 *The Life of Hugh Price Hughes* (1907 edition), pp. 362–3.
32 K. S. Inglis, 'English Nonconformity and Social Reform, 1880–1900', in *Past and Present* (1958), p. 81.
33 Emrys Hughes (ed.), *Keir Hardie's Speeches and Writings* (c. 1925), p. 140.
34 Fenner Brockway, *Socialism over Sixty Years* (1946), p. 41.
35 Henry Pelling, *The Origins of the Labour Party* (1965 edition), p. 135.
36 K. S. Inglis, 'The Labour Church Movement', in *International Review of Social History* (1958), p. 456.
37 D. F. Summers, *The Labour Church and Allied Movements of the Late Nineteenth and Early Twentieth Centuries* (1958 Edinburgh Ph.D. thesis), p. 185.
38 John F. Glaser, 'English Nonconformity and the Decline of Liberalism' in *American Historical Review* (1958), p. 359.
39 Eifion Evans, *The Welsh Revival of 1904* (1969), p. 127.
40 *Bulletin of the Society for the Study of Labour History* (Spring 1970).
41 J. H. S. Kent, 'The Role of Religion in the Cultural Structure of the Late Victorian City', in *Transactions of the Royal Historical Society* (1973), p. 162.

NOTES TO CHAPTER 6

1 Andrew Reid (ed.), *The New Party* (1894), p. 11.
2 John Burnett (ed.), *Useful Toil* (1974), pp. 89–99.
3 Paraphrase by Eunice M. Schofield, 'Food and Cooking of the Working Class about 1900', in *Transactions of the Historic Society of Lancashire and Cheshire*, Vol. 123 (1972).
4 C. Stella Davies, *North Country Bred* (1963), p. 71.
5 *Fortnightly Review* (October 1868), p. 432.
6 J. A. R. Pimlott, *The Englishman's Holiday* (1947), p. 156.
7 Alfred Williams, *Life in a Railway Factory* (1915).
8 Michael Anderson, *Family Structure in Nineteenth-Century Lancashire* (1971), p. 104.
9 Robert D. Storch, 'The Plague of the Blue Locusts', in *International Review of Social History* (1975).
10 George Green, 'A Dock Labourer in the 1880s', in *History Today* (1969), p. 424.
11 D. Rubinstein, *School Attendance in London, 1870–1904* (1969), p. 61.
12 Sally Alexander, *St Giles's Fair, 1830–1914* (c. 1970), p. 20.
13 T. C. Barker, J. C. McKenzie and John Yudkin (eds), *Our Changing Fare* (1966), p. 81.
14 D. J. Oddy, 'Working-Class Diets in Late Nineteenth-Century Britain', in *Economic History Review* (1970), p. 322.
15 George Orwell, *The Road to Wigan Pier* (1937), p. 173.

16   Alec Waugh, *The Lipton Story* (1951), p. 30.
17   E. P. Thompson, *The Making of the English Working Class*, p. 68.
18   Burnett, op. cit., pp. 304–12.
19   Edmund W. Gilbert, *Brighton, Old Ocean's Bauble* (1954), p. 205.
20   T. C. Collings (ed.), *Cricket* (1900).
21   Thomas Wright, *Some Habits and Customs of the Working Classes* (1867), p. 193.
22   N. McCord, 'Some Aspects of North-East England in the Nineteenth Century', in *Northern History* (1972), p. 84.
23   W. J. Halliday and A. S. Umpleby, *The White Rose Garland* (1949), p. 103.
24   Martha Vicinus, *The Industrial Muse* (1974), p. 53.
25   Colin MacInnes, *Sweet Saturday Night* (1967), p. 54.
26   M. Willson Disher, *Winkles and Champagne* (1938), p. 34.
27   Frank Atkinson, 'Yorkshire Miners' Cottages', in *Folk Life* (1965), pp. 92–6.
28   Robert Roberts, *The Classic Slum* (1971), pp. 8–10.
29   R. Q. Gray, 'Styles of Life, the "Labour Aristocracy" and Class Relations in Later Nineteenth-Century Edinburgh', in *International Review of Social History* (1973), p. 447.
30   Paul Thompson, 'Memory and History', in *Social Science Research Council Newsletter*, No. 6 (1969).
31   MacInnes, op. cit., pp. 52–3.
32   Orwell, op. cit., p. 84.
33   John Taylor, *From Self-Help to Glamour* (*c.* 1972), p. 59.
34   Maurice B. Reckitt (ed.), *For Christ and the People* (1968), pp. 53–4.

NOTES TO CHAPTER 7

1   J. B. Leno, *The Aftermath* (1892), p. 86.
2   J. W. Mackail, *The Life of William Morris*, Vol. 11 (1899), p. 69.
3   E. P. Thompson, *William Morris*, p. 304. All subsequent Morris/Socialist League quotations in this Chapter come from Thompson unless otherwise stated.
4   Peter Weiler, 'William Clarke', in *Journal of British Studies* (1974), p. 89.
5   E. J. Hobsbawm (ed.), *Labour's Turning Point* (1948), p. 67.
6   *Karl Marx and Friedrich Engels On Britain*, pp. 22–3.
7   Dona Torr, *Tom Mann and His Times* (1956), p. 180.
8   Ibid., p. 207.
9   Ibid., p. 336.
10   Chushichi Tsuzuki, *H. M. Hyndman and British Socialism* (1961), p. 50.
11   Ibid., p. 42.
12   *The Letters of William Morris*, p. 242.
13   A. L. Morton, 'A French View of William Morris', in *Marxism Today* (1973), p. 152.
14   R. Page Arnot, *William Morris* (1964), p. 62.
15   Stephen Yeo, 'A Phase in the Social History of Socialism, c. 1885–1895', in *Bulletin of the Society for the Study of Labour History* (Spring 1971), p. 7.
16   Lord Snell, *Men, Movements and Myself* (1936), pp. 59–60.
17   A. M. McBriar, *Fabian Socialism and English Politics, 1884–1918* (1962), p. 18.
18   E. J. Hobsbawm, 'Bernard Shaw's Socialism', in *Science and Society* (1947), p. 313.

19 Fabian Tract No. 41, *The Fabian Society: What It has Done; and How It has Done It* (1892), p. 10.
20 Lionel Munby, 'Marxism and the British Labour Movement, 1880–1900', in *Marxism Today* (1957), p. 75.
21 Asa Briggs (ed.), *William Morris: Selected Writings and Designs* (1962), p. 305.
22 Page Arnot, op. cit., p. 108.
23 Margaret Cole, *The Story of Fabian Socialism* (1961), p. 41.
24 A. L. Morton (ed.), *Political Writings of William Morris* (1973), p. 187.
25 Asa Briggs and John Saville (eds), *Essays in Labour History, 1886–1923* (1971), p. 44.
26 H. M. Pelling, 'H. H. Champion', in *Cambridge Journal* (1953), p. 235.
27 Kenneth O. Morgan, *Keir Hardie* (1975), p. 49.
28 Emrys Hughes, *Keir Hardie* (1950), p. 23.
29 Frank Jackson, 'A Welcome Article', in *Marxism Today* (1958), pp. 63–4.
30 Henry Pelling, *The Origins of the Labour Party*, p. 118.
31 Laurence Thompson, *Robert Blatchford* (1951), p. 139.
32 A. E. P. Duffy, 'Differing Politics and Personal Rivalries in the Origins of the Independent Labour Party', in *Victorian Studies* (1962–3), p. 61.
33 A. M. McBriar, op. cit., p. 252.
34 Thompson, op. cit., p. 133.
35 Gwyn A. Williams, 'The Concept of "Egemonia" in the Thought of Antonio Gramsci', in *Journal of the History of Ideas* (1960), p. 596.
36 Thompson, op. cit., p. 96.
37 John Foster, *Class Struggle and the Industrial Revolution* (1974).
38 D. Lockwood, 'Sources of Variation in Working-Class Images of Society', in *Sociological Review* (1966), p. 258.
39 Richard Hyman, *The Workers' Union* (1971), p. 222.
40 John H. Goldthorpe and David Lockwood, 'Affluence and the British Class Structure', in *Sociological Review* (1963), p. 163.

NOTES TO CHAPTER 8

1 Dona Torr, *Tom Mann and His Times* (1956), p. 297.
2 E. J. Hobsbawm (ed.), *Labour's Turning Point*, p. 85.
3 Giles and Lisanne Radice, *Will Thorne* (1974), p. 15.
4 Tom Mann and Ben Tillett, *The New Trades Unionism* (1890), p. 14.
5 E. J. Hobsbawm, *Labouring Men* (1968 edition), p. 189.
6 John Corbett, *The Birmingham Trades Council* (1966), p. 55.
7 H. A. Clegg, *General Union in a Changing Society* (1964), p. 20.
8 A. E. Dingle and B. H. Harrison, 'Cardinal Manning as Temperance Reformer', in *Historical Journal* (1969), pp. 509–10.
9 Paul Thompson, *Socialists, Liberals and Labour* (1967), p. 51.
10 Gareth Stedman Jones, *Outcast London* (1971), p. 320.
11 E. L. Taplin, *Liverpool Dockers and Seamen, 1870–1890* (1974), p. 72.
12 H. A. Clegg, Alan Fox and A. F. Thompson, *A History of British Trade Unions Since 1889*, Vol. 1 (1964), p. 81.
13 Richard Hyman, *The Workers' Union* (1971), p. 10.
14 Zygmunt Bauman, *Between Class and Elite* (1972), p. 155.
15 Ibid., p. 95.
16 Kenneth D. Buckley, *Trade Unionism in Aberdeen, 1878–1900* (1955), p. 68.

17 Henry Pelling, *The Origins of the Labour Party*, p. 87.
18 H. A. Turner, *Trade Union Growth, Structure and Policy* (1962), p. 177.
19 Hobsbawm (ed.), op. cit., p. 9.
20 Raymond Postgate, *The Builder's History* (1923), p. 345.
21 Buckley, op. cit., p. 51.
22 P. F. Clarke, *Lancashire and the New Liberalism* (1971), p. 90.
23 Ibid., p. 43.
24 Hobsbawm (ed.), op. cit., p. 15.
25 David Douglass, *Pit Life in Co. Durham* (c. 1972).
26 J. E. Williams, *The Derbyshire Miners* (1962), pp. 348–9.
27 R. Page Arnot, *The Miners* (1949), p. 292.
28 D. A. Hamer, *Liberal Politics in the Age of Gladstone and Rosebery* (1972), p. 307.
29 Glanmor Williams (ed.), *Merthyr Politics* (1966), p. 67.
30 E. P. Thompson, *William Morris*, p. 702.
31 Laurence Thompson, *The Enthusiasts* (1971), p. 93.
32 Bauman, op. cit., p. 224.
33 Barnard Barker (ed.), *Ramsay MacDonald's Political Writings* (1972), p. 48.
34 Ibid., p. 48.
35 Richard Price, *An Imperial War and the British Working Class* (1972).
36 Laurence Thompson, *Robert Blatchford* (1951), p. 150.
37 Nigel Todd, 'Trade Unions and the Engineering Industry Dispute at Barrow-In-Furness, 1897–1898', in *International Review of Social History* (1975), pp. 37–8.
38 Corbett, op. cit., p. 65.
39 David Cox, 'The Labour Party in Leicester', in *International Review of Social History* (1961), p. 202.
40 Frank Bealey and Henry Pelling, *Labour and Politics, 1900–1906* (1958), p. 24.
41 Philip Snowden, *An Autobiography*, Vol. 1 (1934), p. 90.
42 *Bulletin of the Society for the Study of Labour History* (Spring 1972), p. 84.
43 Kenneth O. Morgan, *Keir Hardie* (1975), p. 109.
44 Peter d'A. Jones, *The Christian Socialist Revival, 1877–1914* (1968), pp. 142–3.
45 Morgan, op. cit., p. 110.
46 *Bulletin of the Society for the Study of Labour History* (Spring 1974), p. 92.
47 P. J. Keating, *The Working Classes in Victorian Fiction* (1971), p. 158.

NOTES TO POSTSCRIPT

1 Frank Bealey and Henry Pelling, *Labour and Politics, 1900–1906* (1958), p. 131.
2 Kenneth D. Brown (ed.), *Essays in Anti-Labour History* (1974), pp. 149–50.
3 Bealey and Pelling, op. cit., p. 75.
4 A. M. McBriar, *Fabian Socialism and English Politics, 1884–1918* (1962), p. 326.
5 Kenneth D. Brown, *Labour and Unemployment, 1900–1914* (1971), p. 53.
6 Asa Briggs and John Saville (eds), *Essays in Labour History, 1886–1923* (1971), p. 9.
7 H. A. Clegg, Alan Fox and A. F. Thompson, *A History of British Trade Unions Since 1889*, Vol. 1 (1964), p. 381.

8   Henry Pelling, *A Short History of the Labour Party* (1972 edition), p. 21.
9   Briggs and Saville (eds), op. cit., p. 134.
10 McBriar, op. cit., p. 340.
11 Roy Gregory, *The Miners and British Politics, 1906–1914* (1968), p. 46.
12 Brown (ed.), op. cit., p. 151.
13 Henry Pelling, *Popular Politics and Society in Late Victorian Britain* (1968), p. 117.
14 Frank Bealey (ed.), *The Social and Political Thought of the British Labour Party* (1970), p. 78.
15 J. M. Winter, *Socialism and the Challenge of War* (1974), p. 25.
16 Richard Hyman, *The Workers' Union* (1971), p. 71.
17 G. A. Phillips 'The Triple Industrial Alliance in 1914', in *Economic History Review* (1971), p. 67.
18 A. R. Griffin, 'The Miners' Lockout of 1893: A Rejoinder', in *Bulletin of the Society for the Study of Labour History* (Autumn 1972), p. 63.
19 The whole debate is contained in the *Bulletin of the Society for the Study of Labour History* (Spring 1975).
20 Bealey (ed.), op. cit., p. 77.
21 Robert E. Dowse, *Left in the Centre* (1966), p. 20.
22 Peter Stansky (ed.), *The Left and War* (1969), p. 61.

Index